Measure milk, buttermilk, Half and Half and whipping cream in glass measuring cups. Check measurement at eye level. 1 quart = 4 cups or 32 ounces volume. 1 pint = 2 cups or 16 ounces volume. ½ pint = 1 cup or 8 ounces volume. Use buttermilk in old-fashioned recipes calling for sour milk ☐ Cream cheese or hoop cheese can usually be measured by cutting the block. 1 8-ounce package = ½ pound or almost 1 cup. Half the 8-ounce package = almost ½ cup. 1 3-ounce package cream cheese = 6 tablespoons or slightly more than ⅓ cup ☐ Eight ounces by volume is usually the same as, or at least similar to, eight ounces by weight. Exceptions include whipped or aerated products and products high in fat or sugar.

Cooking for Compliments

Your Guide to the Fascinating World of Dairy Food Cookery

Knudsen Corporation, Los Angeles, California

Introduction

What does a kitchen counter crowded with groceries mean to a woman? Many things, I'm sure. But I think those vegetables and meats and dairy products and boxes and bags of carefully chosen things are a promise of something to come. She *could* look at them and see only the hours of preparation and cleanup. But if that was all she could see, she could have filled her shopping cart with TV dinners instead. But she didn't. She chose to take the time to select the foods her family likes—along with the ones she knows they need. She carefully sorted through the confusing mélange of cans, boxes and cartons to get the very best value and quality. She even made special trips through crowded aisles to search out a specially requested item. To an outsider that pile of groceries might seem very mundane. But to her it is the promise of compliments to come!—The promise of the appreciation that makes all of her efforts worthwhile.

A woman recognizes a compliment in many forms. It doesn't have to be as direct as, "That was a great meal!" It might be, "Your kids have the rosiest cheeks" or, "May I have your recipe?" Nonverbal compliments count, too. Like when her husband walks through the kitchen just to enjoy the aromas of what she is cooking. Or knowing that the neighborhood children are all in *her* yard because she's baking homemade cookies.

This book is written for that woman who likes to go the extra measure. We think you are that woman. This is a book of recipes, quick and not-so-quick, that all have a special touch. Somewhere in each is a dab or a cartonful of sour cream or cottage cheese or another dairy food to bring a little magic. If you have not yet discovered the excitement that these dairy foods bring to cooking, don't wait.

Special Touches for Familiar Foods is a whole chapter full of quick ideas for using dairy foods right now on the everyday foods you already prepare. The more formal recipes have all been tested, retested and written to be detailed enough for the new cook and concise enough for the experienced one. Many of them are beautifully basic and offer several variations that we hope will suggest others you can dream up just to suit your family. In addition, there is a treasury of information on the hows and whys of cooking with dairy foods so that you can create your very own dishes.

Surrounding the recipe chapters are three others not so directly involved with cooking. They fill in the background that makes cooking a meaningful hobby. The first tells you how and why you should care for dairy foods. At the end of the book is a chapter that explains what good nutrition is and why milk and milk foods are so important. And following that, one on how dairy foods are made—to answer those nagging questions that cross your mind as you are deciding which product to buy or whether you can substitute one for another.

You can expect more from this book than a collection of reliable recipes. These pages are an invitation to a whole new world of cooking and eating experiences for you to create and explore. They are your guide and advisor in turning those bags of newly purchased groceries into a bouquet of compliments.

Barbara Lane
Home Economics Director, Knudsen Corporation

Book design by Richard C. Runyon Design.
Photography by George de Gennaro.
Lithographed in the United States of America by Graphic Press.
Recipes and copy by the Knudsen Corporation Home Economics Staff.

For information on how to get additional copies, write:
Barbara Lane, Home Economics Director, Knudsen Corporation, P. O. Box 2335, Terminal Annex, Los Angeles, California 90051.

Table of Contents

Taking Care of Dairy Foods

Enjoy dairy foods when they are at their very best—FRESH! Freshness starts all the way back with the feeding of the milk cow and continues to the point that the last spoonful or swallow is consumed from the carton. The chapter on HOW DAIRY FOODS ARE MADE, beginning on page 152, will give you an idea of how Knudsen works to give you a fresh product with freshness built in. Your job starts at the market when you reach into the dairy case. Basically there are only two rules to remember. Keep dairy foods cold. Keep dairy foods covered.

Keep Dairy Foods Cold

The last items to be picked up on your market trip should be dairy products and frozen foods. Put them in your own refrigerator or freezer as soon as possible. Car trunks can be very warm!

Keep your refrigerator at a constant temperature between 35°F. and 40°F. The colder your refrigerator the longer your dairy products will stay in peak condition. Don't open the door unnecessarily or leave it open. Turn it to a colder setting in warm weather to accommodate for the warmer outside air and more frequent door openings. Temperatures above 40°F. encourage the growth of yeasts and molds. Acid flavors may develop in the cultured products and fluid milks may develop off-flavors. Don't go as low as 32°F. or dairy products could freeze.

Do not let milk products sit out of the refrigerator unnecessarily. Once these products have warmed to near room temperatures the flavors may change permanently. For this reason don't put product from a serving bowl or pitcher back into the original carton with the fresh product.

It is extremely unlikely that harmful organisms would ever grow in dairy products at refrigeration temperature. But if a product is contaminated from the outside and allowed to warm for a period of time—it could develop undesirable characteristics.

Keep Dairy Foods Covered

The original dairy product carton is designed to protect its contents. Open it only when you are using the product and keep it closed and refrigerated whenever it is not being used. Here's why.

Air carries yeast and mold spores that are looking for a nourishing place to multiply.

Dairy products eagerly absorb other flavors like cantaloupe, onion or whatever. This is another reason for not mixing the product from the table with the fresh product in the original carton.

Uncovered foods dry out—even in the refrigerator. Cover open dishes with plastic wrap.

Light changes the flavor of milk products and destroys the riboflavin (vitamin B$_2$).

Use only clean metal utensils when spooning from the carton. Wooden spoons are porous and very difficult to clean thoroughly.

When is a Dairy Food Fresh?

Appearance, aroma, smell and flavor are the homemaker's tests for freshness. If a dairy product looks and smells normal, the next test is to taste it. Milk products that have been kept cold and covered are safe to taste. If they taste fresh, use them as you normally would.

It is normal for a layer of moisture (whey) to collect on yogurt, sour cream and cottage cheese —especially if the product has warmed up or if some of it has been spooned from the carton. Just stir it up for normal consistency. If the surface of the sour cream, yogurt or cottage cheese is leveled, this moisture does not collect so readily.

Cultured products like yogurt, sour cream and buttermilk are especially resistant to spoilage because of the lactic acid content. Bacteria that ordinarily cause spoilage do not grow well in cultured products.

Yeasts and molds will grow on the cultured dairy products. It is extremely unlikely that they would be harmful—but they *are* unappetizing. Most people just spoon them off and if the product smells and tastes normal, they use it as they normally would. This applies to cream cheese, too.

How long will Knudsen Products stay fresh?

If Knudsen products are kept cold and covered—as described in the previous paragraphs—it is possible to predict an approximate time span of their freshness. Under these conditions, cottage cheese, fluid milks and creams will normally be fresh for a week or ten days. Hoop cheese, because it is unsalted, is more fragile and should be consumed within a few days. It is not unusual for sour cream to be in perfect condition for over two weeks. Yogurt and cream cheese may last even longer. Any of these products may remain fresh for a greater period of time than estimated here. The temperature of the refrigerator plays a most important role in this regard. The closer to 35°F. that your refrigerator maintains, the longer your Knudsen products will last. As the temperature of the refrigerator rises above 40°F. the life of your dairy products, as well as other foods, will be shortened.

About Freezing Dairy Foods

If you find that you have overbought for a party or are leaving town unexpectedly, freezing is a simple, safe and good means of preserving dairy products for a limited time. The nutritional values are not changed and the cultures are not harmed. Because of texture changes, we do not recommend buying large quantities specifically for freezing. In most cases, freezing causes dairy products to become grainy. Because of this, most frozen dairy products find their way into cooked dishes.

Cottage cheese or hoop cheese that has been frozen is actually easier to use in casseroles, egg dishes and baking than fresh product. Freezing breaks down the curd so that it is easily blended into other ingredients. Sour cream, buttermilk and plain yogurt should be used in baking. Thawed cream cheese is fine for casseroles and some baking (not cheese pie). The fluid milks and creams should be used in baking if they are very "flaky." Otherwise they can be used in puddings and sauces. Or for drinking if they show practically no texture change. Whipping cream can be frozen in the carton, thawed and used in baking. (See Fabulous Biscuit recipe, page 99.) Or it can be whipped, frozen in dollops on a foil lined cookie sheet and plastic bagged for freezer storage. Serve the frozen dollops on pudding or pie. Don't try to whip cream that has been frozen. It becomes very heavy and grainy. Fruit-blended yogurt usually shows very little change after it is thawed and vigorously stirred. Use it in recipes or eat it right from the carton.

For the least texture change and the longest storage life, dairy products should be frozen as quickly as possible at temperature below 0°F. Above 0°F., such as in ice cube sections within refrigerators, the food will freeze, but it will have a much less desirable texture after thawing. An overcrowded freezer slows freezing, too.

In most cases the Knudsen carton is a perfect freezer container. It is moisture and vapor proof. Seal opened milk or cream cartons with freezer tape and overwrap cream cheese, hoop cheese and butter with foil. If there is a lot of air space in the cottage cheese, sour cream or yogurt carton because the contents are partly used, press a layer of plastic wrap against the surface of the product and cover. Or transfer the product to a clean glass jar, leaving a half inch of air space at the top for expansion in freezing.

It is not possible to give an exact time limit for freezer storage of dairy products. The condition of the product when it is frozen, how well it is wrapped and the temperature of the freezer all affect the product. Up to one month storage has been very satisfactory for all products except hoop cheese, which should be limited to one or two weeks. Longer storage does not change the safety of the various products, it only exaggerates the texture changes. Butter can be frozen for up to six months.

Frozen dairy products can be thawed in the refrigerator, at room temperature or in warm water. Speed in thawing, as in freezing, helps minimize texture changes. Because the water, protein and fat portions freeze and thaw at different rates, it is important to completely thaw the fluid milks and creams before using any part of them. Vigorously shake or stir any of the dairy products after thawing and plan to use them soon.

Storage and Serving of Ice Cream and Sherbets

Take care that the ice cream you buy is frozen solid and that it does not soften. Hurry it home to your freezer. If you ever find that you are buying ice cream that has been partially melted and refrozen, let the market manager know. The creaminess of Knudsen Ice Cream is a result of super fast sub-zero freezing. Ice cream that has thawed and been refrozen in market or home freezers has an icy texture.

Ice cream, ice milk and sherbets should be stored at 0°F. or below. Like other fresh dairy products, for *best* texture and flavor they should be eaten fresh. In the case of frozen desserts, that means within 3 or 4 weeks. Shorter than you thought?

Freezers tend to draw moisture from foods. On long storage, ice creams may shrink and become sticky. For this reason you may want to overwrap ice cream packages in foil or freezer wrap, or place them in a plastic container for additional protection. Sherbets, especially, are prone to drying.

For the same reason, if the package is only partially full, press a piece of plastic wrap against the surface of the sherbet or ice cream to retard dehydration or the formation of ice crystals. Fluctuating freezer temperatures exaggerate the tendency toward surface ice formation.

Ice cream is easier to serve if taken from a 0°F. freezer to room temperature for about ten minutes, or placed in the refrigerator for about one half hour, before serving. Rinse the scoop, spoon or knife in running tap water between cuts to prevent sticking. Select a scoop with a thin cutting edge.

Breakfast & Brunch

Breakfast—*Webster:* The first meal of the day; a morning meal (to break the fast).
Brunch—*Webster:* A mid-morning meal that serves both as a breakfast and a lunch.

Few dishes smell as good or taste as good as those served at breakfast. No other meal is as simple to prepare or basically as low in calories.

All considered, breakfast-brunch entertaining is an ideal way for a new bride to develop a quick reputation as a superb hostess. It takes a minimum of tableware, time and talent. Practice on the family before going out on an afternoon of sightseeing. Graduate to entertaining the neighbors before taking in a matinee or a shopping trip. A leisurely breakfast or brunch is a great way to start any day.

The difference between a weekday breakfast and a weekend brunch may be only the linens, the dinnerware, the garnishes and the hour. Brunch is served mid-morning. The basic menu is the same.

Fruit or Juice
A Breakfast Meat
An Egg Dish
Cereal — Pancakes — Coffeecake
Milk — Hot Chocolate — Coffee — Tea

Brunch menus would tend to be more fancy and might include creamed dishes, soufflés and perhaps potatoes or other mild flavored hot vegetables.

These breakfast and brunch recipes needn't be reserved just for the hours before noon. Midnight breakfasts and Sunday supper breakfasts are great, too.

Preceding page: Knudsen Buttermilk Pancakes, page 16, served with Whipped Sour Cream Topping, page 141, and sliced peaches.

Eggs and breakfast are almost synonymous. Yet, in spite of the fact that there are endless ways to prepare them, it is so easy to get into a rut. When there is time to enjoy a leisurely breakfast, it is fun to vary from the usual scrambled, fried, poached or soft-cooked eggs. Cottage cheese, cream cheese and sour cream are delicious companions for eggs and can be used in simple or elaborate ways to give new life and interest to your breakfast or brunch. For special brunches or suppers try your hand at a soufflé, a quiche or creamed eggs. It seems such a shame not to enjoy the many aspects of the ubiquitous egg.

Cottage Scrambled Eggs look and taste better than plain scrambled eggs and they have fewer calories per serving, too.

3 eggs
¼ cup Knudsen Cottage Cheese
Salt and pepper to taste
Knudsen Butter

1. Put eggs, cottage cheese, salt and pepper into blender jar; blend until smooth. *OR:* Beat cottage cheese in mixing bowl to mash. Add eggs, salt and pepper; beat until well blended.
2. To a small fry pan, add enough butter to coat bottom and sides. Heat gently until bubbly.
3. Pour eggs into fry pan. Without stirring, gently push cooked portion to center, continuing until eggs are fully cooked but not dry. Serve immediately.

   Makes 2 servings.

ICEBERG EGGS: Fold about ⅓ cup finely shredded iceberg lettuce into eggs as they finish cooking. Serve topped with crumbled crisp bacon.

COTTAGE SCRAMBLED EGGS FOR A CROWD: Double or triple recipe. Cook in large fry pan.

Add a rounded tablespoon of Hampshire Sour Cream to 2 eggs for delicious scrambled eggs.

Delicious! For a special occasion.

6 eggs
½ teaspoon seasoned salt
1 tablespoon fresh or frozen chives (optional)
2 tablespoons Knudsen Butter
1 (3-oz.) package Knudsen Cream Cheese, diced*

1. Beat eggs with seasonings.
2. Heat butter over low heat in large fry pan until bubbly. Add egg mixture and diced cream cheese.
3. Cook over low heat, stirring occasionally, until cheese melts slightly and eggs are cooked. Serve immediately.

   Makes 3 or 4 servings.

KNUDSEN EGGS MARVELOUS: Omit chives. Add ⅓ cup Knudsen Whipping Cream OR ¼ cup Hampshire Sour Cream to beaten eggs. Sauté 1 tablespoon minced green onion in butter. Add 1 to 2 teaspoons minced green pepper, if desired. Proceed as above.

*Cream cheese can be cut quickly and neatly with a piece of strong thread.

There is a conflict in the world of eggs between the plain omelet and the fluffy omelet. There is no need for us to take sides because our favorite omelet filling, cottage cheese, and our favorite topping, Hampshire Sour Cream, work equally well with both types. Here is our recipe for French Omelet and a few of the possible fillings you could use.

French Omelet for One

Although it will be no less delicious, don't expect your first omelet to be beautiful. It takes experience to make one. Once you've mastered it, it will seem like the simplest thing you prepare and will take no more than two minutes. Don't hesitate to serve several people at one time.

One 7- or 8-inch fry pan or omelet pan*

Omelet Filling (see below)
1 to 2 tablespoons Knudsen Butter
2 eggs
1 tablespoon water
Knudsen Hampshire Sour Cream

1. Read complete recipe and get all food and utensils before beginning.
2. Prepare selected Omelet Filling and set aside.
3. Heat fry pan over *medium high* heat. This is one case where eggs should be cooked very fast.
4. Mix eggs and water lightly with fork.
5. Add butter to hot fry pan—tilt pan to coat sides and bottom.
6. When butter is bubbly but not browned, add eggs all at once. Shake pan and quickly stir eggs with fork, keeping tines flat against bottom of pan, until about half cooked.
7. Let pan rest over heat a moment to cook the bottom. Quickly spread or sprinkle no more than 2 tablespoons filling over the eggs on the front half of pan. Lift and fold remaining half semi-cooked eggs over filling, shaping omelet to a semicircle. Work quickly. A French omelet is served slightly undercooked. It can be fully cooked on lower heat, if desired.
8. Loosen omelet with spatula and turn onto warmed plate by inverting fry pan over plate.
9. Rub a little butter over omelet to glaze, if desired. Top with generous dollop of sour cream and appropriate garnish. Serve with salt.

*A seasoned pan—one that is never detergent washed—is the best prevention for sticking omelets. Using Clarified Butter, page 107, helps, too.

Omelet Fillings

FRESH FRUIT: Sugared fresh peach slices, orange sections, blueberries, raspberries or halved strawberries.

COTTAGE: Plain, chive or pineapple cottage cheese.

SMOKED SALMON: Chive cottage cheese and diced smoked salmon.

ROQUEFORT: Cottage cheese and crumbled Roquefort or blue cheese.

À LA RUSSE: Diced leftover baked, hashed brown or boiled potatoes and cottage cheese. Garnish with green onion.

CHILI: Canned chili con carne and chopped green onions.

CHEESE: Grated Cheddar or Swiss cheese.

FINES HERBES: Minced parsley, chives and tarragon.

COLD CUT: Cottage cheese and diced ham, wiener or luncheon meat.

FLORENTINE: Creamed spinach.

CAVIAR: Cottage cheese and red or black caviar.

TACO: Chopped tomato, grated cheese, shredded lettuce and hot sauce.

AVOCADO: Cottage cheese, diced avocado and crumbled bacon.

GREEN CHILI: Cottage cheese and chopped green chilies.

MOCK BLINTZ: Cottage cheese. Garnish omelet with powdered sugar; top with fruit preserves.

Soufflés have a reputation for being difficult. They really are not. A soufflé is simply a baked mixture of beaten egg whites and thick white sauce.

But because of their reputation, you can establish yourself as a "chef extraordinaire" by preparing one successfully. A few props are helpful in creating the image. Most important—a straight sided soufflé pot. The six cup size is the most useful and it can double for the popular molded dessert soufflés such as the Lemon Cheese Soufflé on page 138. A large copper bowl and a balloon wire whip for beating egg whites will absolutely confirm your expertise.

The most important step in making a soufflé is the serving. It must be served popping out of its casserole as soon as it is baked. Take it to the table, pierce it quickly and confidently with a big spoon and dish out a generous serving for each guest. Serve a cheese sauce or mushroom sauce over the soufflé or a creamed vegetable beside it. Fresh fruit would be the ideal appetizer or dessert.

The elegant mood created by a soufflé leaves everyone completely unaware that it is not only very economical but low in calories.

Cottage Cheese Soufflé

There is a variation of this soufflé for any meal of the day. It's full of protein.

One 1½-quart soufflé dish or
round casserole

¼ cup (½ stick) Knudsen Butter
⅓ cup flour
½ cup Knudsen Milk OR ½ cup
chicken broth, fresh or
reconstituted
1 cup (½ pint) Knudsen Cottage
Cheese
¼ teaspoon paprika
½ teaspoon dry mustard
½ teaspoon Worcestershire
sauce
3 dashes Tabasco sauce
6 eggs, separated
1 teaspoon salt
½ teaspoon cream of tartar
(optional for better volume)

1. Butter sides and bottom of soufflé dish. Prepare water bath by placing a large shallow pan of water in center of oven; preheat to 325°F. (Water should be deep enough to come half way up outside of soufflé dish.)

2. Melt butter in stainless steel or enamel saucepan. Stir in flour and cook until mixture froths but does not brown. Stir in milk or broth, cottage cheese, paprika, mustard, Worcestershire and Tabasco sauces; mix well. Heat, stirring constantly, until cheese curd melts and sauce thickens.

3. Whip egg whites with salt and cream of tartar just until whites form short, distinct, moist-looking peaks. Overbeaten whites cause soufflé to shrink.

4. Beat egg yolks slightly in large bowl. Slowly add hot cheese sauce, stirring constantly. Fold one-third of the whites thoroughly into sauce; gently fold in remaining whites.

5. Pour into buttered soufflé dish; run spatula through soufflé about 1 inch in from edge of casserole to assure well formed "top hat." Place in hot water bath and bake 50 to 60 minutes, or until knife inserted in center comes out clean. Serve immediately.

Makes 4 dinner servings or 6 brunch servings.

CHEESE PLUS SOUFFLÉ: For a more pronounced cheese flavor, add ¼ cup grated Parmesan cheese or ½ cup grated sharp Cheddar cheese with cottage cheese in step 2.

CRUSTY COTTAGE CHEESE SOUFFLÉ: For a delicious crispy crust, sprinkle 2 tablespoons grated cheese over soufflé 10 minutes before end of baking time.

MEATY COTTAGE CHEESE SOUFFLÉ: Fold into the cheese-yolk mixture any one of the following: 1 cup diced cooked turkey or chicken; 1 (6½-oz.) can tuna, well-drained and flaked; 1 cup well-drained chopped, cooked broccoli or asparagus; 1 (12-oz.) can well-drained whole kernel corn or Mexican style corn.

COTTAGE CHEESE SOUFFLÉ À LA MER: Fold into the cheese-yolk mixture, 1 (6½-oz.) can crab, well-drained and flaked.

The Quiche

A quiche (pronounced kēēsh) is a savory, rather than sweet, custard pie. It is served as an hors-d'oeuvre in a French meal but is accepted here as a brunch or supper dish. If you are proud of your pastry baking or custard baking ability, this is a great way to show it off.

"Quiche Lorraine" has become accepted as a quiche flavored with Swiss cheese and crisp bacon. Although the original quiche, which is supposed to have originated in the Lorraine province of France, was merely a cream and egg custard seasoned with salt and baked in a crust, the surrounding provinces have adapted it to their own taste. We have taken the same liberty.

The one trick to baking a quiche is to remove it from the oven at exactly the right moment. An egg custard is done when a knife inserted in the center comes out clean. A milky residue indicates *under*baking; a watery residue indicates *over*baking. At just the right stage of doneness the custard will be "set" and tender. It will not "weep."

Cottage Quiche

This is our version of Quiche Lorraine. Find just the delicious variation to suit you.

One 9-inch unbaked pastry crust
Filling:
  8 strips bacon, crisply fried
    and crumbled
  ½ cup grated Cheddar cheese
  3 eggs
  1 cup Knudsen Half and Half
  1 cup (½ pint) Knudsen
    Cottage Cheese
  1 tablespoon flour
  ½ teaspoon dill weed
  ½ teaspoon dry mustard
  ¼ teaspoon salt
2 tablespoons Parmesan
  cheese

1. Preheat oven to 425°F. Prebake pastry crust for 10 minutes or until edges are lightly browned. Remove pastry and reduce oven heat to 350°F.
2. Spread bacon and Cheddar cheese over bottom of pastry crust.
3. Put remaining filling ingredients into blender jar and blend on low speed until smooth. *OR:* Beat cottage cheese in mixing bowl to mash; add remaining filling ingredients and beat until well blended.
4. Pour filling mixture over bacon and cheese; sprinkle with Parmesan cheese.
5. Bake at 350°F. 35 to 45 minutes or until a knife inserted just off center comes out clean. Serve immediately. Leftovers can be reheated later.

Makes 6 servings.

HAM COTTAGE QUICHE: Substitute 4 ounces julienned boiled or baked ham for the bacon.

BEEF COTTAGE QUICHE: Substitute 2 to 2½ ounces shredded, blanched dried beef for the bacon.

SAUSAGE COTTAGE QUICHE: Substitute 5 cooked and sliced smokie link sausages for the bacon.

TUNA COTTAGE QUICHE: Substitute 1 (2¾-oz.) can white tuna, drained and flaked for the bacon.

Tip: ¼ cup Knudsen Cottage Cheese gives as much protein as one egg. Fewer calories, too!

Tip: Top ready-to-eat cereal with fruit flavored yogurt for a change. No cream or sugar necessary. No soggy cereal.

Tip: Top breakfast strawberries with a dollop of plain or whipped sour cream and a sprinkling of brown sugar.

Tip: Top breakfast toast with cottage cheese and apple butter. It's an old Pennsylvania Dutch treat.

Tip: Slice and fry leftover baked potatoes and serve with sour cream as an accompaniment to breakfast ham and eggs.

Creamed eggs never tasted so good. You'll like the variations, too. A recent Gallup survey indicated a strong interest in creamed chipped beef for breakfast from upper income men between 35 and 49 years.

*1 recipe Basic Sour Cream Sauce
made with milk, page 67*
¼ teaspoon salt
6 to 8 hard-cooked eggs, peeled
and sliced*

1. Prepare sauce; fold in salt and most of the eggs.
2. Spoon onto hot buttered toast or biscuits; garnish with reserved egg or "à la goldenrod," sieved hard-cooked egg yolk. For special treat, serve shortcake style over split layers of Buttermilk Cornbread, page 101. Especially good with ham or chipped beef variations.

   Makes 4 to 6 servings.

ASPARAGUS AND EGG LUNCHEON DISH: Arrange hot asparagus spears on toast. Top with Hampshire Creamed Eggs. Garnish with paprika.

HAMPSHIRE CREAMED CHIPPED BEEF: Omit ¼ teaspoon salt and eggs. Loosen contents of 1 (5-oz.) jar dried chipped beef and put in large strainer. Pour about 2 quarts boiling water over beef to blanch. Drain, shred and fold into sauce. Fresh chipped beef does not need blanching.

HAMPSHIRE CREAMED HAM: Omit ¼ teaspoon salt. Substitute 1 cup diced ham for all or part of the eggs.

HAMPSHIRE CREAMED TUNA: Omit eggs. Drain and flake 2 (6½-oz.) cans white tuna. Fold into sauce. Add instant minced onion, chopped pimiento and cooked peas, if desired. Salmon is excellent, too.

CHICKEN À LA KING: Omit eggs. Fold in 1 to 2 cups chunked, skinned and boned, cooked chicken, 2 tablespoons minced pimiento and ½ cup cooked peas.

*For tender hard-cooked eggs without discolored yolks, start in cold water to cover, bring to a boil, reduce heat to a low simmer and cook 12 to 15 minutes. Plunge into ice water immediately. Fast cooling keeps the yolks bright.

An easy, "do-ahead" breakfast meal-in-a-dish. A great reason for using "planned-over" ham and boiled potatoes.

*One 1½ -quart shallow baking
dish, generously buttered*

*1 to 2 medium potatoes, cooked,
peeled and thinly sliced*
*4 hard-cooked eggs, peeled and
sliced*
1 cup diced cooked ham
Salt and pepper to taste
1 egg
*1 cup (½ pint) Knudsen
Hampshire Sour Cream*
*¼ cup Buttered Bread Crumbs,
page 107*

1. Preheat oven to 350°F.
2. Layer potato, egg and ham in baking dish; season with salt and pepper. Bake 10 minutes.
3. Beat egg in medium bowl; blend in sour cream. Pour over casserole and sprinkle with crumbs.
4. Return to oven and bake 5 minutes or until heated through. Serve immediately.

   Makes 4 servings.

HAM 'N' EGG CASSEROLE FOR A CROWD: Triple recipe and bake in 13x9x2-inch baking dish. Allow extra time for heating.

Pancakes

What's more American than pancakes! Actually the light pancakes that Americans make are *strictly* American. The French crêpe, Italian cannelloni and Jewish blintz are all thin egg pancakes. For an example see the blintz recipe on page 17. Baking soda-baking powder leavened cakes—whether they are called griddle cakes, flannel cakes, flap jacks, slapjacks or flatcars—are all-American. Somewhere in this collection there is a recipe—or two or three—for you. There's even one for the weight watchers.

Special Ways to Serve Pancakes

Top pancakes with fresh strawberries and Knudsen Strawberry Fruit-Blended Yogurt. Blueberries and blueberry yogurt. Peaches and peach yogurt.

Top pancakes with fresh fruit and Whipped Hampshire Crème Fraîche, page 142.

Spread pancakes with cottage cheese and apple butter. Roll and dust with powdered sugar.

Knudsen Buttermilk Pancakes

So light and tender, they melt in your mouth. Double or triple the recipe for a crowd. Leftover batter can be refrigerated or frozen in an airtight container for another day.

2 tablespoons Knudsen Butter, melted
1 cup sifted flour
1 tablespoon sugar
½ teaspoon salt
½ teaspoon baking soda
1 egg
1 cup Knudsen Buttermilk

1. Preheat griddle or fry pan. Put butter for pancake batter on to melt.
2. Sift and measure flour; sift again with remaining dry ingredients.
3. Beat egg in medium bowl; blend in buttermilk.
4. Add dry ingredients to liquid, beating until smooth; blend in melted butter. Add up to ¼ cup more buttermilk for thinner cakes.
5. Bake on lightly oiled griddle or fry pan. Turn cakes when surface bubbles begin to break. Serve immediately.

Makes 14 to 16 three-inch pancakes.

BLUEBERRY BUTTERMILK PANCAKES: Stir in ⅔ cup well-drained canned blueberries OR 1 cup fresh or thawed frozen blueberries just before baking. Serve with syrup, sweetened whipped cream or sour cream and additional blueberries.

APPLE BUTTERMILK PANCAKES: Fold 1 cup chopped apple into finished batter OR arrange thin slices of apple over cakes.

STRAWBERRY BUTTERMILK PANCAKES: Fold 1 cup thinly sliced berries into finished batter.

PINEAPPLE BUTTERMILK PANCAKES: Fold in contents of 1 (8¾-oz.) can well-drained crushed pineapple.

BANANA BUTTERMILK PANCAKES: Pour batter into cakes and arrange banana slices over.

PEANUT BUTTER AND BANANA PANCAKES: Blend ⅓ cup creamy style peanut butter into finished batter. Pour batter into cakes and arrange thin slices of banana over.

Family Pancakes

They will never know you started with a mix when they taste these light moist pancakes. The batter is even better the second day.

2 tablespoons Knudsen Butter, melted
2 eggs
1 cup (½ pint) Knudsen Hampshire Sour Cream
2 cups Knudsen Milk
2⅓ cups biscuit mix

1. Preheat griddle or fry pan. Put butter for pancake batter on to melt.
2. Beat eggs in large bowl; blend in remaining ingredients in order given and beat until smooth. Stir in butter.
3. Bake on lightly oiled griddle or fry pan. Turn cakes when surface bubbles begin to break.

Makes about 20 four-inch pancakes.

FAMILY WAFFLES: Prepare Family Pancake batter. Bake in preheated waffle baker.

Cottage Cheese Pancakes

Even the dieters can justify having pancakes with these moist tender gems. Look at all that protein — and so little flour.

2 tablespoons Knudsen Butter, melted
4 eggs, separated
1 cup (½ pint) Knudsen Cottage Cheese
½ cup sifted flour
¼ teaspoon salt

1. Preheat griddle or fry pan. Put butter for pancake batter on to melt.
2. Put all ingredients except egg whites in blender jar and blend on low speed until cheese curd disappears. *OR:* Beat cottage cheese in mixing bowl to mash; add remaining ingredients except egg whites and beat until thoroughly blended.
3. Whip egg whites until stiff but not dry; fold into cheese mixture.
4. Drop by tablespoonfuls onto lightly oiled griddle or fry pan. Shape into circles with back of spoon. Turn when underside is lightly browned.
5. Serve with Knudsen Low Fat Fruit-Blended Yogurt or other low calorie topping.

Makes 16 to 20 three-inch pancakes.

Delightful Yogurt Pancakes

Yogurt gives these pancakes their marvelous flavor and texture. Make enough batter for two days in a row.

1 cup sifted flour
1 tablespoon sugar
¾ teaspoon baking soda
½ teaspoon salt
4 eggs
1 (8-oz.) carton Knudsen Plain Yogurt (1 cup)
¼ cup water

1. Preheat griddle or fry pan.
2. Sift and measure flour; sift again with remaining dry ingredients.
3. In medium bowl, beat eggs until light and lemon colored. Blend in yogurt and water.
4. Add dry ingredients to liquid and beat until well blended.
5. Bake small pancakes on lightly oiled griddle or fry pan. Turn when underside is lightly browned.

Makes 24 three-inch cakes.

Breakfast-Brunch Cheese Blintzes

A blintz is a Jewish version of a pancake. It resembles a French crêpe and can be filled with many things, including cheese and fruit. Fruit preserves and sour cream are essential toppers for cheese blintzes.

One 7-inch fry pan

Pancake:
2 eggs
1 cup water
½ teaspoon salt
1 cup sifted flour

Filling:
2 cups (1 pint) Knudsen Cottage Cheese OR 2 (8-oz.) packages Knudsen Hoop Cheese plus ¼ teaspoon salt
2 eggs
2 teaspoons vanilla
2 teaspoons sugar

Knudsen Butter
Powdered sugar (optional)
Knudsen Hampshire Sour Cream
Jam or preserves

1. Prepare pancake batter: Beat eggs in medium bowl. Blend in water, salt and flour; beat until smooth. *OR:* Combine all ingredients in blender jar. Batter should be very thin. Refrigerate about 1 hour.
2. Combine filling ingredients and blend thoroughly. Set aside.
3. Heat lightly buttered fry pan over medium heat. Pour about 3 tablespoons batter into hot fry pan; quickly swirl batter to form a very thin pancake covering bottom of pan.
4. Return to heat. When bottom is browned and top is set, turn out onto cooling rack. (Fry one side only.)
5. Spread about 2 tablespoons filling on center of browned side of pancake. Fold sides in and roll jellyroll fashion.
6. Melt butter in large fry pan over medium-low heat. Place filled blintzes, lapped edges down, in pan. Brown on both sides.
7. Sift powdered sugar over blintzes, if desired. Serve with sour cream and preserves.

Makes 12 blintzes or 6 servings.

Waffles

Waffles may originally have been a Dutch treat — but everyone enjoys them now! They seem more trouble to make than pancakes, but we think you'll agree that the benefits of these recipes are much greater than the effort. These waffles are delicious with butter and syrup or served in any of the special ways suggested for pancakes on page 16. Fresh fruit and whipped cream topped waffles are an elegant dessert.

If you are fortunate enough to have a little left over batter, refrigerate it and use it within a few days or freeze it for use much later. Even easier, bake it and freeze the waffles for warming in the toaster. They'll be so much better than any you can buy.

Knudsen Buttermilk Waffles

This batter is even better the next day. Make it the night before and sleep in a few more minutes.

½ cup (1 stick) Knudsen Butter,
  melted OR ½ cup cooking oil
2 cups sifted flour
2 teaspoons baking powder
¾ teaspoon baking soda
½ teaspoon salt
1 tablespoon sugar
3 eggs
1½ cups Knudsen Buttermilk

1. Preheat waffle baker. Put butter for batter on to melt.
2. Sift and measure flour; sift again with remaining dry ingredients.
3. In large bowl, beat eggs until light and lemon colored. Mix in buttermilk.
4. Add dry ingredients and blend well. Blend in melted butter or oil.
5. Bake according to waffle baker instructions.

   Makes 8 six-inch square waffles.

FLUFFY BUTTERMILK WAFFLES: Reduce butter to ¼ cup (½ stick). Separate eggs. Whip whites until stiff but not dry. Beat yolks in step 3. Fold whites into finished batter before baking.

Hampshire Sour Cream Waffles

For a very special occasion. These are the most tender moist waffles in the world!

¼ cup (½ stick) Knudsen Butter,
  melted
1½ cups sifted flour
1 teaspoon sugar
¾ teaspoon baking soda
½ teaspoon baking powder
½ teaspoon salt
3 eggs
2 cups (1 pint) Knudsen
  Hampshire Sour Cream

1. Preheat waffle baker. Put butter for batter on to melt.
2. Sift and measure flour; sift again with remaining dry ingredients.
3. In large bowl, beat eggs until light and lemon colored. Blend in sour cream.
4. Add dry ingredients and blend well. Blend in melted butter.
5. Bake according to waffle baker instructions.

   Makes 6 six-inch square waffles.

Coffeecakes and Breakfast Rolls

Moist, flavorful coffeecakes and breakfast rolls are as happily devoured between meals and in the late evening as they are at breakfast. Many people prefer them to frosted cakes at any time. So don't hesitate to bake one of these coffeecakes or rolls whenever you're in the mood — even if it is just for yourself. Cut the leftovers into serving portions, wrap in foil and freeze. Breads and cakes freeze beautifully and can be thawed and refrozen safely. Because of the topping on the Apple-Cream Custard Coffeecake, it should be eaten fresh.

For information about the delights and "how-tos" of baking with buttermilk, sour cream and butter, see pages 116 and 117. You may discover a way to make your favorite coffeecake recipe even better by converting it to buttermilk or sour cream.

We can't say enough for this elegant coffeecake. It's worth baking for the aroma alone.

One 9-inch tube pan OR
   one 13x9x2-inch baking
   pan, buttered and floured

Topping:
   ½ cup chopped nuts
   1 teaspoon cinnamon
   2 tablespoons sugar
2¼ cups sifted flour
2 teaspoons baking powder
½ teaspoon baking soda
½ teaspoon salt
¾ cup (1½ sticks) Knudsen
   Butter, at room temperature
1½ cups sugar
2 eggs
1 teaspoon vanilla
1 cup (½ pint) Knudsen
   Hampshire Sour Cream,
   at room temperature

1. Preheat oven to 350°F. (Reduce to 325°F. for glass pans.)
2. Mix topping ingredients and set aside.
3. Sift and measure flour; sift again with baking powder, soda and salt.
4. Cream butter with sugar. Add eggs and vanilla, beating until light and fluffy.
5. Add flour mixture in three portions alternating with sour cream, beating well after each addition.
6. Spread half of batter in pan. Sprinkle with half of topping. Spoon on remaining batter and sprinkle with remaining topping.
7. Bake cake in tube pan 45 to 50 minutes. Bake oblong sheet cake 40 minutes. Cake begins to pull away from sides of pan when done. Cool 20 minutes before removing from pan.
8. Serve warm or cooled.

   Makes 12 to 16 servings.

FRUIT FILLED SOUR CREAM COFFEECAKE: Place fruit on top of first layer of batter, sprinkle with half the topping. Proceed as in basic recipe. Suggested fruits: ⅔ cup diced dried apricots, peaches, or dates; 1 cup well-drained canned apricots, peaches, pineapple tidbits or blueberries; 1 peeled, cored, thinly sliced, raw baking apple.

LEMON SOUR CREAM COFFEECAKE: Add 1 tablespoon each fresh lemon juice and grated peel to finished batter. Swirl topping through batter with fork instead of layering. Bake as above.

This is bound to become a neighborhood favorite. Don't think you have to eat it all at once. Layered Butter-Milk Crumb Cake will stay fresh for several days if it is well wrapped. Or freeze it!

One 13x9x2-inch baking pan,
   buttered and floured

2½ cups sifted flour
1½ cups firmly packed light
   brown sugar
½ cup granulated sugar
½ teaspoon salt
½ teaspoon cinnamon
¾ cup (1½ sticks) Knudsen
   Butter, at room temperature
1 cup chopped nuts
½ teaspoon cinnamon
¼ teaspoon nutmeg
2 tablespoons sugar
1 teaspoon baking soda
1 egg
1 cup Knudsen Buttermilk

1. Preheat oven to 350°F.
2. Sift and measure flour. In large mixer bowl combine flour, sugars, salt and ½ teaspoon cinnamon. On low speed cut in soft butter until mixture is uniform and crumbly.
3. Remove 1½ cups crumbly mixture and mix with nuts. Combine ¼ cup crumb-nut mixture with cinnamon, nutmeg and 2 tablespoons sugar to make topping; set aside. Press remaining crumb-nut mixture onto bottom of pan.
4. To remaining crumbs in mixer bowl, add soda, egg and buttermilk. Beat at medium speed for one-half minute.
5. Pour batter over crumb layer in pan. Sprinkle with reserved crumb topping.
6. Bake 40 to 45 minutes. Serve warm or cooled.

   Makes 15 to 20 servings.

Apple-Cream Custard Coffeecake

Apple pie à la mode flavors! Apple-Cream Custard Coffeecake makes a delicious dessert, too. Serve it topped with sweetened whipped cream.

One 11x7x2-inch baking dish, buttered

Cake:
1½ cups sifted flour
⅔ cup sugar
2 teaspoons baking powder
½ teaspoon salt
1 teaspoon cinnamon
⅛ teaspoon allspice
½ cup Knudsen Milk
¼ cup (½ stick) Knudsen Butter, at room temperature
1 egg
1 cup diced pared tart apple
Topping:
2 eggs
¾ cup Knudsen Hampshire Sour Cream
⅓ cup sugar
½ cup finely chopped walnuts

1. Preheat oven to 375°F.
2. Sift and measure flour; sift again with remaining dry ingredients into large bowl. Add milk, butter and egg; beat until smooth.
3. Fold in apples and pour into pan.
4. In small bowl, beat eggs for topping; blend in sour cream. Spread evenly over cake batter; sprinkle with sugar and nuts.
5. Bake 30 minutes. Serve warm.

Makes 8 servings.

Fabulous Buttermilk Donuts

Donuts take some practice. Once you've perfected the process no one will let you forget it.

1 egg
2 egg yolks (optional)
1 cup sugar
1 cup Knudsen Buttermilk
1 tablespoon Knudsen Butter, melted
1 teaspoon vanilla
3½ cups sifted flour
2½ teaspoons baking powder
½ teaspoon baking soda
½ teaspoon salt
½ teaspoon ginger
1 teaspoon nutmeg
1 to 2 quarts cooking oil

1. In medium bowl, beat egg and egg yolks until light and foamy; beat in sugar. Blend in buttermilk, melted butter and vanilla. The two egg yolks make an even lighter, more tender donut with almost no fat absorption.
2. Sift and measure flour; sift again with remaining dry ingredients into buttermilk mixture. Mix on low speed just until combined— dough will be quite soft.
3. Turn onto a well-floured board. Dust fingers generously with flour; gently pat dough to ⅜-inch thickness. Cut donuts with floured cutter. If time allows, let cut donuts stand uncovered for 30 minutes before frying. This reduces fat absorption.
4. Begin heating fat to 370°F. or 375°F. Fat should be at least 1 inch deep and maintained throughout cooking.
5. Slide donuts into preheated fat with slotted pancake turner. Turn as soon as they float to the surface. Turn again when one side is medium golden brown. Remove when both sides are equally browned.

   Note: Fry only a few donuts at one time. Make sure fat is hot before beginning each batch. Add fat as necessary.
6. Drain on absorbent paper. When cool, sprinkle with sifted powdered sugar, if desired.

   Makes about 2½ dozen donuts, using a 2¾-inch donut cutter.

Old-Fashioned Cinnamon Rolls

Hampshire Yeast Crescent Dough makes the most delicious cinnamon rolls. They are good and gooey!

Two 9-inch round cake pans OR two 8-inch square baking pans

1 recipe Hampshire Yeast Crescent dough, page 103

Topping:
- *½ cup (1 stick) Knudsen Butter, melted*
- *1 cup dark corn syrup*
- *½ cup firmly packed light brown sugar*
- *⅔ cup finely chopped pecans*

Filling:
- *½ cup (1 stick) Knudsen Butter, melted*
- *1 cup firmly packed light brown sugar*
- *1 tablespoon cinnamon*
- *⅓ to ½ cup raisins (optional)*

1. Prepare Hampshire Yeast Crescent dough according to recipe directions.
2. After refrigerating dough 3 hours, put butter for topping and filling on to melt.
3. Blend topping ingredients and spread in pans.
4. Blend filling ingredients; set aside.
5. On lightly floured board, roll half of dough into a 12x18-inch rectangle; spread evenly with half of filling and roll, jellyroll fashion, beginning with narrow end. Repeat with remaining half of dough and filling.
6. Cut each roll into 12 slices and arrange slices in pan.
7. Place rolls in warm place; allow to rise until doubled in size. Preheat oven to 350°F.
8. Bake 25 to 30 minutes or until golden brown. Invert onto serving plate and serve warm.

Makes 24 cinnamon rolls.

Quick Cheese Danish

Here is a quick Danish pastry for the new cook — or anyone who feels like a quick treat.

Cheese Filling:
- *1 cup (½ pint) Knudsen Cottage Cheese*
- *1 (3-oz.) package Knudsen Cream Cheese*
- *1 egg yolk*
- *3 tablespoons sugar*
- *½ teaspoon vanilla*
- *½ teaspoon grated orange peel*
- *2 packages refrigerated biscuits (20 biscuits)*
- *Orange marmalade or other jam*
- *Powdered sugar*

1. Preheat oven to 400°F.
2. Beat cottage cheese and cream cheese in medium bowl until cheese curd is partially broken; blend in remaining filling ingredients. Refrigerate.
3. On a lightly floured board, using a rolling pin or your hands, flatten each of the biscuits into a 3-inch circle.
4. Put 1 tablespoon cheese filling in center of each circle. Form rim around dough by moistening edge and pinching together at 3 or 4 points.
5. Bake on greased cookie sheet 15 minutes, or until lightly browned. Remove to cooling racks.
6. Spoon orange marmalade onto each Cheese Danish. Garnish with sifted powdered sugar.

Makes 20 pastries.

Hot Chocolate

Hot chocolate is such a treat for a frosty winter breakfast, a rainy day lunch box or an after-the-game snack. Making it is really no problem with the many easy "recipes" around.

The one step always involved in making hot chocolate is heating milk — a simple but sometimes annoying process. The skin that forms on hot milk and causes it to boil over is composed primarily of milk protein. When it is discarded, up to 13% of the milk nutrients are wasted. This loss can be eliminated simply by keeping a lid on the milk while it is heating or by whipping it to a froth and keeping it frothy while heating. In either case, heat gently and stay nearby. You will have no boilovers or unappetizing skin formation.

Appetizers, Dips & Spreads

Five to seven entertaining has a certain charm and sophistication to it. For such a party the hostess wants to be particularly gracious and attractive. Her home must create a welcoming atmosphere and the food she serves should be interesting and appetizing. Creating all of this effect at five o'clock in the afternoon puts a strain on the management ability of the most efficient woman — whether she has spent her day in the office, the yard or the community.

Here is a chapter full of appetizer recipes that will help you give a do-it-yourself "catered" party. Almost all of the ideas presented allow you to do most of the preparation days or even weeks ahead of the big event. The last minute touches can be handled after the guest towels are out.

Whether your party is to precede dinner or almost replace it, the same rules apply to the selection of appetizers to be served. There is just one exception. If a dinner is to follow immediately, a selection of about three not-too-filling appetizers would be perfect. More than this might leave the guests unable to appreciate the dinner. If the party is to last for several hours and dinner is to be eaten elsewhere or not at all, a dozen different appetizers of varying degrees of richness might be served. No matter how simple or elaborate the spread, there must be variety!

There must be variety in flavor. The basic appetizer flavors are seafood, cheese, meats (including chicken, turkey and eggs), fresh vegetables and fruits, onion or garlic and other herbs and spices. Before any one of these flavors is repeated, in any dominant way, there should be a generous assortment of the other flavors served. The importance of sour cream and cream cheese in an appetizer spread is quite clear. Their soft textures and compatible flavors allow stronger appetizer flavors to complement instead of clash.

The texture of the foods you select should vary. Some should be crunchy, some chewy, some soft.

Serve some hot foods and some cold.

There should be lots of shape and size variation. Serve large things, small individual things, chunky things, flat things, cubes, triangles, balls, crescents, sticks, etc., etc.

Color adds a great deal of appetite appeal to food. Choose red and green foods. Select dark and light foods for contrast.

It is possible for just three appetizers to include nearly all the forms of variety mentioned. Here is one party plan.

Hurry Curry Meat Balls	
Nutty Blue Cheese Spread in Cucumber Wedges	Crab and Water Chestnut Dip
Wheat Crackers and Potato Chips	

In addition to all of this variety, it is fun to have one item in the menu that stands out as unusual, a new experience, a surprise, or an unknown quantity. And it needn't be as esoteric as chocolate covered bees. It could be one of the Quick Canapés on page 35 displaying a special gourmet item. Or it could be Petite Pâtes from page 27 with a mystery filling. Items like these can provide conversation for guests who have known each other for years or who have met for the first time.

APPETIZER: A small portion of tasty food or drink served before or as the first course of a meal. Appetizers should not be too filling because they are meant to stimulate the appetite. This general term would include the Slavic "zakooska," the Italian "antipasto" and the French "hors-d'oeuvre."

HORS-D'OEUVRE: Literally—from the French—"outside the main work." Hot or cold appetizers served at the table before the main part of the meal. Unlike canapés they are not served on a bread or cracker base.

ANTIPASTO: Literally—from the Italian—"before the meal." An appetizer of spicy foods served as a first course at the table. Like the French hors-d'oeuvre.

CANAPÉ: From the French word meaning "couch." Small crackers or fresh, toasted or fried shapes of crustless bread spread with spicy bits of meat, fish or cheese. They may be served hot or cold.

PÂTE: A pastry case filled with meat, fish, vegetables or fruit.

ZAKOOSKA or ZAKUSKA: A wide selection of simple, spicy, appetizer tidbits served at a zakooska hour, which is the Russian equivalent of the American cocktail hour. Zakooskas are served from a buffet table. Mingling guests make their selections.

Owning a Bain Marie, or any chafing dish with a water bath, is excuse enough for serving one of these delicious sour cream meat ball or mushroom recipes at each of your parties.

Like Ali Baba, you can open the doors to a wealth of enjoyment with these magic words —

2 tablespoons Knudsen Butter
2 tablespoons flour
¼ teaspoon salt
Dash cayenne pepper
½ cup beef broth
1 teaspoon soy sauce
1 teaspoon Worcestershire sauce
2 tablespoons toasted
   sesame seeds*
1 cup (½ pint) Knudsen
   Hampshire Sour Cream,
   at room temperature
1 recipe Tasty Appetizer
   Meat Balls, below

1. In stainless steel, glass or enamel saucepan, melt butter on medium heat. Blend in flour, salt and cayenne; heat, stirring, until bubbly.
2. Add broth all at once and cook, stirring, until sauce thickens. Stir in soy sauce, Worcestershire sauce and sesame seeds.
3. Empty sour cream into medium bowl; gradually add hot sauce, stirring constantly.
4. Return sauce to pan, fold in meat balls and heat gently to serving temperature. Serve from chafing dish with toothpicks.

Makes 60 to 64 appetizer meat balls.

HURRY CURRY APPETIZER MEAT BALLS: Omit soy sauce, Worcestershire sauce and sesame seeds. Cook 1 teaspoon curry powder in butter 1 minute. Proceed according to recipe directions. Before adding sour cream, fold in 1 tablespoon lemon juice and well-drained contents of 1 (8½-oz.) can crushed pineapple.

*To toast sesame seeds, sprinkle on cookie sheet and bake at 325°F. about 5 minutes or until golden. Toasting develops the character of sesame seed flavor.

A great basic meat ball! Use for Open Sesame Appetizer Meat Balls or with any of your favorite recipes calling for meat balls.

Meat balls:
   1 pound lean ground beef
   ⅔ cup minced onion
   ½ cup soft bread crumbs*
   1 egg
   ¼ cup Knudsen Milk
   ½ teaspoon salt
   1 teaspoon MSG (monosodium
      glutamate)
   ⅛ teaspoon pepper
   1 tablespoon plus 1 teaspoon
      Worcestershire sauce
Cooking oil
1 cup beef broth, bouillon
   or consommé

1. Mix meat ball ingredients and shape into small 1-inch meat balls.
2. Fry in hot cooking oil, at least ¾-inch deep, until lightly browned. The meat balls will hold their shape and brown without turning.
3. Simmer meat balls in broth about 10 minutes or until cooked through. Reserve broth for use in sour cream sauce.
Note: Meat balls may be made in quantity and frozen after simmering for use later. Freeze loose on cookie sheet; when solid, wrap for freezing. Remove as many as you need and thaw completely in chafing dish or 300°F. oven before adding to sauce.

Makes 60 to 64 appetizer meat balls.

*Make soft bread crumbs by tearing one slice of bread at a time into blender jar. Switch motor on and off until bread is torn into small pieces. 1 slice bread = about ½ cup crumbs.

Mushrooms in Sour Cream Sauce

Impressive, delicious and so easy to make! Serve the leftovers, if you have any, with roast beef.

¼ cup (½ stick) Knudsen Butter
1 pound small whole mushrooms
1 small clove garlic, crushed
2 tablespoons flour
½ cup beef broth
½ teaspoon salt
⅛ teaspoon pepper
½ teaspoon dill weed
1½ teaspoons lemon juice
1 tablespoon dry sherry
½ cup Knudsen Hampshire Sour
   Cream, at room temperature

1. Sauté half of the mushrooms in a third of the butter, remove to side plate. Repeat with remaining half of mushrooms and another third of butter. Drain and reserve excess liquid; add later with broth.
2. Melt remaining butter in saucepan. Add garlic and sauté until golden but not browned. Add flour and cook until bubbly.
3. Add broth, seasonings, lemon juice and sherry; cook, stirring, until sauce thickens. (At this point the sauce and mushrooms can be refrigerated separately until an hour before serving. Reheat sauce before proceeding.)
4. Empty sour cream into medium bowl, gradually add hot sauce, stirring constantly. Return to pan and fold in mushrooms.
5. Heat through and serve immediately from chafing dish.

Makes about 50 appetizers.

Miscellaneous Hot Appetizers

Here are several great recipes to serve from a warming tray or right out of the oven on a silver tray.

Serve hot chunks of broiled ham or bologna with a dip of Mustard Sauce for Ham, page 68.

Barbecue miniature kabobs of boned skinned chicken marinated in a sweet oil and vinegar dressing. Serve with Hampshire Orange Sauce, page 68.

Serve chunks of barbecued or deep fried beef (like Fondue Bourguignonne) with Hampshire Roquefort Dip, page 29, or Horseradish Sauce, page 68.

Tiny cubes of Quiche Lorraine make very elegant hors-d'oeuvres. Try our recipe for Cottage Quiche, page 14. It can be made ahead and will hold up beautifully on a warming tray.

Cubes of Herbed Tomato-Cheese Bread, page 104, served from a warming tray are delicious topped with a pepperoni slice. Like little bites of pizza!

Make tiny Fabulous Biscuits, page 99, or make Hampshire Yeast Crescents dough, page 103, into small Parkerhouse rolls. **Serve with thin sliced ham or rare beef.** Men love these appetizer sandwiches.

Tiny Swedish Meat Balls, page 76, can be served as appetizers.

Savory Clam Puffs

Surprise your guests with hot spicy puffs. They are easier to make than they look. Make them in advance. Refrigerate or freeze the batter until preferred cooking time. Finished puffs may be frozen, also.

1 (3-oz.) can minced clams
¼ cup (½ stick) Knudsen Butter
1 teaspoon salt
1 cup sifted flour
4 eggs
1 (3-oz.) package Knudsen
   Cream Cheese, at room
   temperature
½ teaspoon paprika
½ teaspoon caraway seeds
½ teaspoon curry powder
1 to 2 quarts cooking oil

1. Drain clams; reserve broth and add water to make 1 cup.
2. Heat broth, butter and salt in saucepan. When butter melts and a full boil begins, add flour all at once and stir rapidly. Remove from heat as soon as mixture holds together.
3. Beat in 2 eggs, one at a time. Mix well after each addition. Blend in half the cream cheese. Repeat with remaining eggs and cream cheese. Add clams and seasonings; blend thoroughly.
4. Heat cooking oil, at least 1-inch deep, to 375°F.
5. Drop batter by half-teaspoonfuls into hot fat and brown delicately, turning once. Drain on paper towel-lined baking sheet and hold in low oven, about 200°F., until serving time. Salt lightly.

Makes 5 dozen appetizer-size puffs.

Petite Pâtes

Worth every bit of effort you put into them, these tiny elegant pastry turnovers are ready in the freezer for impromptu entertaining. Serve them to your guests personally. You deserve to hear the compliments.

1 recipe Cream Cheese Pastry,
   page 132

Suggested fillings:
   Cocktail franks, wieners or
      bologna, chopped
   Sweet pickles, chopped
   Stuffed olives, chopped or
      sliced
   Deviled ham and horseradish
      or Dijon type mustard
   Liver spread and pickle relish
   Smoked oysters
   Chicken spread and chutney
   Crushed pineapple and
      chopped Macadamia nuts
   Refried beans and diced green
      chilies
   Crumbled bacon and date
      halves
   Seasoned sautéed mushrooms
      (leftover filling from Bacon
      Stuffed Mushrooms, below)

1. Preheat oven to 425°F.
2. Roll cream cheese pastry on generously floured board to about 1/16-inch thickness. Cut into 2½-inch circles with cookie cutter.*
3. Place approximately ¾ teaspoon filling on each pastry circle. Too much filling will cause pastry to burst during baking.
4. Moisten edge of pastry with water. Fold in half, pressing edges together gently to seal.
5. Place sealed pâte on cookie sheet. Crimp curved edge with fork tines. Pierce top with fork tines or knife tip. Inscribe various patterns to identify fillings, if desired. Sprinkle with topping, if desired.**
6. Bake 10 to 12 minutes or until golden.

Makes 35 appetizers.

*A deviled ham can or 8-ounce tomato sauce can makes a perfect 2½-inch cookie cutter.

**Suggested Toppings: Finely chopped nuts, shredded coconut, sesame seeds, caraway seeds, Parmesan cheese.

Bacon Stuffed Mushrooms

Very, very elegant! Leftover Bacon Stuffed Mushrooms can be rewarmed days later.

One 13x9x2-inch baking dish,
   buttered

1 pound small mushrooms
   (about 50)
4 slices bacon, diced
1 medium onion, minced
2 tablespoons minced green
   pepper
1 teaspoon salt
⅛ teaspoon MSG (monosodium
   glutamate)
Dash pepper
1 (3-oz.) package Knudsen
   Cream Cheese, at room
   temperature
½ cup Buttered Bread Crumbs,
   page 107

1. Preheat oven to 375°F.
2. Wash and dry mushrooms. Remove stems; chop and reserve for stuffing.
3. Sauté diced bacon, onion, green pepper, chopped mushroom stems and seasonings; remove from heat when cooked through but not browned.
4. Combine cheese with bacon mixture; press firmly into mushroom caps, mounding slightly. Put buttered crumbs into small bowl. Lightly press filling side of mushrooms into crumbs to coat.
5. Place mushrooms in baking dish, filling side up. (At this point mushrooms may be covered and refrigerated one or two days.)
6. Add ¼ cup hot water to baking dish and bake uncovered 15 to 20 minutes. Garnish each with parsley sprig.

Makes about 50 stuffed mushrooms.

Miscellaneous Cold Appetizers

Have a few of these special cold appetizers ready to bring out of the refrigerator for your next party. See the variations of the cheese spread recipes on page 32 for additional appetizer ideas. Don't overlook the Quick Canapés on page 35, either.

COEUR À LA CRÈME AND CAVIAR: For a very special occasion, surround a Coeur à la Crème mold, page 140, with black or gray caviar and top with tiny slivers of lemon with peel intact. Serve with melba toast. Perfect with champagne.

BEEFY CHEESE BALLS: Cut a 3-ounce package of Knudsen Cream Cheese into 12 cubes. Flatten each cube in fingers and shape around a cocktail onion or stuffed green olive. Roll in finely shredded dried chipped beef. Serve on toothpicks.

DILL CHEESE BALLS: Mix Knudsen Cream Cheese and a little finely minced dill pickle. Roll into small balls and coat with a mixture of chopped hard-cooked egg and parsley.

CREAM CHEESE STACKS: Season Knudsen Cream Cheese with minced green onion and a few drops lemon juice. Spread on luncheon meat slices. Stack 4 cheese frosted slices; top with plain slice. Press together and refrigerate 1 hour. Cut into cubes, spear with toothpicks and serve.

Cherry-O-Crab Appetizers

Beauty is more than skin deep! These tiny tomatoes taste as good as they look!

30 cherry tomatoes
Filling:
   1 (3-oz.) package Knudsen
      Cream Cheese, at room
      temperature
   2 tablespoons Knudsen
      Hampshire Sour Cream
   2 teaspoons dry sherry
   ½ teaspoon salt
   2 teaspoons capers
   ½ teaspoon poppy seeds
   1 (6½ -oz.) can crab meat,
      drained and flaked

1. Remove stems from washed tomatoes; cut off tops to make small caps and scoop pulp from bottoms.
2. In medium bowl, blend cream cheese, sour cream and sherry; stir in remaining filling ingredients.
3. Fill tomatoes with crab mixture. Stick toothpicks into centers of caps and stick securely into filled tomatoes. Garnish with tiny sprigs of parsley and refrigerate until serving time. Will hold several hours.

Makes 30 appetizers.

CRAB PUFFS: Prepare Appetizer Puff variation of Cream Puff recipe on page 131. Omit cherry tomatoes and prepare double recipe of filling. Fill cooled puffs.

Miniature Cornucopias

Crunchy cornucopias can be made days in advance. They will disappear in minutes.

¼ cup (½stick) Knudsen Butter,
   melted
20 slices regular sliced bread
1 recipe Deviled Ham Spread,
   page 33

1. Preheat oven to 350°F. Put butter on to melt.
2. With 3-inch round cookie cutter, cut circle from each bread slice.
3. Flatten each circle with rolling pin, pressing firmly.
4. Brush both sides with melted butter, roll to form cornucopia and fasten with toothpick. Insert small ball of crumpled foil.
5. Bake on ungreased cookie sheet 12 minutes or until toasted.
6. At serving time, fill with spoonful of spread and garnish with parsley sprig at fold of cornucopia. Sprinkle paprika over filling.

Makes 20 miniature cornucopias.

If it hadn't been for Arthur Godfrey combining sour cream with onion soup mix, the open house might never have become as popular as it is. It is the DIP that makes it possible for busy homemakers, working women and bachelors to entertain easily. It is the basic American appetizer.

Most dips improve if they are made and refrigerated a few hours before serving. This time allows the flavors to develop and blend. However, dry herb flavors may become too strong on long storage. Add more sour cream and a little more salt to correct this. Flavors like horseradish, lemon juice, sherry and other liquors become weaker. Add more of these ingredients as needed before serving dips that have been stored for some time. Most dips keep very well. A few exceptions would include such dips as avocado and seafood combinations.

It is very difficult to know how much dip you'll need for a party. There are so many variables—the hour, the diet consciousness of the crowd, the length of the party, the availability of other nibbles. But—as a general rule—plan on one or two ounces of dip per person or one pint of sour cream per ten guests. Remember, there are lots of ways to use leftover dip. See pages 65 and 69 for a few ideas.

A great variety of delicious dips can be made from mixes with practically no time or effort. See page 31. But, many of our favorites just must be made from scratch. Pick some of our recipes or dream up your own concoctions.

Perky Dill Dip

This dip is flavored especially for serving with crunchy vegetable dippers.

1 (3-oz.) package Knudsen Cream Cheese, at room temperature
½ teaspoon grated lemon peel
1 tablespoon lemon juice
¼ teaspoon dill weed
½ teaspoon salt
1 cup (½ pint) Knudsen Hampshire Sour Cream

1. Combine cream cheese, lemon peel, juice, dill weed and salt; beat until fluffy.
2. Blend in sour cream.
3. Chill thoroughly and serve with vegetable dippers.

   Makes about 1¼ cups dip.

Hampshire Roquefort Dip

With lots of fresh vegetable dippers, this dip replaces a salad and pleases calorie conscious guests.

2 tablespoons Roquefort or blue cheese, at room temperature
2 cups (1 pint) Knudsen Hampshire Sour Cream
½ teaspoon salt
1 teaspoon minced green onion
¼ teaspoon Worcestershire sauce
½ teaspoon MSG (monosodium glutamate)
1 clove garlic, crushed

1. In medium bowl, mash Roquefort or blue cheese with fork. Add remaining ingredients and blend thoroughly; refrigerate 1 hour.
2. Serve with mild flavored crackers or chips or vegetable dippers.

   Makes about 2 cups dip.

Tip: VEGETABLE DIPPER SUGGESTIONS: Cauliflower flowerettes, celery fans or sticks, carrot slices or sticks, whole mushrooms, ripe olives, radishes, cherry tomatoes, cucumber slices, green onions, green pepper, broccoli flowerettes, turnip or kohlrabi slices, zucchini squash.

Crab and Water Chestnut Dip

Exotic! You'll mystify your guests with the Oriental touches.

1 (6½-oz.) can crab meat
1 (5-oz.) can water chestnuts
2 cups (1 pint) Knudsen
   Hampshire Sour Cream
2 tablespoons soy sauce
2 tablespoons minced green
   onion

1. Drain and shred crab meat; remove tendons. Mince water chestnuts and drain on paper towels.
2. Combine all ingredients and blend. Refrigerate.
3. Serve with mild flavored chips or crackers.

   Makes 3 cups dip.

Devil's Dip

You can almost taste the smoke and fire of Hades in this deviled ham dip.

1 cup (½ pint) Knudsen
   Hampshire Sour Cream
1 (4½-oz.) can deviled ham
5 teaspoons horseradish
⅛ teaspoon liquid smoke
¼ teaspoon salt

1. Combine all ingredients and blend thoroughly.
2. Serve with mild flavored crackers or chips.

   Makes 1½ cups dip.

Bean Olé Dip

Salud! A California patio party wouldn't be complete without a little touch of Mexico.

1 (3-oz.) package Knudsen
   Cream Cheese, at room
   temperature
1 (8-oz.) can refried beans
½ cup Knudsen Hampshire
   Sour Cream
2 tablespoons minced green
   pepper
1 tablespoon minced onion
2 teaspoons diced green chilies
2 teaspoons chili sauce
1 teaspoon chili powder
½ teaspoon Worcestershire
   sauce

1. In medium bowl, mash cream cheese with fork; blend in refried beans. Add remaining ingredients and blend thoroughly.
2. Refrigerate at least 3 hours. Serve with tortilla chips.

   Makes about 2 cups dip.

Cottage Cheese Dip

A spicy basic dip for the high protein-low calorie group!

1 cup (½ pint) Knudsen Farmer
   Style Cottage Cheese
¼ cup Knudsen Hampshire
   Sour Cream
1 teaspoon horseradish
1 teaspoon grated onion
¼ teaspoon salt
¼ teaspoon Worcestershire
   sauce
⅛ teaspoon celery seed

1. Blend all ingredients thoroughly.
2. Refrigerate 2 to 3 hours to blend flavors.
3. Serve with corn chips.

   Makes about 1¼ cups dip.

DEVILED HAM CHEESE DIP: Add deviled ham to taste to basic dip.

AVOCADO CHEESE DIP: Add mashed avocado to basic dip. Season with lemon juice, Worcestershire sauce, salt and pepper.

ROQUEFORT COTTAGE CHEESE DIP: Crumble Roquefort or blue cheese; add to taste to basic dip.

Festive Avocado Dip

A *MUST* in California! Sour cream makes this dip taste great and inhibits darkening of the avocado, too.

1 large ripe avocado
½ cup Knudsen Hampshire
   Sour Cream
1 tablespoon diced green chilies
1 teaspoon grated onion
½ teaspoon garlic salt
½ teaspoon lemon juice

1. Peel and chunk avocado.
2. Combine all ingredients without completely mashing avocado.
3. Serve immediately or spoon into airtight container, press plastic wrap onto surface, cover and refrigerate.

Makes about 1½ cups dip.

"As Easy as a Mix" Dips

LIVERWURST DIP: Combine 1 (2¼-oz.) can liver spread with 1 cup (½ pint) Knudsen Hampshire Sour Cream. Add salt and pickle relish to taste.

CALCUTTA DIP: Combine 1 (2¼-oz.) can chicken spread with 1 cup (½ pint) Knudsen Hampshire Sour Cream. Add minced chutney and curry powder to taste.

DRIED BEEF DIP: Snip slices of dried beef into 1 cup (½ pint) Knudsen Hampshire Sour Cream. Add horseradish to taste. Refrigerate 2 hours to blend flavors.

HORSERADISH DIP: Add horseradish and salt to taste to 1 cup (½ pint) Knudsen Hampshire Sour Cream. Garnish with minced green onion.

OLIVE DIP: Combine 1 (4½-oz.) can chopped ripe olives, 1 tablespoon instant minced onion, ¾ teaspoon salt and 2 cups (1 pint) Knudsen Hampshire Sour Cream. Refrigerate 2 hours.

RED CAVIAR DIP: Blend 1 (8-oz.) package Knudsen Cream Cheese with ¼ cup Knudsen Hampshire Sour Cream and ½ teaspoon lemon juice. Fold in 1 (2-oz.) jar red caviar.

CREAMY GUACAMOLE: Thaw 1 (6-oz.) can frozen guacamole. Fold in ½ cup Hampshire Sour Cream and ¼ teaspoon salt.

QUICK BEAN DIP: Combine 1 (10½-oz.) can bean dip with 1 cup (½ pint) Knudsen Hampshire Sour Cream, 2 teaspoons minced green onion and ½ teaspoon salt.

GREEN CHILI DIP: Add diced green chilies and salt to taste to Hampshire Sour Cream.

Dips from Surprise Mixes

Some very good dips can be made from many of the mixes you regularly use for their intended purposes. Next time you need a dip on the spur of the moment, look with new imagination at the sauce and seasoning mixes in your pantry. Ignore the mixes with noodles, dried beans or rice, of course.

Dips made with dry mixes, other than dip mixes, are best refrigerated for about two hours before serving. Dehydrated ingredients need time to moisten. After chilling, stir and taste. Add salt or more Hampshire Sour Cream as necessary. Here are some of our discoveries:

CONFETTI DIP: 1 tablespoon Salad Seasoning Mix, 2 cups (1 pint) Knudsen Hampshire Sour Cream.

CUMIN DIP: 1 package Taco Seasoning Mix, 2 cups (1 pint) Knudsen Hampshire Sour Cream, salt to taste.

PINK PANTHER DIP: 1 package Sloppy Joe Seasoning Mix, 2 cups (1 pint) Knudsen Hampshire Sour Cream, salt to taste.

GAUCHO DIP: 1 package Spanish Rice Seasoning Mix, 2 cups (1 pint) Knudsen Hampshire Sour Cream.

BEEFY DIP: 1 package Beef Stew Seasoning Mix, 2 cups (1 pint) Knudsen Hampshire Sour Cream.

MEDITERRANEAN DIP: 1 package Spaghetti Sauce Seasoning Mix, 2 cups (1 pint) Knudsen Hampshire Sour Cream.

EL TORO DIP: 1 package Chili Seasoning Mix, 2 cups (1 pint) Knudsen Hampshire Sour Cream.

Appetizer Cheese Spreads

A cheese spread can be served in so many different ways. Instead of just mounding it in a bowl and surrounding it with crackers, make your next one a little different. Try one of the variations given in the recipes that follow. Variety of shape and size is one of the "spices" that makes your appetizer spread irresistible.

Nutty Blue Cheese Spread

Nutty Blue Cheese Spread takes many forms. A great choice for adding a new shape to your appetizer assortment.

1 (8-oz.) package Knudsen Cream Cheese, at room temperature
1 (3-oz.) package blue or Roquefort cheese, at room temperature
½ cup chopped walnuts (omit if mixture is to be frozen)
2 tablespoons minced parsley
1 tablespoon dry sherry

1. Blend cheeses; stir in remaining ingredients. Thin with sour cream if softer mixture is desired.
2. Serve with crackers.

Makes about 1½ cups spread.

BLUE CHEESE NUGGETS: Increase walnuts to 1 cup. Combine all ingredients except walnuts and form into small balls. Roll in finely minced walnuts. Serve on toothpicks.

STUFFED CELERY: Fill cavity of celery sticks with spread.

STUFFED CUCUMBER: Hollow out a peeled cucumber. Fill with Nutty Blue Cheese Spread. Cut in ½-inch slices; quarter each. Toothpick for serving.

ROQUEFORT STUFFED SHRIMP: Omit walnuts and reserve parsley. Split shrimp half way through on vein side. Fill with cheese mixture and roll backs in parsley. Serve with a squeeze of fresh lemon juice.

ROQUEFORT APPLE SLICES: Spread red skinned apple slices with cheese spread. Serve as a dessert or an appetizer.

Sesame Cheddar Spread

Great flavors! Toasted sesame seeds give an interesting nut-like flavor.

1 (8-oz.) package Knudsen Cream Cheese, at room temperature
1 cup grated sharp Cheddar cheese (4 ounces)
1 tablespoon Knudsen Hampshire Sour Cream
½ teaspoon soy sauce
⅛ teaspoon salt
2 tablespoons toasted sesame seeds, page 25

1. Blend cheeses; stir in remaining ingredients. Add additional sour cream if softer mixture is desired.
2. Serve with crackers.

Makes about 1½ cups spread.

CHEESE DIP: Substitute 1½ cups Knudsen Hampshire Sour Cream for cream cheese and increase salt to ½ teaspoon.

CHEDDAR CHEESE BALLS: Combine all ingredients except sesame seeds. Form into small balls and roll in sesame seeds (use more as necessary).

Cheese Apple

A Knudsen classic. It improves with age.

1 (8-oz.) package Knudsen
   Cream Cheese
4 ounces blue cheese
4 ounces smoked processed
   sharp Cheddar cheese
2 tablespoons finely minced
   green pepper
2 tablespoons finely minced
   pimiento
¼ teaspoon garlic salt
1 cup finely chopped almonds,
   tinted red*

1. Let cheeses warm to room temperature.
2. Combine all ingredients except almonds and blend thoroughly. Chill.
3. Shape into a round ball. Roll in dry tinted almonds.
4. Garnish with stem and leaf from real apple or other fruit. Surround with crackers and serve with spreader.

   Makes 2 cups spread.

CHEESE HOLLY BERRY: Omit stem and leaf; garnish with holly leaves for Holiday Season.

*To tint almonds, dilute several drops red food coloring with a little water. (For brighter red, add a drop or two of yellow coloring.) Add chopped almonds and toss until evenly colored. Spread on paper towels; dry completely. Keep leftover tinted almonds to "repair" Cheese Apple for serving another time.

Corned Beef Spread

Mundane corned beef becomes a spread that draws raves.

1 (3-oz.) package Knudsen
   Cream Cheese, at room
   temperature
1 cup (½ pint) Knudsen
   Hampshire Sour Cream
1 teaspoon soy sauce
⅓ cup minced dill pickle
1 (12-oz.) can corned beef
½ teaspoon paprika

1. Blend cream cheese until smooth; gradually mix in sour cream and soy sauce. Stir in dill pickle.
2. Flake corned beef into cream cheese mixture, removing excess fat; mix well and chill.
3. Serve on wheat crackers; garnish with paprika.

   Makes about 2½ cups spread.

TUNA SPREAD: Omit corned beef. Drain and flake 1 (6½-oz.) can white chunk tuna. Combine with remaining ingredients.

Deviled Ham Spread

"Deviled" or "Diable" refers to foods that have been highly spiced with seasonings like peppers, Worcestershire sauce, mustard, horseradish and garlic. This recipe is just a little devilish.

1 (3-oz.) package Knudsen
   Cream Cheese, at room
   temperature
1 (4½-oz.) can deviled ham
3 tablespoons minced onion
1½ teaspoons well-drained
   horseradish
⅛ teaspoon celery seed
Dash salt and pepper

1. Blend all ingredients thoroughly.
2. Use as filling for Miniature Cornucopias or as canapé spread. Freeze, if desired.

   Makes 1 cup spread.

Dilly Crab Spread

Take your choice of crab spreads. Either one will be a winner.

1 (3-oz.) package Knudsen Cream Cheese, at room temperature
1 (7½ -oz.) can crab, well-drained and flaked
¼ teaspoon salt
2 tablespoons fresh lime juice
¼ teaspoon dill weed

1. Combine all ingredients and blend thoroughly; refrigerate 1 hour. Thin with sour cream if softer mixture is desired.
2. Serve with mild flavored crackers.

Makes about 1½ cups spread.

CRUNCHY CRAB SPREAD: Omit lime juice and dill weed. Add 1 tablespoon minced green onion, 1 teaspoon Worcestershire sauce and ½ cup finely chopped almonds.

Braunschweiger Spread

Liverwurst with a twist.

1 (3-oz.) package Knudsen Cream Cheese, at room temperature
1 (4-oz.) package Braunschweiger
1 hard-cooked egg, chopped
1 teaspoon grated onion
1½ to 2 teaspoons horseradish
¼ teaspoon Worcestershire sauce

1. Blend all ingredients; chill.
2. Serve with pumpernickel bread or hearty wheat crackers.

Makes 1 cup spread.

Tea Sandwiches and Canapés

A tray of beautifully garnished tea sandwiches or canapés instantly conveys a feeling that the hostess cared enough to spend the extra time. That's all it takes to make a hostess' time well spent.

TEA SANDWICHES AND CANAPÉS FOR FREEZING: Many tea sandwiches and canapés can be made completely in advance and frozen. Tiny sandwiches spread with butter or cream cheese spreads will freeze well for up to a month. Other items to complete them must be well chosen for freezing or added at the last.

All varieties of bread freeze well. Bread actually stays fresher in the freezer than in the refrigerator. Because of this, for even short times, freezing is the best way to store bread. Make tea sandwiches or canapés from day old or partially frozen bread — it holds its shape better when being cut into fancy shapes.

Spread softened cream cheese or soft — not melted — butter over each bread shape to prevent other fillings from soaking into the bread. Do not use mayonnaise as a spread or a filling binder because it will separate in freezing and cause the bread to become soggy.

Soften cream cheese by letting it warm to room temperature and mixing a little Half and Half with it. Blend in other appropriate flavorings, if desired, and top with some freezable items to garnish. Here are a few of the foods that freeze very well and can be used in the cream cheese spread or to garnish.

Ham, ground or thinly sliced
Beef, cooked and ground or thinly sliced
Chicken or turkey, cooked and ground or thinly sliced
Cheddar cheese, grated or sliced

Egg yolks, hard-cooked (not the whites!)
Peanut butter
Pieces of crab, lobster or shrimp

Arrange the tiny sandwiches on a foil lined cookie sheet and freeze. When they are frozen solid, place them in airtight containers or wrap in heavy foil. Separate layers with plastic wrap or foil.

Allow 30 minutes to thaw tiny canapés or tea sandwiches. Add fragile or nonfreezable items and serve.

Cream Cheese Tea Sandwiches

Tea sandwiches differ from canapés somewhat, although many spreads would be compatible with either. Tea sandwiches tend to be more bland and sweet.

Cream Cheese Spread:
1 (8-oz.) package Knudsen Cream Cheese, at room temperature
1 tablespoon Knudsen Butter, at room temperature
1 tablespoon Knudsen Hampshire Sour Cream
2 teaspoons sugar
Dash salt
1 or more optional variation ingredients*
Food coloring (optional)
Sliced day-old or partially frozen bread**
Optional garnishes***

1. Beat cream cheese until smooth; blend in remaining spread ingredients, including variation ingredients. Add appropriate food coloring to match party decor, if desired.
2. Cut bread into interesting shapes with knife or cookie cutter. Try rounds, diamonds, sticks, squares, triangles, cloverleafs, hearts, etc.
3. Spread cheese mixture generously over bread shapes, covering completely. Sandwiches may be frozen at this point according to directions on page 34.
4. Just before serving, top with desired garnish.

*OPTIONAL VARIATION INGREDIENTS (Suitable for freezing): Minced crystallized ginger, grated citrus peel, candied fruit or peel, dried fruit, Roquefort or blue cheese (omit sugar), crumbled bacon (omit sugar), chutney, peanut butter, frozen citrus juice concentrate, chives or parsley (omit sugar).

**Select any bread compatible with spread: white, wheat, rye, pumpernickel, fruit, nut, etc. Tinted bread can be ordered from many bakeries. Have it sliced lengthwise for less waste.

***OPTIONAL GARNISHES (Do Not Freeze): Drained, canned fruit chunks; fresh fruit such as grapes, berries; citrus sections; toasted flaked coconut; nuts, halved or chopped; fruit preserves; cranberry sauce; candied fruit or peel; maraschino cherries.

Quick Canapés

Delicious and glamorous ways to stretch precious appetizer ingredients. Prepare these just before the guests arrive — or recruit some help during the party to help replenish.

Spread a layer of Knudsen Cream Cheese softened with Knudsen Hampshire Sour Cream over cracker or toast shapes and add flavorful tidbits and garnishes. Serve immediately.

BASES:
Shapes of crustless bread sautéed in Knudsen Butter
Any small cracker or toast shape in a compatible flavor
Melba toast rounds
"Ritz" type crackers

TOPPINGS:
A small piece of smoked salmon and a tiny piece of lemon with peel.
A small dab of black caviar and a tiny piece of lemon with peel.
A beautiful shrimp or half shrimp and a tiny piece of lemon with peel.
One or two smoked oysters and a tiny sprig of parsley.
A slice of cucumber, a dab of sour cream and a sprinkling of garlic salt.
A slice of cucumber, a dab of sour cream and a bit of caviar or a tiny shrimp.
A slice of avocado, a dab of sour cream and a sprinkling of garlic salt.
A slice of avocado, a sprinkling of crumbled Roquefort or blue cheese and a dab of sour cream.
A slice of avocado, a dab of sour cream and a tiny shrimp.
A thin slice of onion or red apple, a bit of marinated herring and a dab of sour cream.

Snack Foods & Beverages

Adults, teen-agers and children are all consuming more and more food away from the family table. The snack foods they are eating take a significant bite out of the family food budget and total up to an even more noticeable figure on the calorie account. In spite of the cost in money and calories, most provide very little in the way of essential nutrients, being composed mostly of sugar, starch and fat. In too many cases these snack meals end up replacing regular meals or cutting the appetite for them. Because of this, it is important that between-meal-snacks are as nourishing as regular family meals.

A well-balanced snack, like a well-balanced meal, should, as much as possible, include foods from the four Basic Food Groups—fruits and vegetables, cereals, meat and milk. The essential nutrients provided by each of the food groups are more useful to the body when eaten together.

Marketing for snacks should focus on foods that provide protein, such as lunch meats, eggs and cheeses, including cottage cheese. Milk, yogurt, buttermilk and ice cream also provide protein and, in addition, calcium and other minerals and vitamins. Fresh fruits and vegetables are a source of vitamins A and C. Breads and crackers supply essential B vitamins.

There are many dairy foods that are great for snacking because they require no preparation— an important quality for a snack food.

Cottage Cheese: Complete, easy to digest protein, ready to eat right from the carton. It provides more protein for fewer calories than most of the common meat or meat substitute foods.

Yogurt: Yogurt provides all of the protein and calcium of milk and is delightfully filling. It comes in plain and fruit flavors. And it is low fat.

Buttermilk: In spite of the rich sounding name and the creamy texture, buttermilk has fewer calories and less fat than low fat milk. It is famous as a refresher because of its thirst quenching quality. Real fans often season it with a little salt and maybe even some pepper.

Snack foods can be fun, appetizing and quick as well as nutritious. This chapter is full of many suggestions for using cottage cheese, yogurt, buttermilk and other dairy foods in snacks. Dips and cheese spreads from Chapter 3 can be served with vegetable dippers and wheat crackers. The next time you have a party prepare extra dips and spreads just for family snacking. The nutritious and appetizing snacks you plan for your family will let you feel more comfortable when an occasional meal is skipped. And your family will be healthier and happier for it.

Three flavors of Buttermilk Concentrated Coolers, page 38; L.T.B.C.C. Sandwich (Cottage Cheese Sandwich Ideas), page 40.

Buttermilk Coolers

A Buttermilk Cooler is a combination of buttermilk and fruit or vegetable juice. It's a great way to drink buttermilk whether you're a fan or a first-timer.

CONCENTRATED COOLER: Combine 1 quart Knudsen Buttermilk with 1 (6-oz.) can frozen concentrated orange or pineapple juice, lemonade, limeade or Hawaiian punch. Stir to melt. Makes 4 or 5 tall drinks.

GARDEN COOLER: Blend equal parts ice-cold Knudsen Buttermilk and tomato juice or vegetable juice cocktail. Season to taste with Tabasco sauce, Worcestershire sauce, salt, pepper and lemon juice.

FRUIT COOLER: Mix equal parts Knudsen Buttermilk and apple, orange, pineapple or apricot juices.

Lemon Buttermilk Frost

Try our version. Then take off on your own.

1 pint Knudsen Vanilla Ice Cream
1 quart Knudsen Buttermilk
1 (6-oz.) can frozen concentrated lemonade OR ½ cup lemon juice, ½ cup sugar and ¼ teaspoon grated lemon peel

1. In large bowl, beat ice cream to soften.
2. Add buttermilk and remaining ingredients; beat until frothy and serve immediately.

Makes about 2 quarts.

RASPBERRY BUTTERMILK FROST: Substitute 1 pint Knudsen Raspberry Sherbet for ice cream. Add ¼ cup sugar.

SUNSHINE BUTTERMILK FROST: Omit lemonade and add 1 cup orange juice, 1⅓ cups prune juice, 2 tablespoons lemon juice, ⅓ cup sugar and ⅛ teaspoon salt.

Knudsen Chocolate Malt

Rich and creamy! You can't buy a malt this good.

1 pint Knudsen Vanilla Ice Cream or Ice Milk
¼ cup Knudsen Milk
1 to 2 tablespoons chocolate syrup
1 teaspoon instant malted milk powder

1. Combine all ingredients in blender jar or electric mixer bowl. Blend or beat until thickened and smooth. For thinner malt increase milk to ½ cup.
2. Pour into chilled glasses and top with dollop of sweetened whipped cream, if desired.

Makes 2 servings.

VANILLA MALT: Omit chocolate syrup.

STRAWBERRY MALT: Substitute Knudsen Strawberry Ice Cream for vanilla and strawberry topping for chocolate syrup.

CHOCOLATE SHAKE: Omit instant malted milk powder.

Lemon Orange Freeze

Simply a cup each of yogurt and sherbet plus a half cup of fruit juice. Tooth tingling refreshment!

½ cup orange juice
1 (8-oz.) carton Knudsen Orange or Lemon Fruit-Blended Yogurt
1 cup Knudsen Lemon Sherbet*

1. Put ingredients in blender jar in order and blend until smooth. Serve immediately.

Makes 2 or 3 tall drinks.

BOYSENBERRY FREEZE: Substitute cranberry juice and Knudsen Boysenberry Fruit-Blended Yogurt for orange juice and orange yogurt.

*1 cup of sherbet is half the pint carton.

Yogurt Delight

Use any of the soda drinks and fruit flavored yogurts for this light refresher.

1 (8-oz.) carton Knudsen Lime
Fruit-Blended Yogurt
1 (12-oz.) bottle ginger ale

1. Divide yogurt into three tall glasses; add a little ginger ale and stir until smooth.
2. Fill glasses with remaining ginger ale. Stir and serve.

    Makes 3 tall drinks.

FIGURE 8 SODA: Substitute 1 (12-oz.) bottle lemon-lime flavored dietetic soda for ginger ale.

MISCELLANEOUS YOGURT DELIGHTS: Substitute Knudsen Boysenberry, Orange, Cherry, Lemon or Strawberry Fruit-Blended Yogurt for lime yogurt. Vary carbonated beverages.

Tropical Delight Punch

"Punch" comes from the Hindi word, "panch," meaning five—standing for its five basic ingredients: wine or liquor, water, sugar, lemon and spice. No one will guess the ingredients in this one. It is a beautiful blending of flavors!

1½ cups guava nectar
1 small banana
2 (8-oz.) cartons Knudsen
Pineapple Fruit-Blended
Yogurt
1 (1-quart) bottle lemon-lime
soda

1. Have all ingredients well chilled.
2. Blend guava nectar and banana until smooth. Electric blender or mixer may be used.
3. Empty yogurt into punch bowl or large pitcher; blend in banana mixture.
4. Just before serving, stir in soda.*

    Makes 2 quarts.

TROPICAL LIME REFRESHER: Substitute pineapple juice for guava nectar and Knudsen Lime Fruit-Blended Yogurt for pineapple yogurt. Add crushed pineapple, if desired.

*Keep punches cold without diluting them by: Adding scoops of ice cream or sherbet, adding cubes of frozen fruit juices or lining a large bowl with crushed ice—place smaller punch bowl inside.

Very Berry Buttermilk Nog

Eating on the run? Make a buttermilk nog and enjoy a quick breakfast or snack with a delightful fresh fruit flavor. Try our favorites first—then your own with your favorite fresh or frozen fruits. Complete the meal with a piece of toast or a muffin.

2 cups Knudsen Buttermilk
1 (10-oz.) package frozen
strawberries, partially thawed
3 eggs
2 teaspoons lemon juice
Dash salt

1. Combine ingredients in blender jar and blend until smooth.

    Makes 3 servings, 241 calories each.

Orange Buttermilk Nog

The classic breakfast combination — orange juice, egg and milk. Serve it with a muffin or cinnamon toast.

2 cups Knudsen Buttermilk
½ can (6-oz. size) frozen
orange juice concentrate
2 eggs
2 teaspoons sugar or honey
Dash salt
½ teaspoon lemon juice
(optional)

1. Combine ingredients in blender jar and blend until smooth.

    Makes 2 servings, 289 calories each.

Islander Buttermilk Nog

Exotic island flavors blend right into another version of buttermilk nog.

1 cup Knudsen Buttermilk
½ cup papaya or guava nectar
1 banana
2 eggs
1 teaspoon sugar
1 teaspoon lemon juice
Dash salt

1. Combine ingredients in blender jar and blend until smooth.

   Makes 2 servings, 275 calories each.

Cottage Cheese Sandwich Ideas

A well planned sandwich is a small balanced meal in itself. It includes bread, a protein food, lettuce and perhaps tomato. A glass of milk, or one of the snack drinks in this chapter, completes the nutritional picture.

L.T.B.C.C. SANDWICH: Add cottage cheese to your next lettuce-tomato-bacon sandwich. Top with avocado slices for a glamor touch.

PEANUT SANDWICH: Add chopped peanuts to cottage cheese for a delicious sandwich spread. It doesn't stick to the roof of your mouth!

OPEN FACE COTTAGE-AVOCADO SANDWICH: Mash ripe avocado with garlic salt and pepper; blend with cottage cheese. Spread on toasted English muffin half, sour dough slice or French bread slice. Cottage cheese enhances the flavor of avocado.

EGG, TUNA OR HAM SALAD SANDWICHES: Mix cottage cheese with egg salad, tuna salad or ham salad sandwich fillings. Add additional seasonings to taste. Cottage cheese adds low calorie protein and moistness. Cuts down the need for higher calorie salad dressings.

AVOCADO AND BACON SANDWICH: Give a protein boost to an avocado sandwich with a thick layer of cottage cheese. It complements the avocado and bacon—and holds it together at the same time.

COTTAGE CHEESE SALAD SANDWICH: Mix chopped vegetables with cottage cheese. Vegetables to try include cucumber, radish, green onion, carrot, celery, ripe or green olives, etc. Spread on toasted wheat bread.

A Carton of Yogurt is:

A QUICK BREAKFAST: A carton of fruit flavored Knudsen Yogurt really improves a toast and coffee breakfast.

A BAG LUNCH: Carry a carton of frozen Knudsen Fruit-Blended Yogurt to school, the office or the beach. By noon it is thawed and ready to eat. Stir well.

AN AFTER SCHOOL SNACK: A half carton of fruit flavored Knudsen Yogurt provides real satisfaction and still leaves room for dinner. Serve it with a cookie.

A BED-TIME SNACK: A half carton of fruit flavored Knudsen Yogurt keeps you from going to bed hungry. It's easy to digest and doesn't keep you awake.

Mid-Morning Snacks

Whether you need a morning wake up or pick up, these snack ideas are great. Lots of energy to keep you going the rest of the morning.

Heat frozen Knudsen Buttermilk Waffles or Hampshire Sour Cream Waffles, page 18, in toaster. Serve topped with Knudsen Fruit-Blended Yogurt.

Spread cottage cheese on toasted Boston Brown Bread, page 102. Garnish with fresh or well-drained canned fruit.

Serve warmed Buttermilk Bran Muffins, page 101, with butter.

Prepare Quick Cheese Danish, page 21.

Spread cottage cheese on toast and top with apple butter.

Special afternoon treats for your family—or for you.

Spear bananas with wooden skewers or ice cream sticks and freeze. Coat with Knudsen Vanilla or Fruit-Blended Yogurt; roll in coconut, shaved chocolate or chopped nuts and freeze until solid. Other "frostings" can be sweetened Hampshire Sour Cream or Knudsen Chocolate-at-Bottom Yogurt, stirred.

Fill packaged taco shells with cottage cheese, lettuce, tomato, avocado and taco sauce. Or spread crisp tortillas, tostada fashion, with the same ingredients.

Mix cottage cheese and other condiments with hard-cooked egg yolk for deviled eggs.

Stuff celery or cucumbers with cottage cheese. Sprinkle with seasoned salt.

Vegetable dippers and sour cream dips make a nutritious snack food for teen-agers. See page 29 for dipper suggestions. Dip recipes appear on pages 29 to 31.

Spread plain cottage cheese or Cottage Cheese Dip, page 30, on wheat crackers or wheat toast.

Spread wheat crackers with cheese spread and enjoy them with an apple. Cheese spread recipes appear on pages 32 and 33.

Serve boysenberry or apple pie with a generous scoop of Knudsen Vanilla Yogurt. Pie à la Yogurt.

After School Snacks

These snacks are as special in the morning as they are late in the evening. Good protein energy.

Make individual pizzas by spreading cottage cheese on English muffin halves. Top with pizza topping and pepperoni slices. Place under broiler to warm.

Layer fruit flavored gelatin with cottage cheese and fruit in a parfait glass.

Serve chunks and spears of fresh fruit with fruit-blended yogurt as a dip.

Apple slices with cottage cheese are crisp and appetizing.

Spread cottage cheese on graham crackers—top with jelly.

Make Yogurt Popsicles: Spoon Knudsen Fruit-Blended Yogurt into paper cups. Spear with a plastic spoon and freeze. Do it for the children—then indulge yourself.

Anytime Snacks

Dinner's planned-overs can become nutritious, delicious snacks. Make an extra portion of these dishes for the between-meal-eaters and for those who eat on the run.

Cold pieces of Buttermilk Fried Chicken, page 66. Add bread, fresh fruit and milk.

Broiled or barbecued ham, bologna or hot dog chunks served with Mustard Sauce, page 68. Serve with wheat crackers, crisp vegetable finger foods and a glass of milk.

Cold sliced Cottage Meat Loaf, page 88, makes a delicious sandwich.

Gelled salads made with cottage cheese, such as the Lemon-Lime Ring Mold on page 54, are refreshing and nourishing snacks. A good way to pacify a nagging sweet tooth.

Warmed Crusty Cheese Bread, page 103, with lots of fresh creamy butter.

Planned-Over Snacks

Desserts don't have to be forbidden snack foods. Here's a list of particularly nutritious ones right from the pages of this book. Yogurt and cottage cheese provide the body building bonus.

Mock Tapioca, page 70.
Traditional Cheesecake, page 112.
Buttermilk Custard Pie, page 126.
Strawberry Parfait Pie, page 130.
Lemon Cheese Soufflé, page 138.

Strawberry Yogurt Shimmy, page 138.
Cool Orange Sherbet, page 144
Lime Sherbet, page 144.
Buttermilk Pineapple Sherbet, page 144.
Orange Freeze, page 145.

Special Dessert Snacks

Salads

Defining "SALAD" in five easy words is a difficult task. Webster says it is "a dish of lettuce or other vegetables, herbs, or meat or fowl, fish, eggs, fruit, etc. prepared with various seasonings or dressings and usually served cold. Herbs or plants used in salads are usually eaten raw." A salad can be served as an appetizer, a side dish to an entrée, a main dish or a dessert, depending on its ingredients. We have complicated the issue further by adding another variation to our chapter, chilled soups—or could we say, liquid salads. With this almost limitless definition it hardly seems possible that one could get in a rut. But nevertheless, Westerners are inclined to be in a "tossed salad" rut.

Variety in salad dressings could be the first step out of the rut. In the section on salad dressings that follows, there are many dressings made of sour cream, yogurt and cottage cheese. In using these dairy dressings you'll discover the full flavor of salad ingredients. The creamy compatible flavors of dairy foods enhance the delicate highlights of fresh fruit and vegetable flavors. No heavy masking effect. On potato, macaroni, bean, seafood and chicken salads, sour cream dressings preserve that fresh "just mixed" look. The right new dressing can make the same old ingredients taste like a new salad.

Broadening the choice of salad ingredients could be next. The always widening selection of fruits, vegetables and condiments in the market place provides constant possibilities for new salad experiences. Familiar ingredients used in new ways are just as good. Add a scoop of cottage cheese for a protein boost. It is equally compatible with fruit, vegetable, seafood or even potato salads. Garnish a lovely arranged salad with cream cheese balls like the ones on page 49. Cottage cheese, sour cream, yogurt or buttermilk added to a gelled salad for part of the liquid completely change the look and the taste.

Varying the form of the salad is another way out of the rut. Instead of tossing ingredients together, try arranging them, molding them, freezing them or liquifying them. Cut pieces into interesting shapes. Use your imagination.

Imagination is the key to making interesting salads and getting out of the "tossed salad" rut. Outside of keeping liquid-gelatin proportions in gelled salads, there are no limits to exploration. Your own taste, your knowledge of your family's preferences and your imagination can lead you anywhere. These recipes are patterns that you can alter and refine over and over to suit your mood, the season, the menu, and, most of all, the whims of those you like so much to please.

Preceding page: Lemon-Lime Ring Mold, page 54; Chilled Potavocado Soup, page 59.

There are multitudes of ready-made salad dressings in the supermarket but none can match the flavor of a fresh dressing "whipped up" just for the occasion. Sour cream, yogurt and cottage cheese can be the beginnings of a tremendous number of dressings made just to suit your taste and to lower your calorie intake, too.

CALORIC VALUES OF COMMON SALAD DRESSINGS:

	Calories per 2 tablespoons
Knudsen Low Fat Plain Yogurt	18
Knudsen Plain Yogurt	22
Knudsen Hampshire Sour Cream	62
Salad dressing (mayonnaise type)	113
French, commercial	118
Homemade oil and vinegar	172
Mayonnaise	184

Basic Sour Cream Dressing

Remember the calories you have saved when you toss a salad with these creamy dressings. Only ⅓ the calories of mayonnaise or oil and vinegar dressing.

1 cup (½ pint) Knudsen Hampshire Sour Cream
½ teaspoon salt
⅛ teaspoon pepper
1 to 2 tablespoons lemon juice
1 teaspoon sugar (optional)

1. Blend all ingredients and refrigerate 1 to 2 hours to blend flavors.

Makes about 1 cup.

HERBED SOUR CREAM DRESSING: Add ¼ to ½ teaspoon of any one or a combination of the following dry herbs or ¾ to 1½ teaspoons fresh:

Tarragon, marjoram, beau monde seasoning, savory, chervil, dill weed (for cucumbers or coleslaw), basil (for tomatoes), oregano (for tomatoes), thyme (for tomatoes or beets).

CREAMY HORSERADISH DRESSING: Add about 1 teaspoon horseradish.

CREAMY GARLIC DRESSING: Add 1 crushed garlic clove.

OLIVE DRESSING: Add ¼ cup chopped ripe or stuffed olives.

SOUR CREAM FRENCH DRESSING: Stir in ¼ cup French dressing.

CHEESE 'N' CREAM DRESSING: Add ¼ cup grated Parmesan or Cheddar cheese.

MISCELLANEOUS VARIATIONS OF SOUR CREAM DRESSING: Use the following in combination with the above or alone in the basic dressing:

Worcestershire sauce	Prepared mustard
Soy sauce	Catsup
Tabasco sauce	Cottage cheese
Capers	Crumbled bacon
Pickle relish	Paprika
Minced pimiento	Celery seed
Chives	Caraway seed
Anchovy fillets or paste	Toasted sesame seeds

Roquefort Cheese Dressing

A creamy "spoonable" version of this California favorite.

1 (3-oz.) package Knudsen
  Cream Cheese, at room
  temperature
1 teaspoon fresh lemon juice
½ teaspoon garlic salt
1½ ounces Roquefort or blue
  cheese, at room temperature
1 cup (½ pint) Knudsen
  Hampshire Sour Cream

1. Blend cream cheese with lemon juice, garlic salt and Roquefort or blue cheese.
2. Gradually blend in sour cream and refrigerate 2 hours to blend flavors.

Makes about 1½ cups.

Creamy Roquefort Dressing

You may have been served this dressing in a famous restaurant!

2 tablespoons Roquefort cheese
  (1 ounce)
½ cup mayonnaise
½ cup Knudsen Hampshire Sour
  Cream
⅓ cup Knudsen Buttermilk
1 teaspoon lemon juice
¼ teaspoon onion salt
¼ teaspoon garlic salt
Fresh ground pepper

1. In small bowl, crumble Roquefort cheese with fork.
2. Blend in mayonnaise, sour cream and remaining ingredients; refrigerate 3 to 4 hours to blend flavors.

Makes about 1½ cups.

CREAMY ROQUEFORT DRESSING FOR A CROWD: Use 4 ounces Roquefort or blue cheese, 1 pint mayonnaise, 2 cups (1 pint) Knudsen Hampshire Sour Cream, 1⅓ cups Knudsen Buttermilk plus quadrupled seasonings. Makes about 6 cups.

Green Goddess Dressing

This San Francisco creation is a Western favorite. It's tangy!

2 tablespoons tarragon vinegar
  OR 2 tablespoons white
  vinegar and ⅛ teaspoon
  tarragon
1 small clove garlic
4 small green onions with fresh
  tops (about ¼ cup chunked)
1 tablespoon anchovy paste
¼ cup coarsely chopped parsley
  (packed)
⅛ teaspoon tarragon
⅛ teaspoon salt
½ cup mayonnaise
1 cup (½ pint) Knudsen
  Hampshire Sour Cream

1. Combine all ingredients except mayonnaise and sour cream in blender jar; blend until *nearly* smooth.
2. Fold blended mixture into mayonnaise and sour cream; refrigerate several hours to blend flavors.

Makes 2 cups.

Hampshire Thousand Island Dressing

For a quick Thousand Island Dressing, just mix chili sauce and Hampshire Sour Cream. But for the real thing, try this recipe to please all tastes.

¼ cup chili sauce
1½ teaspoons minced pimiento
1 tablespoon minced green
   pepper
1 tablespoon minced onion
1 hard-cooked egg, finely
   chopped or grated
1 cup (½ pint) Knudsen
   Hampshire Sour Cream
Salt and pepper to taste

1. Blend all ingredients and refrigerate several hours to blend flavors.

   Makes about 1½ cups.

Knudsen Cottage Dressing

A spicy dressing for dieters.   Only 21 calories per tablespoon.

1 cup (½ pint) Knudsen Farmer
   Style Cottage Cheese
⅔ cup Knudsen Hampshire
   Sour Cream
½ medium clove garlic, crushed
2 teaspoons tarragon vinegar
1 teaspoon dry mustard
¼ to ½ teaspoon salt
¼ teaspoon pepper
¼ teaspoon paprika
¼ teaspoon sugar
½ teaspoon Worcestershire
   sauce

1. Combine all ingredients in blender jar or electric mixer bowl. Blend or beat until smooth and refrigerate to blend flavors.

   Makes about 1⅔ cups.

Salad Dressings from Dry Mixes

Many salad dressing mixes give directions for mixing with sour cream. The results are not only delicious but significantly lower in calories. The mixes made up with sour cream will cut the calories to ⅓ or even ¼ of the original oil and vinegar or mayonnaise versions.   To cut calories and fat even lower, try them with plain yogurt instead of sour cream. Try mixes for Caesar dressing, French dressing or bacon dressing.

Basic Hampshire Dressing for Fruit Salad

Fruit flavors come alive when dressed with Hampshire Sour Cream. You'll never use mayonnaise on fruit salads again.

2 tablespoons fresh lemon
   or lime juice
2 tablespoons sugar or honey
Dash salt
1 cup (½ pint) Knudsen
   Hampshire Sour Cream

1. Blend juice, sugar or honey and salt; gradually blend in sour cream and refrigerate several hours to blend flavors.

   Makes about 1¼ cups. 28 calories per tablespoon.

TANGY YOGURT DRESSING: Substitute 1 (8-oz.) carton Knudsen Plain Yogurt for Hampshire Sour Cream. Only 12 calories per tablespoon. For even fewer calories, substitute artificial sweetener for sugar. Only 9 calories per tablespoon.

See next page for additional variations.

MISCELLANEOUS VARIATIONS FOR HAMPSHIRE DRESSING FOR FRUIT SALAD: Add one or more of the following ingredients:

Finely minced crystallized ginger	Grated citrus peel	Cinnamon
Frozen concentrated fruit juices	Wine	Rosemary
Grenadine syrup for part of the sugar or honey	Ginger ale	Tarragon
Jelly or jam for the sugar or honey	Poppy seed	Curry powder
Maraschino cherry juice	Toasted sesame seed	
Bitters	Mint	

Miscellaneous Dressings for Fruit Salads

Dairy products are perfect flavor complements for canned or fresh fruit salads.

Whipped Cream Topping, page 123.
Whipped Sour Cream Topping, page 141.
Cottage Cheese Fluff, page 142.
Whipped Hampshire Crème Fraîche, page 142.
Knudsen Sherbet
Knudsen Cottage Cheese
Kundsen Fruit-Blended Yogurts—pineapple, lemon and lime especially.

Fruit Salads

A fruit salad can be an appetizer, a main dish, a main dish accompaniment or even a dessert. The warm weather and the wide variety of fruits available in California make fruit salads welcome and appealing year-round.

Make your own creations. The possibilities are endless.

Selection and Preparation of Fruit

Select several compatible fruits. Consider color, flavor and texture. Supplement with canned fruits when fresh fruit supplies are short.

YEAR-ROUND FRUITS: *(One variety or another)* Apples, Avocados, Bananas, Grapefruit, Oranges, Papayas, Pears, Pineapples.

FALL AND WINTER FRUITS: Persimmons, Tangelos, Pomegranates, Grapes.

SPRING AND SUMMER FRUITS: Apricots, Strawberries, Blueberries, Raspberries, Cherries, Figs, Thompson Seedless Grapes, Loquats, Mangos, Cantaloupes, Honeydew melons, Watermelons, Nectarines, Peaches, Plums.

Try these exotic fruits for fun when they appear in your produce market: Kiwi, Cheremoya, Cactus Fruit, Lychee.

Cutting the fruit into small pieces and dressing or sugaring it in advance, will make a juicy flavorful salad or fruit cocktail. For an arranged fruit salad, the fruit is best cut into larger pieces and dressed just before serving. Cutting fruit with melon ballers and interesting blades adds to the excitement. The short period between cutting and serving the fruit is long enough to cause some fruits to darken. Avocados, pears, bananas, peaches, apples, nectarines, apricots and plums are common offenders. To inhibit darkening, dip the cut fruit in citrus juice, honey or sour cream. Or use one of the ascorbic acid products on the market.

Serve fruit salads well chilled.

Combination Hampshire Fruit Salad

A year-round fruit salad prepared in minutes from a pint of Hampshire Sour Cream and items on your pantry shelf. Wonderful for a buffet menu featuring ham or chicken.

2 cups (1 pint) Knudsen
   Hampshire Sour Cream
2 cups miniature marshmallows,
   plain or fruit flavored
1 (3½ -oz.) can flaked coconut
5 to 6 cups well-drained chunked
   fruit.* Select 2 or more of the
   suggested fruits.**

1. Combine sour cream, marshmallows and coconut; fold in well-drained *canned* fruit except dark bleeding fruit like Bing cherries. Refrigerate several hours or overnight to soften marshmallows and blend flavors. Add powdered sugar to taste for immediate serving.

2. At serving time, fold in *fresh* fruits and any dark canned fruits. Make certain apples, bananas and other fruits that darken are well coated with dressing.

   Makes 8 to 10 servings.

2 (1-pound 13-oz.) cans equal about 5 cups of chunked, drained fruit.

**SUGGESTED FRUITS: Canned pineapple chunks (essential), canned or fresh apricots, canned or fresh mandarin orange segments, fresh strawberries or blueberries, canned or fresh pears, canned Bing cherries (rinsed and well-drained), canned or fresh peaches or nectarines, canned fruit cocktail or fruits for salad, fresh apples, canned or fresh seedless grapes, fresh bananas, fresh cantaloupe, chopped dates. Do not use fresh pineapple or fresh papaya in this recipe.*

Waldorf Salad

If you have never tried Waldorf Salad made with Hampshire Sour Cream, you have never tasted it at its best.

1 cup (½ pint) Knudsen
   Hampshire Sour Cream
1 tablespoon sugar
½ teaspoon salt
1 tablespoon lemon juice
2 medium-large red eating
   apples (about 3 cups diced)
1 cup chopped celery
½ cup chopped walnuts

1. Combine sour cream, sugar, salt and lemon juice. Refrigerate.
2. Core and dice unpeeled apples; fold immediately into dressing. Fold in celery and walnuts. Serve immediately.

   Makes 6 servings.

TROPICAL WALDORF SALAD: Substitute 1 cup diced banana or well-drained pineapple tidbits for 1 cup of apple.

CALIFORNIA WALDORF SALAD: Add a few raisins or chopped dates.

PARTY WALDORF SALAD: Substitute 1 cup miniature marshmallows for sugar.

Tropical Medley

Coat chunks of fresh banana in Hampshire Sour Cream and roll in coconut. Arrange on lettuce lined salad plates with pineapple spears and papaya or cantaloupe wedges. A beautiful and delicious salad.

Fruit Salad Garnishes

Garnish fresh or canned fruit salads with one of the following.

DANISH CHEESE BALLS: Blend 1 (4-oz.) package blue cheese with 1 (8-oz.) package Knudsen Cream Cheese. Soften with cream or a little lemon juice, if desired. Form into balls and roll in finely chopped walnuts. Especially good with pineapple or pears.

GINGER CHEESE BALLS: Combine 1 (8-oz.) package Knudsen Cream Cheese with 1 tablespoon plus 1 teaspoon minced crystallized ginger and ¼ teaspoon salt. Soften with cream, if desired. Form into balls and roll in finely chopped walnuts. Try with pears, peaches, pineapple, apples or apricots.

Frozen Fruit Delight

In many formal menus a sherbet is served between or following rich courses to refresh the palate. The cold sweet-tart flavor of a frozen fruit salad provides a similar refreshing quality. Here is a salad that will be equally welcome with a warm weather dinner or a winter holiday feast.

One 9-inch square baking dish

1 (1-pound) can apricot halves
1 (1-pound) can pineapple tidbits
1 (11-ounce) can mandarin orange segments
1½ teaspoons unflavored gelatin
1 (3-oz.) package Knudsen Cream Cheese, at room temperature
1 cup (½ pint) Knudsen Hampshire Sour Cream
⅓ cup sugar
1 cup (½ pint) Knudsen Whipping Cream, whipped
⅔ cup diced pecans (optional)

1. Turn freezer to coldest setting. Drain canned fruits; reserve syrup. Dice apricots.
2. Soften gelatin in ¼ cup syrup in a cup; place cup in pan of simmering water until gelatin is dissolved.
3. Beat cream cheese until smooth; gradually blend in sour cream, sugar, dissolved gelatin and additional ¼ cup syrup.
4. Fold in whipped cream, drained fruits and pecans, if desired.
5. Spoon into baking dish; cover tightly with foil and freeze.
6. Move salad from freezer to refrigerator 1 hour before serving.

Note: If this salad is to be frozen more than 2 days, omit pecans.

Makes 12 servings.

FROZEN YOGURT DELIGHT: Omit sugar. Substitute 1 (8-oz.) carton Knudsen Pineapple Fruit-Blended Yogurt for Hampshire Sour Cream. Substitute 1 (3½-oz.) can flaked coconut for pecans.

MISCELLANEOUS VARIATIONS OF FROZEN FRUIT DELIGHT: Substitute bananas, maraschino cherries, seedless grapes or fruit cocktail for all or part of the fruit. Toasted almonds may be substituted for pecans.

Vegetable Salads

The next time a vegetable salad seems the best choice in a menu, resist the urge to serve your "old standard" tossed salad. Try a new green salad combination or look to some of our favorite vegetable salad recipes. Side advantage: Most of these vegetable salads actually improve if the dressings are added several hours ahead. Leafy green salads, of course, must be dressed at the last minute.

Some Green Salad Combinations

Westerners usually serve the green salad as an appetizer — to heighten the appetite for the courses to follow. The Frenchman serves it after the entrée — to clear the taste buds for the desserts and wines to come. For many of us it is eaten with the main dish, "family style."

Whenever it is served, the difference between an ordinary green salad and a superb one depends on attention to detail in the preparation of the greens and the choice and application of the dressing. Above all, serve them *well* chilled.

SALADE ITALIANO: Assorted greens, salami triangles, marinated garbanzo beans, Bermuda onion rings and a garlic version of Basic Sour Cream Dressing or a French dressing mix made with Knudsen Hampshire Sour Cream.

MUSHROOM GREEN SALAD: Butter lettuce, sliced fresh mushrooms, chopped green onions, chopped parsley and Basic Sour Cream Dressing.

AVOCADO CUCUMBER GREEN SALAD: Romaine lettuce, sliced cucumber, chopped green onion, chunked or sliced avocado, crumbled crisp bacon and the garlic version of Basic Sour Cream Dressing.

CAESAR SALAD: Romaine lettuce, croutons, Parmesan cheese and Basic Sour Cream Dressing or Caesar dressing mix made with Knudsen Hampshire Sour Cream.

See next page for more ideas.

SPINACH SALAD: Fresh spinach, shoestring beets, chopped hard-cooked eggs, crumbled bacon and Basic Sour Cream Dressing or bacon dressing mix made with Knudsen Hampshire Sour Cream.

FAMILY TOSSED SALAD: Assorted greens, tomatoes, chopped celery, cucumber, onion, green pepper, sliced radishes, shredded red and green cabbage, grated carrot and Thousand Island, Roquefort or Basic Sour Cream Dressing.

CITRUS GREEN SALAD: Assorted mild greens, tangerine or orange wedges, Bermuda onion rings and French variation of Basic Sour Cream Dressing or a French dressing mix made with Knudsen Hampshire Sour Cream.

Hampshire Carrot and Raisin Salad

Orange and nutmeg flavors highlight this nutritious and crunchy year-round salad. It keeps for days so make a whole recipe even if your family is small.

Dressing:
½ teaspoon salt
2 tablespoons sugar
¼ to ½ teaspoon nutmeg
1 to 2 teaspoons grated
*   orange peel*
1 tablespoon plus 1 teaspoon
*   lemon juice*
1 cup (½ pint) Knudsen
*   Hampshire Sour Cream*
4 cups grated carrot (about 5
*   medium)*
1 (8¾-oz.) can crushed pine-
*   apple, well-drained*
½ cup raisins (packed)

1. Combine dressing ingredients; refrigerate to blend flavors.
2. Fold carrots, pineapple and raisins into dressing. The dressing becomes light and bubbly.

   Makes 8 servings.

Hampshire Cole Slaw

Keep this favorite in your cooking repertoire.

Dressing:
2 tablespoons lemon juice
1 teaspoon salt
2 tablespoons sugar
¼ teaspoon pepper
¼ to ½ teaspoon celery seed
¼ teaspoon paprika
1 pimiento, minced (about 2
*   tablespoons)*
1 cup (½ pint) Knudsen
*   Hampshire Sour Cream*
1 small head cabbage
*   (5 to 6 cups shredded)*
¼ cup chopped parsley
*   (packed)*
3 tablespoons chopped green
*   onion*

1. In large bowl, blend dressing ingredients; refrigerate.
2. Shred or chop cabbage and add to dressing with parsley and onion; mix and refrigerate.
3. Just before serving, toss lightly and sprinkle with paprika.

   Makes 6 servings.

Farmer's Chop Suey

Cold, crunchy and swimming in dressing. It's delicious as an accompaniment salad or as the main attraction of a summer lunch.

1 large firm cucumber, pared
   and cubed
1 medium green pepper,
   chunked
1 cup sliced red radishes
6 green onions with tender
   tops, sliced
3 medium tomatoes
½ teaspoon salt
⅛ teaspoon pepper
1 cup (½ pint) Knudsen
   Cottage Cheese
1½ cups Knudsen Hampshire
   Sour Cream
1 teaspoon lemon juice

1. Combine cucumber, green pepper, radishes and green onion in large bowl; refrigerate.
2. Just before serving, seed and chunk tomatoes; add with remaining ingredients to vegetables; mix well and serve.

Makes 6 servings.

Fresh Mushroom Salad

Mushrooms *can* be eaten raw. Try this for an eating experience you'll want to repeat.

Dressing:
   1 cup (½ pint) Knudsen
      Hampshire Sour Cream
   1 tablespoon lemon juice
   1 teaspoon salt
   1 teaspoon sugar
¼ pound very fresh mushrooms,
   washed and thinly sliced
2 green onions, thinly sliced
1 small head iceberg lettuce
2 hard-cooked eggs, grated

1. Blend dressing ingredients and refrigerate.
2. Wash and thinly slice mushrooms and green onions; refrigerate.
3. Cut lettuce into quarters and arrange on 4 salad plates.
4. *Just* before serving, fold mushrooms and onion into dressing. Spoon over lettuce and sprinkle generously with egg.

Makes 4 servings.

Cucumbers in Sour Cream

Serve sliced cucumbers simply with Hampshire Sour Cream, salt and pepper or season them in this refreshing way.

2 tablespoons lemon juice
½ teaspoon salt
⅛ teaspoon pepper
½ teaspoon paprika
½ small onion, minced
1 small clove garlic, crushed
1 cup (½ pint) Knudsen
   Hampshire Sour Cream
2 medium cucumbers, peeled
   and sliced

1. Combine all ingredients in large bowl; mix and refrigerate.
2. Toss lightly before serving.

Makes 4 to 6 servings.

CUCUMBERS AND APPLE IN SOUR CREAM: Substitute ½ apple, chopped, for onion.

CUCUMBERS IN YOGURT: Substitute Knudsen Plain Yogurt for Hampshire Sour Cream, omit paprika and add 1 teaspoon dried mint.

A salad that can be made from items on the pantry shelf is a real boon for an impromptu meal—or any time the refrigerator is bare.

Chill and drain cooked or canned vegetables. Add compatible fresh vegetables like green onion, green pepper, cucumber, radishes, celery or tomatoes, if they are available. Top or toss with a dressing selected from pages 45 to 47. Or simply add Hampshire Sour Cream seasoned with salt, pepper and herbs.

Suggested Vegetables:
Artichokes—serve with Calorie Counters' Mayonnaise, page 84
Asparagus tips
Beets, plain or pickled—cucumbers add nice contrast
Brussels sprouts
Carrots
Cauliflower—nice with beets
Corn—Mexican style or whole kernel
Sauerkraut—add green onion, apple, caraway seed, green pepper

You won't be sorry you tried this one. It's a great make-ahead salad.

Dressing:
*⅓ cup Knudsen Hampshire
  Sour Cream*
1 teaspoon lemon juice
¼ teaspoon marjoram
⅛ teaspoon Tabasco sauce
¼ teaspoon salt
Dash pepper
*1 pound zucchini, cut in
  ½-inch slices*
1 tablespoon diced pimiento
½ cup bottled Italian dressing
*½ pound fresh mushrooms,
  sliced*
2 tablespoons minced onion
½ clove garlic, crushed
Shredded Parmesan cheese

1. Blend dressing ingredients and refrigerate to blend flavors.
2. Cook zucchini in boiling salted water 3 to 5 minutes or until *just* tender; drain.
3. Marinate zucchini and pimiento in Italian dressing about 1 hour, tossing often; drain dressing into large fry pan.
4. Boil dressing until only oily portion remains. Add mushrooms, onion and garlic; sauté until tender. Drain and add to zucchini; refrigerate.
5. At serving time, toss dressing with zucchini mixture; serve and garnish with Parmesan cheese.

Makes 4 or 5 servings.

A molded salad can be very simple or it can be a highly decorative work of art. Either way, the beauty of it is that it is a do-ahead salad that can be completely ready to serve hours before you bring it to the table. If you enjoy exploring your artistic talents and experimenting with your own recipes, a molded salad is a great medium. The shape of the mold, the ingredients, their arrangement and their colors are things you can vary endlessly. The wide range of fruits, vegetables, nuts, meats, eggs and cheeses are yours to choose. There is only one caution: Do not use either fresh pineapple or fresh papaya in a molded salad. They contain enzymes that destroy the ability of gelatin to gel. Another word of caution: Serve molded gelatin salads cold and firm.

CHOOSING THE MOLD: Choose a metal mold in a size and shape that will best display the ingredients you plan to use. To make unmolding easier, oil the inside of the mold or spray it with a non-stick frying compound. Do not use glass or plastic containers as molds. They do not conduct heat well enough to unmold successfully.

MOLDING AND UNMOLDING: Here are a few tips to insure a mold that will keep its shape and have a pleasing texture:

1. One 3-ounce package of flavored gelatin or 1 envelope of plain gelatin will gel 2 cups of liquid. The first cup must be water and/or liquid that can be boiled such as fruit or vegetable juice, carbonated drink, canned fruit syrup or broth. If the liquid is too sweet the gelatin will be very soft.

   If a recipe calls for more than two 3-ounce packages of gelatin, allow only 1¾ cups liquid per package instead of the usual 2 cups. Large molds require a firmer gel.

2. Thoroughly dissolve the flavored gelatin in 1 cup of boiling liquid. This is important!

3. Part or all of the second cup of liquid can be one or more of these Knudsen Dairy Products. All dairy products should be added to liquid that is *cool* but not set.

Knudsen Cottage Cheese:	1 cup replaces ½ cup liquid.
Knudsen Hampshire Sour Cream:	1 cup replaces ½ cup liquid.
Knudsen Plain Yogurt:	1 cup replaces ¾ cup liquid.
Knudsen Fruit-Blended Yogurt:	1 cup replaces ⅔ cup liquid.
Knudsen Milk, Buttermilk, or Cream:	1 cup replaces 1 cup liquid.

4. Before adding other ingredients, allow gelatin to thicken to consistency of unbeaten egg white. Otherwise the ingredients will tend to float or sink.

5. Add up to 2 cups of other *well-drained* ingredients (such as fruit, nuts, vegetables, eggs or meat) per 3-ounce package of gelatin. Pieces should be small or salad will be fragile and difficult to serve.

6. Pour into mold and refrigerate for several hours or until firm.

7. To unmold:

   a. Pull edges of gelatin away from mold with fingers or dip a small pointed knife in warm water and run it around edge to loosen.

   b. Moisten top of mold as well as surface of chilled serving plate.

   c. Gently shake gel to loosen from mold. If the mold has not been oiled or treated, first dip it to the rim in *warm* water for about 5 seconds. Hot water will melt the gel.

   d. Place moistened plate over mold and invert. The mold should drop into place. Slide into position.

Lemon-Lime Ring Mold

One of our most requested recipes.

One 9-inch ring mold OR
one 1½-quart mold

Salad:
1 (3-oz.) package EACH lime
and lemon gelatin
2 cups boiling water
1 (8¾-oz.) can crushed
pineapple
1 cup (½ pint) Knudsen
Cottage Cheese
1 cup (½ pint) Knudsen
Hampshire Sour Cream
½ cup finely chopped walnuts
Dressing:
1 cup (½ pint) Knudsen
Hampshire Sour Cream
2 teaspoons horseradish
(optional)
Salt to taste

1. Dissolve gelatins in boiling water; add entire can of crushed pineapple and chill to consistency of unbeaten egg white.

2. Fold cottage cheese, sour cream and walnuts into thickened gelatin; pour into mold and chill until set.

3. Combine dressing ingredients; refrigerate.

4. Unmold onto lettuce lined serving platter and serve with dressing.

Makes 8 to 10 servings.

Layered Perfection Salad

For easy buffet service, the dressing is built right into this classic salad.

One 9-inch square baking dish

Salad Layer:
- 1 (3-oz.) package lemon gelatin
- 1 cup boiling water
- 1 teaspoon beef stock base
- 1 cup cold water
- 1 tablespoon white vinegar
- ¼ teaspoon salt
- ½ cup finely shredded cabbage
- ½ cup minced celery
- 2 tablespoons minced green pepper
- 2 tablespoons minced pimiento

Dressing Layer:
- 1½ teaspoons unflavored gelatin
- ¼ cup cold water
- ¾ cup boiling water
- 1 tablespoon white vinegar
- 1 teaspoon sugar
- Pinch salt
- 1 cup (½ pint) Knudsen Hampshire Sour Cream

1. Prepare salad layer. Dissolve lemon gelatin in boiling water; stir in beef stock base until dissolved. Add cold water, vinegar and salt; chill to consistency of unbeaten egg white.
2. Fold in vegetables and pour into baking dish; chill until *almost* set.
3. Meanwhile, soften gelatin for dressing layer in cold water; add boiling water and stir until dissolved. Add remaining dressing ingredients except sour cream. Cool to room temperature and blend in sour cream.
4. Pour dressing onto *almost* set salad. Chill until firm. Cut in squares and serve.

Makes 6 servings.

Snow Capped Cranberry Mold

This sweet and spicy gelatin mold should not be reserved only for the Holiday Season. Serve it with pork, game or poultry.

One 9-inch square baking dish

Salad:
- 2 envelopes unflavored gelatin
- 1 cup water
- 2 (1-pound) cans whole cranberry sauce
- 2 teaspoons grated orange peel
- ¼ teaspoon salt
- ½ cup diced walnuts

Topping:
- 2 teaspoons unflavored gelatin
- ¼ cup water
- 2 cups (1 pint) Knudsen Hampshire Sour Cream
- ¼ cup orange marmalade
- ¼ teaspoon cinnamon
- Dash salt

1. Soften gelatin for salad in ½ cup water.
2. Blend remaining ½ cup water with cranberry sauce and bring to boiling point. Add softened gelatin, orange peel and salt, stirring until gelatin is dissolved; chill to consistency of unbeaten egg white.
3. Fold in walnuts and pour into baking dish; refrigerate until almost set.
4. Soften gelatin for topping in water in a cup; place cup in pan of simmering water until gelatin is dissolved.
5. Combine sour cream, marmalade, cinnamon and salt; gradually blend in dissolved gelatin.
6. Pour topping over *almost* set cranberry gelatin. Refrigerate until set.
7. Cut into squares and serve garnished with twist of orange peel.

Makes 9 servings.

Molded Pineapple-Chutney Salad

This very sweet and spicy mold will serve as a condiment to a roast or a curried dish. A favorite with men.

One 1½ -quart mold

1 (11-oz.) can mandarin
orange segments
1 (8¾-oz.) can crushed
pineapple
2 (3-oz.) or 1 (6-oz.) package(s)
orange-pineapple gelatin
½ (10-oz.) jar mango chutney
2 (3-oz.) packages Knudsen
Cream Cheese, at room
temperature
½ cup Knudsen Hampshire
Sour Cream
1 (3½ -oz.) can flaked coconut

1. Drain fruit well; reserve syrup and add water to make 2 cups.
2. Heat syrup in medium saucepan; sprinkle gelatin over surface and stir just until gelatin is dissolved. Remove ½ cup dissolved gelatin and let stand at room temperature. Chill remaining gelatin to consistency of unbeaten egg white.
3. Mince chutney. Fold with well-drained fruit into thickened gelatin; pour into mold and chill until *almost* set.
4. Meanwhile, beat cream cheese until smooth; gradually blend in reserved gelatin and sour cream; fold in coconut. Spoon onto almost set gelatin; refrigerate until firm.
5. Unmold on lettuce lined plate and serve.

Makes 12 servings.

Fruit Ring Mold With Dressing

A most attractive buffet mold.

One 1½ -quart ring mold

Fruit Ring:
1 (11-oz.) can mandarin
orange segments
1 (1-pound) can pineapple
chunks
2 (3-oz.) or 1 (6-oz.)
package(s) orange gelatin
1 cup boiling water
1¼ cups ginger ale
2 (3-oz.) packages Knudsen
Cream Cheese
½ cup minced walnuts
12 maraschino cherries
1 recipe Basic Hampshire
Dressing for Fruit Salad made
with honey, page 47

1. Drain orange segments and pineapple chunks; reserve 1 cup syrup.
2. In large bowl, dissolve gelatin in boiling water; add reserved syrup and ginger ale; chill until slightly thickened.
3. Form cream cheese into 24 small balls; roll in nuts and chill. Drain cherries on paper towels.
4. Arrange cheese balls and cherries in bottom of ring mold. Spoon over just enough thickened gelatin to hold in place; refrigerate. Fold well-drained fruit into remaining gelatin; let stand at room temperature.
5. When gelatin in mold is *almost* set, fill with remaining gelatin-fruit mixture; chill until set.
6. Combine dressing ingredients and serve from small bowl in center of unmolded Fruit Ring Mold.

Makes 8 servings.

Molded Citrus Crunch Salad

Buttermilk gives the surprise tang in this molded salad.

One 1-quart mold

1 (1-pound) can grapefruit
sections
1 (3-oz.) package lemon gelatin
1 cup Knudsen Buttermilk
½ cup minced celery
¼ cup diced walnuts
1 (11-oz.) can mandarin orange
segments, well-drained

1. Drain grapefruit; reserve syrup and add water to make 1 cup.
2. Heat syrup in medium saucepan; add gelatin, stirring until dissolved. Cool to room temperature.
3. Blend buttermilk into cooled gelatin and chill to consistency of unbeaten egg white.
4. Fold celery, walnuts and drained fruits into thickened gelatin; spoon into mold and chill until set.
5. Unmold; serve with Hampshire Sour Cream and grated citrus peel.

Makes 4 to 6 servings.

California Fruit-Yogurt Mold

Use our plentiful California fruits in this appetizing salad.

One 1½ -quart mold OR
  six individual molds

Salad:
  ¾ cup orange juice
  1 (3-oz.) package orange
    gelatin
  ¼ teaspoon salt
  1 (8-oz.) carton Knudsen
    Orange Fruit-Blended Yogurt
  1 tablespoon lemon juice
  1 avocado, peeled and diced
  1 (11-oz.) can mandarin
    orange segments, drained
  1 (1-pound) can grapefruit
    sections, drained
  2 tablespoons chopped
    pistachio nuts (optional)
Dressing:
  Knudsen Hampshire Sour
    Cream
  Grated orange peel

1. Heat orange juice in glass, enamel or stainless steel saucepan. Add gelatin and salt, stirring until dissolved. Cool to room temperature.
2. Blend in yogurt and lemon juice; chill to consistency of unbeaten egg white.
3. Fold in remaining salad ingredients and spoon into mold; refrigerate until set.
4. Unmold on lettuce lined plate and serve with Hampshire Sour Cream, salted to taste. Garnish with orange peel.

Makes 6 servings.

Stuffed Iceberg Lettuce

Here is a different look in lettuce salads. The dressing is built right in.

1 head iceberg lettuce
1 (3-oz.) package Knudsen
  Cream Cheese, at room
  temperature
3 tablespoons Knudsen
  Hampshire Sour Cream
¼ teaspoon Worcestershire
  sauce
1 teaspoon lemon juice
½ teaspoon salt
3 tablespoons minced, peeled
  and seeded tomato
2 tablespoons grated carrot
1 tablespoon minced green pepper
1 tablespoon minced green onion
1 tablespoon minced celery
2 teaspoons minced parsley

1. Core and hollow out center of lettuce; drain on paper towels.
2. Blend cream cheese, sour cream, Worcestershire sauce, lemon juice and salt; mix in remaining vegetables.
3. Stuff lettuce with vegetable-cream cheese filling and wrap in plastic wrap. Refrigerate 5 or 6 hours.
4. Slice into wedges and serve.

Makes 6 servings.

Chilled Soups or "Liquid Salads"

The idea of serving cold soup is still a new one for most people. In spite of that, converts are not difficult to recruit. Iced soups are appetizing and refreshing. And they give freshness to a menu full of old favorites. Serve them in chilled mugs in the living room or in elegant icers at the table. Don't forget that final dollop of sour cream, particularly if you are serving Gazpacho, Danish Fruit Soup, Jellied Madrilène or any of your favorite hot soups.

Elegant Jellied Consommé

Fill a chilled cup or icer with jellied consommé; arrange a crab leg or shrimp on top, if desired. Mix Knudsen Hampshire Sour Cream with lemon juice and salt to taste. Dollop over consommé and garnish with fresh dill sprig or minced chives.

"Chili" Tomato Soup

Tomato soup never tasted like this before! And it's easy, too.

1 slice onion, about ⅛-inch
  thick
2 tablespoons sherry
1 teaspoon horseradish
¼ teaspoon salt
¼ teaspoon chili powder
¼ teaspoon Worcestershire
  sauce
1 (10½-oz.) can tomato soup
¾ cup water
1 cup (½ pint) Knudsen
  Hampshire Sour Cream

1. Put all ingredients, except sour cream, in blender jar; blend until onion is puréed. Add sour cream and blend on low speed just until well mixed.
2. Refrigerate 3 to 4 hours to blend flavors.

Makes 4 or 5 servings, ½ cup each.

Iced Middle East Cucumber Soup

Great with Shish Kabob on a warm summer evening!

1 medium cucumber
1 cup chicken broth, fresh or
  reconstituted
½-inch slice medium onion
¾ teaspoon salt
¼ to ½ teaspoon dry mint
  leaves
Dash garlic powder
½ teaspoon lemon juice
1 cup (½ pint) Knudsen
  Hampshire Sour Cream
1 (8-oz.) carton Knudsen
  Plain Yogurt

1. Peel cucumber and remove seeds; cut into thick slices. Put in blender jar with broth, onion, seasonings and lemon juice.
2. Blend until cucumber is grated fine but not liquefied. (If blender is not available, cucumber and onion can be put through food grinder.)
3. Combine sour cream and yogurt in bowl, gradually stir in cucumber mixture. Blend well and refrigerate 1 hour to blend flavors. Serve in chilled cups or bowls, garnish with chopped onion and/ or a cucumber slice.

Makes 4 to 6 servings.

Borsch à la Crème

The flavor is delightful—but it's the bright pink color that's really oustanding.

1 (8-oz.) can diced beets
1 tablespoon lemon juice
3 tablespoons minced onion
¼ teaspoon dill weed
½ teaspoon salt
1 cup (½ pint) Knudsen
  Hampshire Sour Cream

1. Put all ingredients except sour cream in blender jar; blend until smooth.
2. Empty sour cream into medium bowl; gradually blend in beet mixture.
3. Refrigerate several hours to blend flavors; salt to taste.
4. Serve in well chilled cups or bowls; garnish with sour cream and minced chives.

Makes 4 servings, ½ cup each.

Crème Vichyssoise Glacé

You'll not find Vichyssoise in a French cookbook. It was created to celebrate the opening of the Roof Garden at the Ritz Carlton Hotel in New York City in 1910. The chef patterned it after his French mother's Leek and Potato Soup.

1½ cups chicken broth, fresh
  or reconstituted
1½ cups diced raw Russet
  potato (about 1½ medium)
1 small onion, chopped
½ teaspoon salt
⅛ teaspoon dill weed
Dash white pepper
1 cup Knudsen Half and Half
1 tablespoon fresh minced
  parsley
1 cup (½ pint) Knudsen
  Hampshire Sour Cream

1. Cook potato, onion, salt, dill and pepper in chicken broth until potato is tender and breaks when pierced with a fork. Add Half and Half and parsley and blend in blender or put through a food mill. Chill.
2. Just before serving, blend in sour cream. Serve in chilled cups or bowls. Top each serving with a dollop of sour cream and sprinkle with minced chives.

Makes 4 servings, ¾ cup each.

Quick Vichyssoise

In blender jar, combine 1 (10-oz.) can frozen potato soup with 1 can buttermilk; blend until smooth. Add garlic and onion salt to taste. Serve and garnish with sour cream and minced chives.

Chilled Potavocado Soup

Add 1 peeled and chunked ripe medium avocado, ½ cup Hampshire Sour Cream, 2 teaspoons lemon juice, 3 drops Tabasco sauce and dash Worcestershire sauce to Quick Vichyssoise. Blend until smooth. Makes 6 servings, ½ cup each.

Picnic Salads

Potato, macaroni and bean salads are traditionally made with mayonnaise. Enjoy a fresh new flavor and appearance as well as lower calories by dressing these salads with half Knudsen Hampshire Sour Cream and half mayonnaise. Try our recipes or your own favorites. You'll be pleased with the difference.

Knudsen Kidney Bean Salad

An old-fashioned salad that is too often forgotten.

3 (15-oz.) cans kidney beans,
  rinsed and drained
1 cup sweet pickle relish, drained
½ cup chopped celery
4 hard-cooked eggs, minced
⅓ cup minced green onion
½ cup chopped cucumber
1 tablespoon minced pimiento
½ cup Knudsen Hampshire Sour
  Cream
½ cup mayonnaise
1 tablespoon prepared mustard
1 teaspoon champagne vinegar
1 teaspoon salt

1. Combine all ingredients; mix well and refrigerate 1 to 2 hours.
2. Just before serving, toss lightly and garnish with additional chopped green onion or red onion rings.

Makes about 8 cups or 12 to 16 servings.

Three Way Potato Salad

Depending on how much time you have—make this salad with macaroni, mashed potatoes or boiled potatoes. It is delicious all three ways.

Salad:
1¼ pounds boiling potatoes
½ cup sweet pickle juice
⅓ cup diced celery
¼ to ⅓ cup minced green onion
2 tablespoons minced pimiento
2 tablespoons minced sweet pickle
2 tablespoons sliced ripe olives, well-drained
2 hard-cooked eggs, chopped

Dressing:
¼ cup Knudsen Hampshire Sour Cream
¼ cup mayonnaise
½ teaspoon prepared mustard
½ teaspoon champagne vinegar
1 teaspoon salt
Dash white pepper

1. Cook whole potatoes in boiling salted water until fork tender; peel and cube into pickle juice; marinate 1 hour.
2. Combine dressing ingredients; refrigerate to blend flavors.
3. Drain potato; mix in remaining salad ingredients and dressing. Refrigerate until well chilled.

Note: If this salad seems dry, more dressing should be added.

Makes 4 cups or 4 to 5 servings.

MASHED POTATO SALAD: Substitute 3 cups prepared instant mashed potatoes for 1¼ pounds potatoes. (To prepare, substitute ½ cup sweet pickle juice for ½ cup of the water.) Omit step 1.

SMÖRGASBORD POTATO SALAD: Substitute dill pickle juice for sweet pickle juice and dill pickle for sweet pickle. Add 3 tablespoons minced parsley. In dressing substitute 2 teaspoons horseradish for prepared mustard.

MACARONI SALAD: Substitute 4 ounces salad macaroni, cooked and drained, for 1¼ pounds potatoes.

Main Dish Salads

When the weather is warm—and the kitchen is, too—nothing sounds more appealing or perks up sluggish appetites faster than a cool refreshing salad.

The fringe benefits of serving a main dish salad are many. They tend to be low in calories, fat and carbohydrate. They are usually relatively uncomplicated in that they don't demand that the cook has a lot of experience. They can be prepared and even garnished long before serving.

The feature that makes a main dish salad different from an appetizer or accompaniment salad is *protein*. A main dish salad will contain cottage cheese, meat, seafood or eggs to provide the protein nourishment necessary in every main dish.

Most main dish salads need only a bread and beverage to complete the menu. Then, of course, a luscious dessert, well earned by the calories saved.

Baja Shrimp Salad

We love this. Serve it from a sea shell with refried beans and tortillas. Or for a more formal luncheon, in large individual cream puff shells, page 131.

½ cup Knudsen Hampshire Sour Cream
2 tablespoons mayonnaise
1 cup diced cucumber
¼ cup minced celery
2 tablespoons minced green onion
2 tablespoons lemon or lime juice
2 teaspoons sweet pickle relish
½ teaspoon salt
¼ teaspoon oregano
¼ teaspoon tarragon
¾ pound fresh cooked medium shrimp OR 2 (6½- or 7-oz.) cans medium, deveined shrimp, well-drained
1 large avocado, peeled and diced

1. Blend all ingredients except shrimp and avocado; refrigerate 1 to 2 hours.
2. Just before serving, fold in shrimp and avocado; spoon onto lettuce lined plates and garnish with twist of lime or whole shrimp.

Makes 4 servings.

Confetti Egg Salad

Like eating delicious deviled eggs by the slice. A very economical main dish!

One 3-cup mold
1 envelope unflavored gelatin
½ cup cold water
1 tablespoon champagne vinegar or distilled vinegar
½ teaspoon salt
¾ cup Knudsen Hampshire Sour Cream
¼ cup sandwich spread
2 teaspoons prepared mustard
4 hard-cooked eggs, finely chopped*
1 cup minced celery
¼ cup minced green pepper
2 tablespoons sliced ripe olives, well-drained
2 tablespoons radish slices, halved
2 teaspoons minced green onion

1. Soften gelatin in water in a cup. Place cup in pan of simmering water until gelatin is dissolved.
2. Add vinegar and salt to dissolved gelatin; cool to room temperature.
3. Blend sour cream, sandwich spread and mustard into cooled gelatin; fold in remaining ingredients and pour into mold.
4. Chill until firm. Unmold onto lettuce lined serving platter.

Makes 4 servings.

*Use pastry blender to chop hard-cooked eggs quickly.

Crab Louis

Believed to have originated in San Francisco, Crab Louis has become a California favorite. Simply arrange chunks of cooked crab, wedges of tomato and quarters of hard-cooked egg over lettuce. Serve with a generous quantity of Hampshire Thousand Island Dressing (omit the chopped egg), page 47.

Singapore Chicken Salad

A delightful salad for a very special luncheon.

Dressing:
*¾ cup Knudsen Hampshire
    Sour Cream*
½ teaspoon salt
½ teaspoon curry powder
1 teaspoon lemon juice
*1 tablespoon minced mango
    chutney with syrup*
*2 cups chunked, skinned and
    boned cooked chicken*
*1 (1-pound 4-oz.) can pine-
    apple chunks, well-drained*
1½ cups diagonally sliced celery
½ cup toasted slivered almonds

1. Combine dressing ingredients and refrigerate to blend flavors.
2. Prepare and combine chicken, pineapple, celery and almonds; refrigerate.
3. At serving time, mix dressing with chicken mixture; spoon onto lettuce lined serving plate. For a special touch, surround with peeled cantaloupe wedges. Or use small hollowed-out pineapple halves as individual servers.

Makes 4 to 6 servings.

New England Corned Beef Mold

Don't scratch this idea until you have tried it.

One 9x5x2¾-inch loaf pan

2 envelopes unflavored gelatin
½ cup cold water
1 tablespoon beef stock base
2 cups boiling water
*1 cup (½ pint) Knudsen
    Hampshire Sour Cream*
2 tablespoons horseradish
1 teaspoon prepared mustard
½ teaspoon seasoned salt
1 (12-oz.) can corned beef
3 cups finely shredded cabbage
½ cup sliced, stuffed olives
¼ to ⅓ cup minced green onion
¼ cup diced green pepper

1. Soften gelatin in cold water. Add stock base and boiling water, stirring until gelatin dissolves; cool.
2. Blend next four ingredients into cooled gelatin; chill to consistency of unbeaten egg white.
3. Dice corned beef and add with remaining ingredients to gelatin mixture. Fold until blended; pour into pan and chill until firm.
4. Unmold and garnish with parsley. Serve with sour cream, salted to taste.

Makes 8 servings.

Salmon Mousse

If you have a fish shaped copper mold, this is the time to use it.

One 1-quart mold

1 envelope unflavored gelatin
¼ cup water
1 (1-pound) can red salmon
*1 cup (½ pint) Knudsen
    Hampshire Sour Cream*
¼ cup chili sauce
½ cup minced celery
2 tablespoons grated onion
2 tablespoons sweet pickle relish
1 tablespoon prepared mustard
1 tablespoon lemon juice
½ teaspoon salt

1. Soften gelatin in water in a cup. Place cup in pan of simmering water until gelatin is dissolved.
2. Remove skin and bones from salmon. Combine with remaining ingredients in large bowl; blend in dissolved gelatin.
3. Pour into mold and chill until firm.
4. Unmold onto lettuce lined serving platter and serve with dressing of half sour cream and half mayonnaise, salted to taste.

Makes 4 to 6 servings.

Special Touches for Familiar Foods

New thoughts and new experiences make life more fun and exciting. This joy of "discovery" can come from even very simple things. Ever think of a carton of sour cream or cottage cheese —or even leftover sour cream dip—as a source of new life and interest to your everyday cooking and eating? See what happens to familiar foods when you combine them in unexpected ways with a little sour cream or cottage cheese. Such an easy way to make mealtime more exciting! There will never again be a reason for even one spoonful of these versatile foods to go to waste.

Discover the magic that a few spoonfuls of sour cream or cottage cheese will work in many packaged, takeout or frozen convenience dishes. They immediately lose their standardized and mass-produced look and take on a fresh new flavor. These little touches will bring back that I-did-it-myself pride.

Our overscheduled life pushes us into a rut of preparing the same tried and true, quick and economical dishes that the whole family likes. Let dairy foods bring new interest to them. The simple addition of a spoonful of sour cream to everyday hamburgers, for instance, gives them a gourmet glow—whether it is mixed into the meat or spooned on top of the cooked pattie.

Think of sour cream too, as a condiment or a garnish that you use to make simple foods more attractive. Dishes will not only look better but they will taste better, too. From soup to dessert, there isn't a course in the meal that doesn't benefit. And you get all of this flavor and glamor for only 31 calories a level tablespoon.

This chapter is full of discoveries you can make right now to help you catch the brass ring on a merry-go-round of cooking and eating fun. Once you get the swing of it you'll be ready to start exploring the classic recipes in the chapters that follow.

Preceding page: Rare roast beef served with Horseradish Sauce, page 68.

Discover the newness that sour cream can add to familiar soups and salads. For only ⅓ the calories of mayonnaise!

Serving soup?

Top individual servings of canned or frozen soups with a dollop of Hampshire Sour Cream. Especially good with tomato, potato, green pea, cream of shrimp, clam chowder. Choose a garnish of crushed herbs, grated Parmesan cheese, croutons, minced chives or crumbled bacon.

If serving soup from a tureen, put a heaping spoonful of Hampshire Sour Cream in the bottom of the tureen—stir while adding the hot soup. Good for almost all soups, cream or otherwise.

Buttermilk adds a tang to canned cream soups. Blend 1 soup can of buttermilk into the concentrated soup and heat just to serving temperature. *Do not boil.* Try cream of tomato, celery, chicken or potato soups. Buttermilk has all the protein and calcium of whole milk and only half the fat.

Salad dressings simplified

Leftover or "planned-over" dips make interesting salad dressings. Or make up recipes on pages 45 to 48— especially for salads.

A little cottage cheese or sour cream can bring new life to many of your favorite but all-too-familiar main dishes.

Hamburgers

Top with leftover Roquefort Dip. Or make up the recipe on page 68, especially for hamburgers.

Steak or roast beef

Garnish with leftover horseradish dip or make up a recipe, page 68, especially for roast beef.

A new disguise for fried liver

The next time you fry liver, stir a little sour cream or leftover onion dip into the pan brownings. It makes a delicious gravy you'll really appreciate. Particularly if you're eating liver only for your health.

Meat loaf

Ground beef, meat loaf mixture, veal loaf all will have a special flavor, be more moist, and have more protein if made with cottage cheese instead of milk. Substitute cottage cheese, measure for measure, for milk in your favorite recipe or start by trying our recipe for Cottage Meat Loaf on page 88.

A can of tuna or salmon on the shelf?

Try our Tuna Noodle Favorite on page 89. Or, if you have an au gratin potato mix, try the All-In-One Dinner, page 94.

Some canned chili on the shelf?

Try our Chilimex Casserole on page 92. So easy the teen-agers can fix it themselves.

Casseroles

The most ordinary casserole takes on a party flavor when sour cream is added. Try it with some of your family favorites. Add about ½ cup Hampshire Sour Cream and 2 teaspoons flour for 4 servings. Refer to the rules for preventing curdling, page 73.

Try some of our casseroles on pages 80 to 82. Casserole Italiano, page 82, starts with a noodle mix.

For Instant Stroganoff

Blend 1 heated (14-oz.) package frozen Mushroom Sauce with Sirloin Tips into ¼ to ½ cup Hampshire Sour Cream. Heat gently and serve over hot noodles. Check tips for preventing curdling on page 73.

Beef stew

Canned or frozen beef stew makes Instant Hungarian Goulash with Hampshire Sour Cream and a generous dash of paprika. Or start from scratch with Hampshire Caraway Goulash on page 78.

Enchiladas

Enchiladas really go native topped with the cool contrast of Hampshire Sour Cream.

To make a heartier main dish out of frozen enchiladas, heat according to directions on package. Serve on heated plate; top each serving with a layer of hot green chili salsa, if desired, then a layer of Knudsen Cottage Cheese, a layer of diced avocado, a sprinkling of chopped green onion. Top with Hampshire Sour Cream. Scrumptious!

Other Mexican treats

A glass of buttermilk with any hot Mexican food will cool tender palates. It's a great flavor combination, too. A dollop of Hampshire Sour Cream will do the same on a bowl of chili, in a taco, etc., etc.

Like to marinate meat? Game meats and fowl, especially.

Sour cream and buttermilk have been used by game hunters for years to tenderize meat and to mellow flavors. Marinate meat or fowl overnight. Try sour cream with pheasant.

Buttermilk Fried Chicken

If you're a supermarket hunter, try the recipe for Garlic Fried Chicken, page 78, or this buttermilk marinated chicken with a subtle spicy flavor twist.

1 (2½ - to 4-pound) frying chicken, cut in pieces
2 to 3 cups Knudsen Buttermilk
1 cup flour
1 teaspoon curry powder
1 teaspoon salt
1 teaspoon paprika
½ teaspoon white pepper
¼ cup (½ stick) Knudsen Butter
¼ cup cooking oil
1 clove garlic, crushed

1. Place chicken pieces in deep casserole and add buttermilk to cover. Refrigerate 1 to 4 hours.
2. Combine flour, curry powder, salt, paprika and pepper in small paper bag.
3. Combine butter and oil in fry pan over medium heat; add garlic and sauté.
4. Toss lightly-drained chicken in flour mixture and brown slowly in hot fat a few pieces at a time.
5. Place browned chicken, skin side up, on shallow sided baking sheet. Bake uncovered at 350°F. 30 minutes or until tender.

Makes 4 to 6 servings.

Sauces

A carton of sour cream in the refrigerator is a beginning for an endless number of sauces. Hot and cold. Spicy and mild.

Cottage Hollandaise Sauce

A fail-proof hollandaise with a bonus of fewer calories for weight watchers.

¼ cup (½ stick) Knudsen Butter
1 cup (½ pint) Knudsen Cottage Cheese
2 eggs
1 tablespoon lemon juice
¼ teaspoon dry mustard
¼ teaspoon salt

1. Melt butter in saucepan on low heat. Add cottage cheese and heat, stirring, until curd melts slightly and mixture is warmed through.
2. Add remaining ingredients to blender jar and blend on low speed for five seconds.
3. Gradually add heated cottage cheese mixture to blender while still operating on low speed. Blend just until completely smooth.
4. Put blender jar in pan of hot water on range until serving time to keep sauce warm. Stir occasionally. Blend briefly before serving.

Makes about 1½ cups.

Basic Sour Cream Sauce

Hampshire Sour Cream right out of the carton is a delicious sauce and a beautiful garnish for so many different dishes. It is so easy to spoon onto meats, vegetables and fruits right at the table. But for a large dinner party, when there are many projects demanding attention, a sauce that can be applied in advance is a blessing.

The Basic Sour Cream Sauce can be made, and even reheated, without fear of curdling. Even if it accidentally comes to a boil, there is no disaster. It is made by simply combining a cup of white sauce with a cup of Hampshire Sour Cream. The secrets to why this sauce does not curdle are found on page 73. The sooner you make this sauce, the more delightful uses you'll find for it. Try the Can-Opener Sour Cream Sauce for a fast start. The possibilities for variation are endless.

White Sauce:
  2 tablespoons (¼ stick)
    Knudsen Butter
  2 tablespoons flour
  ½ teaspoon salt
  Dash cayenne pepper
  1 cup Knudsen Milk OR
    1 cup chicken broth
1 cup (½ pint) Knudsen
  Hampshire Sour Cream, at
  room temperature

1. On medium heat, melt butter in stainless steel, enamel or glass saucepan. Stir in flour and cook until bubbly.
2. Add milk or broth all at once and cook, stirring, until thickened and smooth. Stir in seasonings. (Omit salt if broth is used.) Add variation ingredients, if desired.
3. Empty sour cream into medium bowl; gradually add hot sauce, stirring constantly.
4. Return to pan and heat gently to serving temperature. Taste and correct seasoning.

Makes 2 cups sauce.

Can-Opener Sour Cream Sauce

1 (10½ -oz.) can white sauce
  or cream of mushroom soup
¼ teaspoon salt
1 cup (½ pint) Knudsen
  Hampshire Sour Cream,
  at room temperature

1. Combine white sauce or soup with salt in saucepan. Add variation ingredients, if desired, and heat.
2. Empty sour cream into medium bowl; gradually add hot sauce, stirring constantly. Return to pan and heat gently to serving temperature.

Makes about 2¼ cups sauce.

Variations for Sour Cream Sauces

Vary the Basic Sour Cream Sauce or Can-Opener Sour Cream Sauce in any of these ways.

PIQUANT: For tuna loaf and fish. Blend ⅛ teaspoon pepper, 2 tablespoons lemon juice, 1 teaspoon grated lemon peel and 2 teaspoons prepared mustard into sauce before adding to sour cream. Fold in 2 chopped hard-cooked eggs, if desired.

HORSERADISH: For roast beef, ground meat patties and ham. Add 1 teaspoon instant minced onion with liquid; blend 1 tablespoon prepared horseradish into thickened sauce before adding to sour cream.

CHEESE: For potatoes, cauliflower and broccoli. Blend 1 teaspoon Worcestershire sauce and 1 to 2 cups grated Cheddar cheese into sauce before adding to sour cream.

MUSTARD: For broccoli, green beans, cauliflower and ham. Use chicken broth for liquid. Add ¼ teaspoon dill weed and 4 teaspoons prepared mustard to broth.

CURRY: For carrots, onions, zucchini and green beans. Add 1 teaspoon curry powder to butter and cook for ½ minute before adding flour. Use chicken broth for liquid.

Instant White Sauce Mix

Cook 1 stick Knudsen Butter over low heat until watery portion boils off. Stir in ½ cup flour and cook until frothy; do not brown. Divide evenly into 4 small paper cups and refrigerate until firm; wrap in foil. Keeps several weeks in refrigerator; months in the freezer. *To make Instant White Sauce:* scald 1 cup milk and add 1 portion mix. Cook, stirring, until thick and smooth. Add salt and cayenne pepper to taste.

Mustard Sauce

Serve this tangy sauce with barbecued, baked, fried or broiled ham or Fondue Bourguignonne.

1 cup (½ pint) Knudsen
  Hampshire Sour Cream
2 teaspoons prepared mustard
1 teaspoon horseradish
¼ teaspoon salt

1. Blend ingredients and refrigerate.

Makes 1 cup sauce.

Roquefort Sauce

Try this on broiled or barbecued steaks or hamburger patties.

1 cup (½ pint) Knudsen
  Hampshire Sour Cream
¼ cup (1½-oz.) crumbled
  blue or Roquefort cheese
¼ teaspoon salt

1. Blend ingredients and refrigerate.

Makes 1 cup sauce.

Hampshire Orange Sauce

Serve baked or broiled chicken "à l'orange" with this simple sauce.

1 cup (½ pint) Knudsen
  Hampshire Sour Cream
¼ cup orange marmalade
¼ teaspoon salt

1. Blend ingredients in glass, enamel or stainless steel saucepan; warm slightly over very low heat.

Makes 1 cup sauce.

Horseradish Sauce

The perfect accompaniment for Roast Beef!

1 cup (½ pint) Knudsen
  Hampshire Sour Cream
1 tablespoon horseradish
¼ teaspoon salt

1. Blend ingredients and refrigerate.

Makes 1 cup sauce.

Sour Cream Sauces on Vegetables

Any compatible vegetable can be served with a sour cream sauce at the table—but not all vegetables are at their best cooked "en casserole" with sour cream. The color of the vegetable decides.

White Vegetables

White vegetables stay white when they are cooked or served in a sour cream sauce. They taste great, too.

Cauliflower, Turnips, Onions, Parsnips.

Yellow and Orange Vegetables

Yellow and orange vegetables can be cooked in a sour cream sauce or sauced at serving time. Either way they keep their beautiful color and taste great, too.

Carrots, Corn, Crookneck squash, Winter squash.

Green Vegetables

Green vegetables are the most sensitive. Long cooking causes them to gray. The presence of acid ingredients speeds this reaction. In most cases, it is best to add a sour cream sauce to green vegetables at serving time. In the case of casseroles using canned vegetables, there is no problem because the canning process has already changed their color.

Artichokes, Asparagus, Green beans, Broccoli, Brussels sprouts, Green cabbage, Peas, Celery, Zucchini.

Red Vegetables

Beets look and taste wonderful with sour cream. If they get together too soon it is the sour cream that changes color.

Sour cream belongs on tomatoes not with. It takes a great deal of care to mix tomatoes with sour cream without curdling.

Pecan Dressing

Make this elegant dressing or stuffing for Cornish game hens or pork chops.

One 3-cup casserole, buttered

1 tablespoon Knudsen Butter
¼ cup minced onion
1 egg
1½ cups soft bread crumbs, page 25
¾ cup diced pecans
½ cup finely chopped celery
1 cup (½ pint) Knudsen Cottage Cheese
½ teaspoon salt
¼ teaspoon thyme
⅛ to ¼ teaspoon rosemary
⅛ teaspoon garlic salt
Buttered Bread Crumbs, page 107 (optional)

1. Sauté onion in butter.
2. Beat egg in medium bowl; blend in onion and remaining ingredients except Buttered Bread Crumbs.
3. Spoon into casserole. Sprinkle with crumbs, if desired.
4. Bake at 325°F. 45 minutes.

   Makes about 2½ cups dressing.

Vegetables, Noodles, Potatoes

When a strikingly plain entrée heads the menu, plan to serve a sauce on the potato, noodle or vegetable accompaniment.

Baked potato
Any leftover dip? Top a baked potato with it for a nice change. Onion, blue cheese, horseradish, avocado are particularly good. Or try any of the toppings especially for baked potatoes listed on page 82.

Broiled tomatoes
Give a lift to broiled tomatoes by topping them with Hampshire Sour Cream and a few minced chives.

Green vegetables
Leftover Cheddar cheese dip is great on broccoli, asparagus and Brussels sprouts. Also leftover blue cheese or onion dips are good with vegetables.

Leftover frozen or canned vegetables?
Make them into a meatless main dish—Vegetable Bake, page 96.

Cook-out?
Barbecue vegetable kabobs of mushrooms, cherry tomatoes, chunked green peppers, quartered onions and zucchini slices. Baste with oil and vinegar dressing and serve with Hampshire Herb Sauce: Mix 1 cup (½ pint) Knudsen Hampshire Sour Cream with ½ teaspoon each dill weed, tarragon and salt.

Corn on the cob
Next time try sour cream instead of butter on corn-on-the-cob. It doesn't run off—it clings! Tastes great, too!

Instant sauce for dieter's vegetables:
Heat Knudsen Cottage Cheese in saucepan over low heat. Stir until curd melts slightly and forms a sauce. Serve immediately over hot vegetables. Broccoli, asparagus, potatoes, cauliflower, Brussels sprouts are especially good. Less than 30 calories per 2 tablespoons. And a bonus of 4 grams protein!

Tip: Extended boiling may cause a flour-thickened sauce, such as Can-Opener Sour Cream Sauce or Basic Sour Cream Sauce, to thin. It is better to rewarm a cooled sauce than to continue boiling.

Quick Sour Cream Scalloped Potatoes

Improve on packaged scalloped and au gratin potatoes with Hampshire Sour Cream. Gives a fresh flavor.

One 1½ -quart baking dish

*1 (6½ -oz.) package
  scalloped potato mix*
*½ cup Knudsen Hampshire Sour
  Cream, at room temperature*
2 teaspoons flour
Buttered Bread Crumbs, page 107

1. Prepare scalloped potatoes according to package directions EXCEPT mix flour with dry sauce mix and blend into sour cream before adding to potatoes and water.
2. Sprinkle with crumbs and bake according to package directions.

   Makes 4 to 6 servings.

QUICK SOUR CREAM AU GRATIN POTATOES: Substitute 1 (6¼ - or 6½ -oz.) package au gratin potato mix for scalloped potato mix.

Instant Hampshire Mashed Potatoes

Prepare 4 servings of instant mashed potatoes according to package directions EXCEPT substitute ½ cup Hampshire Sour Cream or Knudsen Buttermilk for milk. Or start from scratch with the recipe on page 83.

Try the Secret Treasure Potato Casserole, page 95, if you still have some instant mashed potato mix.

Quick Noodles Romanoff

If a mix isn't handy, make your own from fresh ingredients from the recipe on page 94.

*1 (4-serving) package Noodles
  Romanoff mix*
*1 cup (½ pint) Knudsen Cottage
  Cheese*
*¼ cup crushed cheese and
  garlic croutons*

1. Prepare Noodles Romanoff according to package directions EXCEPT reduce milk to ¼ cup.
2. Add cottage cheese and stir until melted. Garnish with crushed croutons and serve.

   Makes 4 servings.

Desserts

A spoonful of sour cream is the Fairy Godmother that can make a glamorous Cinderella out of an everyday dessert.

Instant pudding mix available?
Make Mock Tapioca. Prepare a 3¼ -ounce package of instant coconut cream pudding according to package directions. Fold in up to 1 cup (½ pint) Knudsen Farmer Style Cottage Cheese and serve.

Why not an Instant Cheese Pie, page 111? More time? Make the classic version on the same page.

Try a Tropical Banana or Coconut Cream Pie, page 131.

Planning a simple fruit dessert? Make it glamorous!
Simply spoon Hampshire Sour Cream right from the carton onto any fresh, canned or frozen fruits. Or go one more step by making one of the easy sour cream toppings on pages 141 and 142.

A can of peaches on the shelf?
How about a Quick Hampshire Brûlée for dessert, page 140?

New twist on strawberry or peach shortcake
Spoon sugared cut strawberries or peaches over sponge cakes or split biscuits. Top with the *perfect* complement—Whipped Hampshire Crème Fraîche, page 142. It's even better than whipped cream.

Thompson seedless grapes in the refrigerator?
Make Grapes à la Suisse. Sweeten Hampshire Sour Cream with brown sugar. Serve over seedless grapes. Try Strawberries à la Suisse next.

Sour Cream Main Dishes & Vegetables

To explore any of the great cuisines of the world in any depth means to uncover some equally great sauces. In France and China, for example, where cooking has reached a fine art, the sauce is probably the most treasured expression. For it is the sauce that is the bearer of the subtle spice and broth flavors. In this medium these flavors are so ready to escape and tantalize the tastebuds. Actually, the enjoyment of a sauce begins before it touches the tongue. Visually it gives a moistness and softness to a dish. And the delicate flavors escape as teasing aromas to suggest the experience to come. No meal is at its very best without a sauce.

The sauce on a dish is the tattletale of its origin. In each ethnic cuisine certain sauces dominate. The sour cream sauce is the foundation of the cookery of many peoples. What would Hungarian cookery be without goulash? Russian cookery without Stroganoff? Sour cream sauces are basic throughout the Middle East, the Balkan countries and into Austria and Switzerland. They are enjoyed as far North as Scandinavia and as far East as India. And deservedly so! What more harmonious companion could meats, pastas and vegetables have? The mild tartness of the sour cream enhances subtle flavors and tempers strong ones at the same time.

Here is a chapter of recipes with roots reaching from all over the globe. Before you begin your exploration, take time to read the next page and find out how to treat sour cream sauces. They are precious and deserve a little special attention. Then—welcome to the world of saucery!

Preceding page: Fillet of Sole Gourmet, page 77.

The satisfaction of having served your friends a Stroganoff, a Goulash or a Chicken Paprika that hasn't curdled—and won't be curdled when it is reheated a few days later—is tremendous. By being aware of a few rules—it can happen to you. First it is necessary to understand when and why the sensitive proteins in dairy products will curdle.

There is normally more than one cause for curdling—usually too much heat in combination with one of the other possibilities. Here are the factors that can cause milk, or in this case, sour cream, to curdle.

1. Heat—too much, too fast or too long.
2. Acid—from foods such as tomatoes, citrus juices, vinegar, pickles.
3. Salt—too much or all in one spot.
4. Alcohol—from wines or liquors used.

Most sour cream recipes can be made safe, without changing ingredients, by simply adjusting the procedure. Here are some rules to follow. The time taken to understand these rules will be well worth it because they apply to all milk sauces, cream soups, scalloped potatoes and such eating delights as Chicken Paprika and Hungarian Goulash.

1. Bring the sour cream from the refrigerator before you start preparing the dish so that it will be at room temperature before being combined with hot ingredients.
2. Have all acid, spice, salt, and alcohol ingredients added to the meat sauce or white sauce before it is combined with the sour cream.
3. Salt lightly. Ham and dried beef are sources of salt.
4. After wine or liquor are added, boil the sauce a while to evaporate the alcohol before combining it with the sour cream.
5. The addition of flour actually guards against curdling. Add 2 tablespoons per cup of sour cream. It should be blended with fat or cold water and fully cooked in the sauce before combining with sour cream. Or it can be added directly to the sour cream. Egg yolk also inhibits curdling somewhat.
6. *Most important: Remove the white sauce or meat sauce from the heat and gradually add it to the room temperature sour cream—not the reverse.* This way, if there is excessive salt, alcohol or acid in the gravy it will not overwhelm the sour cream. Repeat: *Do not add cold sour cream directly to a bubbling hot sauce!*
7. Add the hot sauce to the sour cream just before serving and warm gently. *Always use low heat when warming or holding a milk or sour cream sauce.*
8. Do not cover the pan once the sour cream is added. The heat and steam held under the lid can encourage curdling.
9. A false curdling may occur if there is free fat in the gravy. Avoid this by pouring excess fat from the meat or skimming it from the sauce before adding it to the sour cream. If there is still some fat floating on the surface and if the sauce is quite thick, add a little water and both problems will be solved.
10. Observing all of these rules will not absolutely guarantee a perfect sauce but it is very good insurance. Foods are natural products and therefore vary in subtle ways from day to day, season to season. These changes affect the very delicate balance of a sour cream sauce. There will even be days when you can break many of these guides and still have a smooth sour cream sauce.

Beef Stroganoff

Count Paul Stroganoff is better known for the dish named after him than he is for the service he did for Ivan the Terrible in conquering Siberia. It was in St. Petersburg around the Gay Nineties that he flourished and gave his name to this world loved beef dish—made with a Russian sauce and a French technique. It is believed that the original recipe contained neither tomato paste nor mushrooms but a dash of mustard instead. Here is a classic American Stroganoff to suit American tastes. If you wish to prepare it in advance for freezing, leave out the sour cream. Add it just before serving.

¼ cup (½ stick) Knudsen Butter
½ pound fresh mushrooms
¾ cup finely chopped onion
¼ cup flour
¾ teaspoon salt
1½ pounds beef sirloin tip, cut in strips ½-inch thick by 2-inches long
Cooking oil as necessary
1 (10½-oz.) can or 1⅓ cups beef bouillon
3 tablespoons tomato paste (optional)
1 teaspoon Worcestershire sauce
½ teaspoon MSG (monosodium glutamate)
1 cup (½ pint) Knudsen Hampshire Sour Cream, at room temperature

1. Melt butter in fry pan. Wash, drain and slice mushrooms. Sauté mushrooms and onion separately until golden. Using slotted spoon, remove to side plate.
2. Combine flour and salt in paper bag; add beef strips and shake to dredge.
3. Brown meat, a few pieces at a time, in butter remaining in pan. Remove to side dish as soon as browned on both sides. Add oil as necessary.
4. Pour off excess fat. Return meat and onions to fry pan, add bouillon, tomato paste, Worcestershire sauce and MSG; blend.
5. Cover and simmer gently until meat is tender, 30 to 45 minutes. Stir occasionally to prevent sticking. Add water, if necessary, to make about 1 cup sauce before going to next step.
6. At serving time, add mushrooms to sauce and remove from heat. Empty sour cream into medium bowl; gradually add hot sauce, stirring constantly. Return to fry pan and heat gently to serving temperature.
7. Serve over hot noodles*. Garnish with chopped parsley.

   Makes 4 to 6 servings.

ORIGINAL BEEF STROGANOFF: Omit mushrooms and tomato paste. Use beef tenderloin and reduce cooking time in step 5 to just until sauce thickens. Add ½ teaspoon mustard, if desired.

HAMBURGER STROGANOFF: Substitute about 1½ pounds ground beef for sirloin. Reduce flour to 3 tablespoons and add to hamburger after draining excess fat. Add bouillon and cook just until thickened.

Quick Hamburger Stroganoff

This quick family version is sturdy enough to stand up under boiling and extended holding. You'll enjoy the turkey and calorie conscious versions on the next page, too.

1 medium onion, chopped
2 tablespoons cooking oil
1 pound lean ground beef
1 (10½-oz.) can cream of mushroom soup
2 tablespoons catsup or chili sauce
1 small can sliced mushrooms, drained (optional)
1 cup (½ pint) Knudsen Hampshire Sour Cream, at room temperature
Salt

1. Sauté onion in oil until transparent; add beef and cook until browned. Drain excess fat.
2. Blend in soup, catsup and sliced mushrooms; heat through.
3. Remove from heat; add sour cream all at once and blend well. Heat gently to serving temperature. Salt to taste.
4. Serve over hot noodles* or rice.

   Makes 4 servings.

4 ounces of dry noodles makes 2 to 3 hearty or 4 moderate servings.

QUICK TURKEY STROGANOFF: Omit ground beef. Add 2 tablespoons sherry with soup and heat to boiling. Add 2 cups chunked leftover turkey with sour cream.

CALORIE-CONSCIOUS STROGANOFF: Stir 2 tablespoons flour into ground beef after draining excess fat. Substitute 1 cup Knudsen Buttermilk or 1 cup Knudsen Plain Yogurt for sour cream. Trims about 75 calories from each serving. Yogurt version is tangy.

Veal Strips in Hampshire Sauce

The delicious flavor of the sour cream is predominant here.

⅓ cup flour
1½ teaspoons salt
¼ teaspoon pepper
2 pounds thin veal cutlets, cut in strips
¼ cup (½ stick) Knudsen Butter
½ cup chicken broth, fresh or reconstituted OR ½ cup dry white wine
2 teaspoons minced parsley
½ teaspoon basil
1½ cups Knudsen Hampshire Sour Cream, at room temperature

1. Combine flour, salt and pepper in paper bag; add veal strips and shake to dredge.
2. Brown veal in butter. A little more butter may be added, if necessary, to complete browning.
3. Add broth, parsley and basil; cook, stirring, until thickened. Cover and simmer *very* slowly about 30 minutes or until veal is tender.
4. Empty sour cream into large bowl; gradually add hot sauce, stirring constantly. Return mixture to pan and heat gently to serving temperature.
5. Serve over hot noodles or rice. Garnish with minced parsley.

Makes 6 to 8 servings.

LAMB STRIPS IN HAMPSHIRE SAUCE: Substitute 6 to 8 shoulder lamb chops, cut in strips, for veal cutlets.

PORK STRIPS IN HAMPSHIRE SAUCE: Substitute 6 to 8 pork chops, cut in strips, for veal cutlets.

Hampshire Lobster Newburg

Wonderful aroma! Delightful flavor! Not at all difficult to make.

2 (9-oz.) packages frozen lobster tails
3 tablespoons Knudsen Butter
2 tablespoons flour
1 cup Knudsen Milk
¼ cup dry sherry
½ teaspoon salt
2 teaspoons lemon juice
2 egg yolks
1 cup (½ pint) Knudsen Hampshire Sour Cream, at room temperature

1. Thaw lobster according to package directions. Remove from shell; cut into bite-size pieces.
2. On medium heat, melt butter in stainless steel or enamel saucepan. Sauté lobster briefly in butter; remove to side plate.
3. Stir flour into remaining butter and cook until bubbly; add milk all at once and cook, stirring, until thickened. Slowly add sherry, salt and lemon juice to sauce and cook 2 minutes.
4. Beat egg yolks in small bowl and blend in sour cream; gradually add hot sauce, stirring constantly. Return to pan and cook gently 2 minutes. *Do not boil!*
5. Fold in lobster; heat gently to serving temperature. Serve over fluffy rice or in puff pastry shells.

Makes 4 servings.

Tip: Glass, enamel or teflon-lined pans are wonderful for cooking sour cream sauces. The sauce remains appetizingly white. Stainless steel pans, as long as you use a wooden spoon or a rubber spatula, are satisfactory. An unlined aluminum pan will invariably turn any milk or sour cream sauce gray.

Swedish Meat Balls

With the subtle spice flavor in these meat balls, they'll be gone in minutes.

Meat balls:
1 pound ground beef
1 egg
1 cup soft bread crumbs (1½ slices bread), page 25
1 teaspoon brown sugar
½ teaspoon salt
¼ teaspoon pepper
¼ teaspoon ginger
¼ teaspoon ground cloves
¼ teaspoon nutmeg
¼ teaspoon cinnamon
½ cup Knudsen Milk
Sauce:
2 tablespoons Knudsen Butter
2 tablespoons flour
1 cup beef broth
½ teaspoon salt
Dash cayenne
½ teaspoon Worcestershire sauce
1 cup (½ pint) Knudsen Hampshire Sour Cream, at room temperature

1. Blend meat ball ingredients thoroughly; form into 12 meat balls.
2. Fry in hot fat, about 1-inch deep, until fully cooked, turning only once. Drain on paper towels.
3. Pour off all frying fat and add butter for sauce to brownings. Stir in flour and cook until bubbly.
4. Add broth, salt, cayenne and Worcestershire sauce; cook, stirring, until thickened and bubbly.
5. Empty sour cream into large bowl, gradually add hot sauce, stirring constantly. Fold in meat balls.
6. Spoon into chafing dish, stainless steel pan or enamel pan; heat gently to serving temperature.
7. Serve with boiled potatoes or hot noodles; garnish with minced parsley.

   Makes 4 servings.

SWEDISH APPETIZER MEAT BALLS: Form 50 one-inch diameter meat balls and fry. Serve in sauce from chafing dish.

Chicken Divan

Hampshire Sour Cream adds a special touch to an already special dish.

One 13x9x2-inch baking dish

4 frying chicken breasts, halved
2 (10-oz.) packages frozen broccoli spears OR 2 to 3 pounds fresh broccoli
2 tablespoons Knudsen Butter
2 tablespoons flour
1 cup chicken broth, fresh or reconstituted
1 teaspoon Worcestershire sauce
1¼ cups grated mild Cheddar cheese
1 cup (½ pint) Knudsen Hampshire Sour Cream, at room temperature
Paprika

1. Simmer chicken in lightly salted water to cover for 25 minutes or just until cooked through. Skin and bone cooked chicken.
2. Cook broccoli and drain.
3. Over medium heat, melt butter in stainless steel, glass or enamel saucepan. Stir in flour and cook until bubbly. Add broth and Worcestershire sauce; cook, stirring, until thickened.
4. Reduce heat and stir in 1 cup of the cheese, heating gently until melted.
5. Empty sour cream into medium bowl; gradually add cheese sauce, stirring constantly. Salt to taste.
6. Arrange broccoli in 8 portions in baking dish. Top each with half a chicken breast, pour sauce over all. Sprinkle with remaining cheese and paprika.
7. Bake at 325°F. 20 minutes or until heated through. Brown under broiler, if desired.

   Makes 8 servings.

A party touch for fish fillets. A handsome buffet all-in-one main dish.

Fillet of Sole Gourmet

One 11x7x2-inch baking dish, buttered

1 (6-oz.) package white and wild rice mix
1 (10-oz.) package frozen asparagus spears OR 1½ pounds fresh asparagus
1 cup finely chopped celery
3 tablespoons Knudsen Butter
3 tablespoons flour
1 cup Knudsen Milk
½ teaspoon salt
1 teaspoon Worcestershire sauce
1 tablespoon fresh lemon juice
1 cup (½ pint) Knudsen Hampshire Sour Cream, at room temperature
6 sole fillets (1½ to 2 pounds)
½ fresh lemon
2 tablespoons Parmesan cheese
2 tablespoons sliced almonds, lightly toasted, page 95

1. Cook rice according to package directions; spoon into baking dish. Cook asparagus according to package directions; drain.

2. Meanwhile, sauté celery in butter. Stir in flour and cook 1 minute; add milk all at once and cook, stirring, until sauce thickens. Add salt, Worcestershire sauce and lemon juice.

3. Empty sour cream into medium bowl; gradually add hot sauce, stirring constantly.

4. Sprinkle fillets lightly with juice of half a lemon; salt to taste. Roll each fish fillet around 2 or 3 asparagus spears; arrange roll-ups on top of rice, lapped edge down.

5. Spoon sour cream sauce over fish; sprinkle with cheese and almonds.

6. Bake at 350°F. 25 minutes or just until fish becomes milky white and flakes easily.

Makes 6 servings.

Sour cream and paprika are ingredients that most typify Hungarian cookery. Paprika is the Hungarian word for sweet pepper. The red spice that we use so sparingly and the Hungarians use so generously is the ground red sweet pepper. It is generally accepted that the best paprika comes from Hungary. Here are these two flavors wrapped up in one delicious dish.

Hampshire Chicken Paprikash

One 11x7x2-inch baking dish

2 tablespoons flour
1 teaspoon salt
1 (2½ -pound) frying chicken, cut in pieces
2 to 3 tablespoons Knudsen Butter
1 medium onion, finely chopped
½ medium green pepper, finely chopped
1 small clove garlic, crushed
1 tablespoon flour
1 tablespoon paprika
¼ teaspoon salt
¾ cup chicken broth, fresh or reconstituted
1 cup (½ pint) Knudsen Hampshire Sour Cream, at room temperature

1. Combine 2 tablespoons flour and 1 teaspoon salt in paper bag; add chicken pieces and shake to dredge.

2. In large stainless steel, enamel or teflon-lined fry pan, brown chicken in butter; remove to side plate.

3. In same pan, sauté onion, green pepper and garlic until tender. Stir in flour, paprika and salt; cook 1 minute. Add chicken broth and cook, stirring, until thickened.

4. Return chicken to pan and simmer, covered, about 45 minutes or until tender. Remove chicken and arrange in baking dish.

5. Empty sour cream into medium bowl; gradually add hot paprika sauce, stirring constantly. Spoon sauce over chicken.

6. Place chicken under broiler a few minutes or until sauce begins to bubble.

7. Serve with hot noodles or rice. Garnish with parsley.

Makes 4 servings.

Hampshire Caraway Goulash

To say that goulash is simply beef stew does not do it justice. The paprika and sour cream give a flavor and character that have made it a world favorite. Your own home will be your favorite little Hungarian restaurant once you try this.

*2 pounds stewing beef
1 tablespoon cooking oil
6 tablespoons (¾ stick) Knudsen
  butter
3 medium onions, chopped
1 clove garlic, crushed
6 tablespoons flour
4 teaspoons paprika
1 teaspoon salt
1 cup beef broth, fresh or
  reconstituted
½ teaspoon caraway seed
½ teaspoon marjoram
1 cup (½ pint) Knudsen
  Hampshire Sour Cream,
  at room temperature*

1. Cut beef into 1-inch cubes. Brown in oil in large saucepan; remove to side plate.
2. In same pan, add butter and sauté onion and garlic until tender.
3. Stir in flour, paprika and salt; cook 1 minute. Add broth, caraway seed and marjoram; cook, stirring, until thickened.
4. Return meat to pan, cover and simmer *very* slowly 1 hour. Remove cover and simmer 2 hours longer or until meat is tender.
5. Empty sour cream into large bowl; gradually add hot meat sauce, stirring constantly. Return to pan and heat gently to serving temperature.
6. Serve over hot noodles or rice. Garnish with minced parsley.

Makes 8 servings.

Easy Hamburger Wellington

Meat loaf goes incognito — and elegant!

*Meat loaf:
  1 egg
  2 pounds lean ground beef
  1 cup (½ pint) Knudsen
    Hampshire Sour Cream
  ½ cup dry bread crumbs
  ¼ cup hamburger relish
  ¼ cup finely chopped onion
  1½ teaspoons salt
  ⅛ teaspoon pepper
  1 teaspoon Worcestershire
    sauce
1 recipe Fabulous Biscuit dough,
  page 99*

1. Preheat oven to 425°F.
2. Beat egg lightly in large bowl; mix in remaining loaf ingredients. Shape into log about 12 inches long.
3. Prepare Fabulous Biscuit dough. On well floured board, roll dough into a 12-inch square.
4. Center meat loaf on dough and wrap dough around. Moisten overlapping edges to seal.
5. Place ''log,'' overlapped edge down, on shallow-sided baking sheet. Cut several small vents in top.
6. Bake at 425°F. 10 minutes. Reduce heat to 325°F. and continue baking 1 hour.
7. Serve whole on platter. Garnish with parsley.

Makes 8 servings.

Garlic Fried Chicken

This is home fried chicken at its best.

*Marinade:
  1 cup (½ pint) Knudsen
    Hampshire Sour Cream
  2 cloves garlic, crushed
  1 tablespoon lemon juice
  1 teaspoon Worcestershire
    sauce
  1½ teaspoons seasoned salt
  ¼ teaspoon pepper
1 (2½ -pound) frying chicken
Flour and cooking oil*

1. Blend marinade ingredients in medium bowl.
2. Cut chicken into serving pieces. Dip pieces in marinade to coat; put in refrigerator dish, spoon on remaining marinade, cover and refrigerate overnight.
3. Dredge sour cream coated chicken pieces in flour and fry in hot cooking oil, 1-inch deep, until browned and crisp on both sides. Reduce heat and fry slowly until tender, about 40 minutes total. Do not crowd chicken in pan and do not cover.

Makes 4 servings.

Curry

A savory curry on fluffy rice with an assortment of condiments makes one of the most exotic and yet simple meals a hostess can serve. It is truly a one dish meal. Curry can be made with sour cream, yogurt, plain milk or coconut milk. The acid of the sour cream or yogurt enhances the curry flavor. Curry is actually a combination of spices, the variety and amounts of which vary with the locale and the cook. Turmeric, fenugreek, cumin seed, coriander and peppers are basic.

THE CONDIMENTS: Chutney is the essential condiment. Molded Pineapple-Chutney Salad, page 56, would replace the chutney and coconut condiments and it is very attractive. Select additional condiments to complement the meat in the curry. Choose from this list or add your own. Chopped peanuts, cashews or almonds; raisins; shredded coconut; chopped hard-cooked eggs; crumbled crisp fried bacon; chopped peeled and seeded tomato; chopped green pepper; chopped green onion or chives; chopped banana tossed in lemon juice.

Chicken Curry

A delicious curry with some of the condiments included.

¼ cup (½ stick) Knudsen Butter
¼ cup blanched, slivered almonds
½ cup chopped onion
½ cup chopped celery
1 tablespoon curry powder
½ teaspoon salt
¼ teaspoon pepper
¼ cup flour
1 cup chicken broth, fresh or reconstituted
½ cup seedless raisins
1 (8-oz.) can tomato sauce
1 teaspoon Worcestershire sauce
1 cup (½ pint) Knudsen Hampshire Sour Cream, at room temperature
3 to 4 cups chunked, skinned and boned, cooked chicken

1. On medium heat, sauté almonds in butter until golden. Add onion and celery; cook until onion is transparent. Add curry powder, salt and pepper; cook 1 minute.
2. Stir in flour and cook 1 minute. Add broth and cook, stirring, until sauce thickens. Mix in raisins, tomato sauce and Worcestershire sauce.
3. Combine sour cream and chicken in large bowl. Gradually add hot sauce, stirring constantly.
4. Return to pan and heat gently to serving temperature. Serve with hot rice and an assortment of condiments.

Makes 4 to 6 servings.

California Shrimp Curry

A strictly local version. It's out of this world!

¾ pound fresh or frozen shrimp
1 large tomato
1 ripe avocado
2 tablespoons fresh lime juice
3 tablespoons Knudsen Butter
1½ teaspoons curry powder
½ teaspoon salt
1 medium onion, chopped
3 tablespoons flour
½ cup chicken broth, fresh or reconstituted
1 cup (½ pint) Knudsen Hampshire Sour Cream, at room temperature

1. Cook and clean shrimp; cut into bite-size pieces. Peel, seed and chop tomato. Peel and chunk avocado; toss gently with lime juice. Set all aside.
2. Melt butter with curry powder and salt on medium heat. Add onion; sauté until transparent. Stir in flour and cook 1 minute. Add broth and cook, stirring, until sauce thickens.
3. Empty sour cream into medium bowl, gradually add hot sauce, stirring constantly; return to pan.
4. Just before serving, fold in tomato and shrimp. Heat *just* to serving temperature. Overheating at this point toughens shrimp and thins sauce.
5. Fold in avocado and lime juice and serve *immediately* over hot rice.

Makes 4 servings.

Casseroles with Sour Cream Sauces

The most ordinary casserole takes on a party flavor when sour cream is added. Try it in some of your own favorites. Follow the rules for preventing curdling on page 73.

Hearty Beef 'n' Corn Casserole

Hampshire Sour Cream adds a quality touch to a great "potluck" casserole.

One 13x9x2-inch baking dish

8 ounces extra wide egg noodles
1 pound lean ground beef
1 medium onion, chopped
½ teaspoon basil
½ teaspoon MSG (monosodium glutamate)
¾ teaspoon salt
½ teaspoon pepper
1 (12-oz.) can whole kernel corn, well-drained
1 (10½ -oz.) can cream of mushroom soup
1 cup (½ pint) Knudsen Hampshire Sour Cream, at room temperature
¼ cup chopped pimiento
1 cup Buttered Bread Crumbs, page 107

1. Cook noodles according to package directions, adding 1 tablespoon butter or oil to water; drain.
2. Brown beef with onion and basil in 4-quart pot; drain excess fat. Fold in noodles and remaining ingredients except crumbs.
3. Pour into baking dish and sprinkle with crumbs.
4. Bake at 375°F. 30 minutes or until bubbly. Let stand 10 minutes before serving.

Makes 6 servings.

Tortilla Chip Casserole

California kids love these flavors.

One 2½ - or 3-quart casserole, buttered

1 medium onion, finely chopped
2 tablespoons Knudsen Butter
2 (8-oz.) cans tomato sauce
1 (4-oz.) can diced green chilies
2 teaspoons leaf oregano
1 teaspoon salt
1 (8-oz.) package tortilla chips
½ pound Monterey Jack cheese, cut in ½ -inch cubes
2 to 3 cups chunked, skinned and boned, cooked chicken
1 cup (½ pint) Knudsen Hampshire Sour Cream, at room temperature
⅓ cup grated Cheddar cheese

1. Sauté onion in butter until transparent. Add tomato sauce, chilies, oregano and salt. Simmer, uncovered, for 10 minutes; remove from heat.
2. Layer in casserole, in order, half the following: tortilla chips, Jack cheese, chicken and sauce. Repeat with remaining half of ingredients.
3. Bake at 325°F. 20 minutes.
4. Remove from oven and spread sour cream over top; wreath with grated cheese. Broil just until cheese melts. Serve immediately.

Makes 6 to 8 servings.

Tip: It is possible to substitute plain yogurt or buttermilk for sour cream in most sour cream sauces. Make an exact substitution and add 2 tablespoons of flour for each cup of plain yogurt or buttermilk. The additional flour will thicken the sauce and also protect the tangier yogurt version from curdling.

Mellow Macaroni Cheese Bake

Macaroni and cheese fit for a king — and maybe even the boss and his wife.

One 2-quart casserole, buttered

8 ounces elbow macaroni
1 small onion, finely chopped
¼ cup (½ stick) Knudsen Butter
¼ cup flour
1 cup Knudsen Milk
½ teaspoon salt
1 teaspoon Worcestershire sauce
*1½ cups grated sharp Cheddar
cheese (6 ounces)*
*1 cup (½ pint) Knudsen
Hampshire Sour Cream, at
room temperature*
*½ pound bacon, crisply fried and
crumbled OR ¼ cup Buttered
Bread Crumbs, page 107 OR
½ cup grated Cheddar cheese
(optional)*

1. Cook macaroni according to package directions; drain.
2. In stainless steel, glass or enamel saucepan, sauté onion in butter until transparent; stir in flour and cook 1 minute.
3. Add milk and cook, stirring, until sauce thickens. Add salt, Worcestershire sauce and cheese; heat, stirring, until cheese melts.
4. Empty sour cream into large bowl; gradually add hot sauce, stirring constantly. Fold in macaroni.
5. Pour into casserole and sprinkle with bacon, crumbs or cheese, if desired.
6. Bake at 375°F. 25 to 30 minutes or until bubbly.

Makes 6 servings.

Tuna Noodle Casserole

New life for an old favorite.

One 3-quart casserole, buttered

*8 ounces egg noodles
or elbow macaroni*
*1 cup (½ pint) Knudsen
Hampshire Sour Cream,
at room temperature*
3 tablespoons Knudsen Butter
3 tablespoons flour
½ teaspoon salt
⅛ teaspoon pepper
*1 (10½ -oz.) can cream of
mushroom soup*
⅛ teaspoon tarragon or basil
¼ cup chopped pimiento
*2 (6½ -oz.) cans white chunk
tuna, well-drained*
*½ cup Buttered Bread Crumbs,
page 107*

1. Cook noodles or macaroni according to package directions, adding 1 tablespoon butter or oil to cooking water; drain. Empty sour cream into large bowl; fold in noodles.
2. Melt butter in saucepan. Stir in flour, salt and pepper; cook until bubbly.
3. Add mushroom soup and tarragon; cook, stirring, until mixture thickens.
4. Gradually add hot sauce to noodles and sour cream, folding continuously; fold in pimiento and tuna.
5. Pour into casserole, sprinkle with crumbs and bake at 350°F. about 20 minutes or until piping hot. Garnish with chopped parsley and serve.

Makes 6 servings.

Tip: Don't hesitate to create your own sour cream casserole. Start with one of the curdle-proof Basic Sour Cream Sauces, quick or regular, on page 67. Add leftover cooked meat, poultry, fish, eggs, cheeses, rice, potatoes, vegetables, bread crumbs, dressings, herbs, spices, condiments and other non-liquid in-gredients. Top with Buttered Bread Crumbs on page 107 and bake until heated through. Voilà! Hampshire Casserole à la You!

Casserole Italiano

A noodle mix never tasted so good!

One 11x7x2-inch baking dish

1 (6-oz.) package Italian noodle casserole mix
1 pound lean ground beef
1 tablespoon minced onion
½ cup Knudsen Hampshire Sour Cream, at room temperature
1 tablespoon flour
1 teaspoon paprika
2 tablespoons shredded Parmesan cheese
¼ teaspoon marjoram
¼ teaspoon parsley flakes
½ cup garlic and cheese croutons, crushed

1. Preheat oven to 375°F.
2. Cook noodles from mix according to package directions; drain.
3. Brown beef with onion; drain excess fat.
4. Combine noodles, beef and cheese filling mix in baking dish.
5. In medium bowl, combine sour cream, flour, paprika and tomato sauce, from mix, prepared according to package directions; blend and pour over noodles.
6. Sprinkle with Parmesan cheese, marjoram and parsley flakes. Bake 20 to 25 minutes.
7. Garnish with crushed croutons and serve.

Makes 4 servings.

Sour Cream Potato Dishes

There is no nicer flavor complement to the potato than Knudsen Hampshire Sour Cream. It needn't be limited only to baked potatoes, either. Try these ideas and look for more on page 70 of Special Touches for Familiar Foods.

Baked Potato with Sour Cream

The easiest and most nutritious way to prepare the mundane potato can be the most glamorous.

1. Select mature baking potatoes of uniform size and regular shape. Idaho Russets are the classic choice. However, the large red potato is an interesting change.
2. Wash, dry and rub potatoes with butter, shortening, oil or bacon fat. Contrary to its popularity, a potato baked in foil is not as fluffy because foil holds in moisture.
3. Stick each potato with fork to allow steam to escape; place on baking sheet.
4. Bake at 425°F. 40 to 60 minutes.* Potatoes are done when they yield easily to squeezing.
5. To serve, roll potato under hand, slash top lengthwise and, using both hands, press ends toward center until potato pops open. Fluff with fork.
6. Sprinkle salt and pepper into potato. Serve with selected toppings and garnishes listed below.

TOPPINGS:

Hampshire Sour Cream—½ pint will serve about 4
Leftover sour cream dips
Knudsen Cottage Cheese—Farmers, Velvet, Low Fat or Chive
A mixture of cottage cheese and sour cream
Hampshire Thousand Island Dressing, page 47
Knudsen Plain Yogurt, herbed and seasoned
Basic Sour Cream Sauce with cheese, page 67—1 recipe will serve about 8

GARNISHES:

Chopped chives or green onions
Crumbled crisply fried bacon
Crumbled blue cheese
Grated Cheddar cheese
Chopped parsley

Chopped green pepper
Minced pimiento
Dry or fresh herbs
Poppy, caraway or toasted sesame seeds

For baking potatoes in half the time, stick an aluminum nail through each potato from end to end. These nails can be purchased from housewares departments or novelty mail order houses.

Stuffed Baked Potatoes

Great for serving a crowd. A do-ahead recipe.

2 large baking potatoes
1 cup (½ pint) Knudsen
   Hampshire Sour Cream
2 tablespoons Knudsen Butter
½ teaspoon salt
Fresh ground pepper
2 tablespoons minced green
   onion (optional)
Salt
Grated Cheddar cheese

1. Bake potatoes according to directions on page 82.
2. Slice potatoes in half lengthwise.
3. Cup potato half in potholder protected hand. Gently scoop insides of potato into bowl, leaving just enough pulp next to skin to keep from breaking. Repeat with remaining potato halves.
4. Add sour cream, butter, salt, pepper and green onion, if desired; blend with fork until well combined but not necessarily smooth. Add salt as necessary.
5. Fill shells with potato to heaping; place on baking sheet and sprinkle with grated cheese. Potatoes may be refrigerated at this point for up to 24 hours.
6. Bake at 375°F. 10 to 15 minutes (longer if refrigerated). Brown cheese under broiler, if desired.

   Makes 4 servings.

Hampshire Mashed Potatoes

For mashed potatoes that melt in your mouth, whip them with Knudsen Hampshire Sour Cream instead of milk.

1½ pounds Russet potatoes
   (about 3 medium)
¾ cup Knudsen Hampshire Sour
   Cream
2 tablespoons Knudsen Butter
Salt to taste

1. Peel and quarter potatoes; cook in boiling salted water until potatoes break apart when pierced with fork.
2. Drain liquid from potatoes (reserve for gravy if desired); return potatoes to low heat to dry any remaining moisture.
3. Add sour cream and butter to potatoes and heat slightly.
4. Whip potatoes with electric mixer until smooth and fluffy. Salt to taste.

   Makes 4 to 6 servings.

BUTTERMILK MASHED POTATOES: Subsitute ½ cup Knudsen Buttermilk for Hampshire Sour Cream.

INSTANT HAMPSHIRE MASHED POTATOES: See page 70.

Sour Cream Scalloped Potatoes

Delicious scalloped potatoes—and they don't curdle.

One 11x7x2-inch baking dish,
   buttered

2 pounds boiling potatoes, pared
   and thinly sliced
1 medium onion, chopped
1 recipe Basic Sour Cream
   Sauce, page 67
⅛ teaspoon paprika
1 cup Buttered Bread Crumbs,
   page 107

1. Gently parboil potato and onion in salted water to cover until *just* tender, about 5 or 10 minutes. Drain.
2. Prepare Basic Sour Cream Sauce and add paprika.
3. Layer half the potato-onion mixture and half the sauce in baking dish. Repeat with remaining halves. Sprinkle with crumbs.
4. Bake uncovered at 350°F. 30 minutes or until potatoes are very tender and sauce is bubbling.

   Makes 6 to 8 servings.

SOUR CREAM AU GRATIN POTATOES: Substitute Basic Sour Cream Sauce with cheese for Basic Sour Cream Sauce.

Vegetable and Sour Cream Recipes

An interesting vegetable is a perfect complement to a steak or a roast. Sour cream is certain to add interest. Try one of these recipes or a quick add-on sauce like those found on page 67.

Artichokes California Style

Serve antichokes hot or cold with a quick and easy "dip."

TO COOK ARTICHOKES: Trim artichoke by cutting 1 inch from top and all but 1 inch from stem. Snip off tips of all exposed leaves, if desired. Drop into boiling salted water. Add ½-inch slice of lemon, 1 tablespoon oil and 1 clove garlic for each artichoke, if desired. Cook 20 to 45 minutes or until stem can be easily pierced with fork. Drain upside down. Cut off remaining stem to serve in upright position. Serve hot or cold with one of the following dips.

HAMPSHIRE DIP: Knudsen Hampshire Sour Cream, salt and pepper to taste.

LEMON HAMPSHIRE DIP: ½ cup Knudsen Hampshire Sour Cream, 2 tablespoons lemon juice, salt and pepper to taste, 1 teaspoon prepared mustard (optional).

DRAWN BUTTER: Melt Knudsen Butter and serve with hot artichokes.

CALORIE COUNTERS' MAYONNAISE: Equal parts Knudsen Hampshire Sour Cream and mayonnaise, lemon juice and salt to taste.

MISCELLANEOUS DIPS: Caesar, onion, cheese, horseradish or your choice of dip or salad dressing mix made according to package directions with Knudsen Hampshire Sour Cream.

Emerald and White Vegetable Delight

A glamorous vegetable for a buffet dinner. It tastes as good as it looks.

1 small head cauliflower
1 recipe Basic Sour Cream Sauce made with chicken broth, page 67
1 or 2 (10-oz.) packages frozen peas
Paprika
Chopped pimiento

1. Wash cauliflower; remove green outer leaves and leave whole. Cook, covered, in 1 inch of boiling water to which ½ teaspoon salt and 1 teaspoon vinegar have been added.* Cook just until tender when tested with fork, about 20 to 30 minutes.
2. Prepare Basic Sour Cream Sauce. Cook peas and drain.
3. Center cauliflower on serving platter; surround with peas and top with sauce. Garnish with paprika and chopped pimiento. Serve with remaining sauce.

Makes 4 to 6 servings.

*Vinegar added to cooking water keeps cauliflower white and firm textured.

Spinach à la Crème

The very nicest way to serve cooked spinach.

1 (10-oz.) package frozen chopped spinach
2 tablespoons Knudsen Butter
¼ cup minced onion
1 small clove garlic, crushed
1 tablespoon flour
¼ teaspoon salt
½ cup Knudsen Hampshire Sour Cream, at room temperature
1 or 2 slices bacon, crisply fried and crumbled (optional)

1. Cook spinach according to package directions; drain thoroughly in strainer.
2. Sauté onion and garlic in butter until tender; stir in flour and cook 1 minute.
3. Add drained spinach and salt; cook, stirring, over low heat until very thick.
4. Remove from heat; add sour cream all at once and blend. Fold in crumbled bacon, if desired.
5. Heat gently to serving temperature. Serve.

Makes 3 to 4 servings.

BUTTERMILK CREAMED SPINACH: Substitute ½ cup Knudsen Buttermilk for sour cream.

VERY SPECIAL SPINACH À LA CRÈME: Substitute ½ cup whipping cream for sour cream.

Broccoli en Casserole

For a green vegetable with a different twist, try broccoli this way.

One 11x7x2-inch baking dish, buttered

1 bunch fresh broccoli (about 1½ pounds) OR 2 (10-oz.) packages frozen broccoli spears
½ recipe Basic Sour Cream Sauce, page 67
1 teaspoon instant minced onion
2 to 4 tablespoons Buttered Bread Crumbs, page 107
Lemon wedges or lemon juice

1. Cook broccoli in boiling salted water until tender; drain and arrange in baking dish.
2. Prepare Basic Sour Cream Sauce; add instant minced onion.
3. Pour sauce over broccoli; sprinkle with crumbs.
4. Bake at 350°F. 15 minutes.
5. Serve with a squeeze of fresh lemon juice or lemon wedges.

Makes 4 to 6 servings.

Very Special Creamed Carrots

Carrots are wonderful for a meal with unpredictable timing. They always keep their color.

One 1-quart casserole, buttered

1 pound carrots
½ recipe Basic Sour Cream Sauce, page 67
2 tablespoons chopped parsley
1 teaspoon instant minced onion
Pepper to taste
2 to 4 tablespoons Buttered Bread Crumbs, page 107

1. Peel carrots; slice on diagonal and cook in small amount of boiling salted water until tender. Drain.
2. Prepare Basic Sour Cream Sauce; fold in carrots, parsley, onion and pepper.
3. Turn into casserole; sprinkle with crumbs.
4. Bake at 350°F. 15 minutes.

Makes 3 to 4 servings.

Zucchini with Sour Cream Topping

A most attractive way to serve zucchini.

One 11x7x2-inch baking dish

8 small zucchini
2 tablespoons Knudsen Butter, melted
1 cup (½ pint) Knudsen Hampshire Sour Cream, at room temperature
Salt and pepper to taste
½ cup shredded sharp Cheddar cheese

1. Wash and trim ends from zucchini. Cook whole zucchini in boiling salted water to cover until tender, about 10 minutes.
2. Brush zucchini with melted butter and place in baking dish.
3. Blend salt and pepper into sour cream and spread over zucchini; sprinkle with cheese.
4. Broil just until cheese melts and begins to brown. Serve immediately.

Makes 4 to 6 servings.

Spirited Sprouts

A savory, saucy vegetable for any time of year.

2 (10-oz.) packages frozen Brussels sprouts OR 2 pounds fresh Brussels sprouts
6 strips bacon
½ cup minced onion
1 teaspoon salt
¼ teaspoon Tabasco sauce
1 cup (½ pint) Knudsen Hampshire Sour Cream, at room temperature

1. Cook Brussels sprouts; drain and keep warm.
2. Fry bacon until crisp; remove and drain on paper towels.
3. Sauté onion in bacon fat until tender; drain *all* excess fat.
4. Crumble bacon and blend with onion and remaining ingredients; fold into Brussels sprouts and heat gently just to serving temperature. Serve garnished with paprika.

Makes 6 servings.

Cottage Cheese Main Dishes & Vegetables

The Chilimex Casserole shown on the preceding page contains an invisible ingredient. An ingredient that makes it more moist, more flavorful and more nutritious. It is cottage cheese. You may not think of cottage cheese as a main dish ingredient, but when you discover what advantages it brings, and how versatile it is, you will quickly accept it in this new role.

When you plan a meal, you almost automatically select a main dish that is a generous source of protein—like meat, fish, fowl, eggs or cheese. This happens whether you think of it in terms of nutrition or not. Cottage cheese, as an excellent source of complete body building protein, fits right into this company. In addition, it provides more protein for fewer calories than most common "diet" foods. Compare these figures. And the costs, too.

PROTEIN AND CALORIE CONTENTS OF COMMON LOW CALORIE MAIN DISHES

	Grams Protein	Calories
¾ cup Knudsen Farmer Style or Velvet Cottage Cheese	22.5	174
¾ cup Knudsen Low Fat Cottage Cheese	23.6	150
¼ of a broiler chicken, fried	22.4	232
1 broiled hamburger patty (¼ pound raw)	21.8	224
3 hard-cooked eggs, large size	20.7	240
2 broiled lamb rib chops, fat trimmed (½ pound raw)	21.0	238

Cottage cheese can be added to a meatless casserole to make it more hearty, to a potato or pasta dish to add flavor and replace some of the starch, or to a meat ball or meat loaf to add moisture and flavor. No matter how you plan to use it, you should be aware that when it is heated cottage cheese becomes a liquid. For this reason it must be measured as carefully as any liquid ingredient. See the inside front cover for instructions on measuring dairy foods accurately. Hot dishes, like the ones presented in this chapter, are wonderful for using any cottage cheese that you may have in the freezer. Thawed cottage cheese blends into casseroles and batters easily and gives all the benefits of fresh.

You'll find recipes in this chapter that are wonderful for calorie counters, budget watchers, protein boosters, vegetarians and all others who enjoy good cooking. Discover this whole new world of cottage cheese cookery and enjoy the raves you'll get.

Chilimex Casserole, page 92.

Main Dishes and Casseroles

Cottage cheese fits right into favorite family entrées made with hamburger and canned seafood. Mexican and Italian dishes, too. It is a perfect food to "beef" up popular meatless casseroles and packaged dinner entrées.

Cottage Meat Loaf

Meat loaf takes on a new moistness and flavor.

One 9x5x2¾-inch loaf pan

Loaf:
1 egg
1 pound lean ground beef
½ cup Knudsen Cottage Cheese
½ medium onion, minced
½ cup cracker crumbs
¼ cup minced celery
¼ cup minced green pepper
2 tablespoons toasted sesame seeds, page 25.
½ clove garlic, crushed
1 tablespoon Worcestershire sauce
½ teaspoon salt
¼ teaspoon basil
⅛ teaspoon pepper
Topping:
¼ cup catsup
2 teaspoons brown sugar
2 teaspoons prepared mustard

1. Preheat oven to 350°F.
2. Beat egg lightly in large bowl; add remaining loaf ingredients and mix thoroughly.
3. Shape into loaf; place in pan.
4. Blend topping ingredients; spread over loaf.
5. Bake 1 hour or until done. Let stand 10 minutes before slicing.

   Makes 4 to 6 servings.

Hamburger Noodle Bake

This casserole will be a family and potluck supper favorite. Cut in half for smaller groups.

One 13x9x2-inch baking dish, buttered

1 (8-oz.) package medium or wide egg noodles
1 pound lean ground beef
2 (8-oz.) cans tomato sauce
1 (8-oz.) package Knudsen Cream Cheese, at room temperature
1 cup (½ pint) Knudsen Cottage Cheese
¼ cup Knudsen Hampshire Sour Cream
⅓ cup minced green onion
1 tablespoon minced green pepper

1. Cook noodles according to package directions adding 1 tablespoon butter or oil to water; drain.
2. Brown beef in large fry pan, breaking into small pieces. Drain excess fat. Stir in tomato sauce and remove from heat.
3. Blend cream cheese to smooth; blend in cottage cheese, sour cream, onion and green pepper.
4. Spread half of noodles over bottom of baking dish; cover with cheese mixture and then remaining noodles. Top with meat sauce.
5. Bake at 350°F. 20 to 25 minutes.

   Makes 6 to 8 servings.

HAMBURGER NOODLES ITALIANO: Sauté 1 clove crushed garlic with hamburger. Add 1 teaspoon chili powder, ½ teaspoon basil, ½ teaspoon leaf oregano and a pinch ground cloves to meat sauce. Serve with shredded Parmesan cheese.

Meal-in-a-Pot

This is a delicious one-dish-meal. It could be described as a thin stew or a hearty soup. Cole slaw and French bread are perfect companions.

One 4-quart Dutch oven, buttered

2 teaspoons salt
½ teaspoon pepper
1 teaspoon paprika
2 medium potatoes
1 cup chopped celery
4 medium carrots
1 large green pepper
3 medium onions
2 pounds ground beef
1½ cups Knudsen Cottage Cheese
1 (1-pound) can stewed tomatoes

1. Combine the seasonings; set aside. Peel and thinly slice potatoes; chop celery and carrots; mince green pepper; chop or slice and ring onions. Set all aside.
2. Chunk hamburger into fry pan and brown. Drain excess fat and blend in cottage cheese.
3. In Dutch oven, layer the following in order, sprinkling seasonings over each: potatoes, celery and carrots, hamburger mixture, green pepper and onion; top with tomatoes and juice.
4. Cover and bake at 350°F. 1½ hours. Uncover for last half hour.
5. Serve in individual casseroles or soup bowls.

Makes 8 to 10 servings.

Knudsen Tuna Casserole

By request. Many Southern Californians have raised their families on this casserole.

One 1-quart casserole, buttered

2 eggs
2 cups (1 pint) Knudsen Cottage Cheese
1 (6½-oz.) can light tuna, drained and flaked
⅛ teaspoon pepper
½ teaspoon Worcestershire sauce
¼ cup soft bread crumbs, page 25
Buttered Bread Crumbs, page 107 OR crushed potato chips

1. Prepare water bath by placing large shallow pan of water in center of oven; preheat to 375°F. (Water should be deep enough to come half way up side of casserole.)
2. Beat eggs in large bowl, blend in cottage cheese, tuna and remaining ingredients except Buttered Bread Crumbs.
3. Pour into casserole and sprinkle with crumbs.
4. Set in water bath and bake 35 minutes or until just set.

Makes 4 to 6 servings.

Tuna Noodle Favorite

The kind of dish you get a craving for.

4 ounces egg noodles
1 (1⅜- or 1½-oz.) package cheese sauce mix
½ cup Knudsen Milk
1 cup (½ pint) Knudsen Cottage Cheese
½ (10-oz.) package frozen peas
1 (6½-oz.) can white chunk tuna, drained and flaked
Crushed cheese or garlic croutons

1. Cook noodles according to package directions adding 1 tablespoon butter or oil to water; drain.
2. In large saucepan, blend cheese sauce mix and milk until smooth. Add cottage cheese and cook, stirring often, until sauce boils.
3. Break up peas; add to sauce. Cook until peas are tender and sauce is smooth and thick.
4. Fold in tuna and noodles. Heat to serving temperature.
5. Turn into serving dish, sprinkle with crushed croutons and serve immediately.

Makes 4 servings.

Knudsen Crab Casserole

Everyone likes this crab and cottage cheese custard. They will never guess it's so low in calories.

One 1½ -quart casserole,
  buttered

3 eggs, separated
2 teaspoons flour
½ teaspoon salt
2 tablespoons finely minced
  onion
1½ cups Knudsen Cottage
  Cheese
1 (7-oz.) can crab, drained
1 recipe Buttered Bread Crumbs,
  page 107
Paprika

1. Prepare waterbath by placing large shallow pan of water in center of oven*; preheat to 325°F. (Water should come up 1 inch on outside of casserole.)
2. Mix egg yolks, flour, salt and onion; fold in cottage cheese.
3. Reserve several large chunks of crab. Flake remainder and fold into cheese mixture.
4. Beat egg whites until stiff but not dry; fold into crab-cheese mixture.
5. Pour into casserole and sprinkle with crumb topping. Arrange reserved crab chunks on top and dust lightly with paprika.
6. Place casserole in waterbath and bake 45 minutes or until set.

Makes 4 to 6 servings.

INDIVIDUAL CRAB CASSEROLES: Bake in buttered individual shells as directed above from 20 to 30 minutes or until set.

TUNA-CHEESE CASSEROLE: Substitute 1 (6½-oz.) can light chunk tuna, drained, for crab.

*When preparing a waterbath in an aluminum pan, put a tablespoon of vinegar in the water to prevent darkening of the metal.

Salmon Cheese Casserole

The delicate flavor of salmon combines with "planned-over" rice and Knudsen Cottage Cheese.

One 1½ -quart casserole,
  buttered

2 tablespoons Knudsen Butter,
  melted
1 (7¾-oz.) can salmon
2 eggs
2 cups cooked rice
1 cup (½ pint) Knudsen Cottage
  Cheese
2 tablespoons minced onion
2 tablespoons minced green
  pepper
2 tablespoons minced pimiento
  (optional)
1 tablespoon lemon juice
2 teaspoons prepared mustard
¼ teaspoon salt
⅛ teaspoon pepper
⅛ teaspoon rosemary, crushed
Buttered Bread Crumbs,
  page 107

1. Preheat oven to 350°F. Put butter on to melt.
2. Drain salmon and flake, removing bones and skin.
3. In medium bowl, beat eggs until fluffy; fold in salmon, melted butter and remaining ingredients except crumbs.
4. Pour into casserole; sprinkle with crumbs and bake 30 minutes or until set.

Makes 4 servings.

Tip: It takes 2⅔ quarts of milk to make 1 pint of creamed style cottage cheese.

Cottage Enchiladas

This dish is so tasty that no one will be aware that it is deliberately meatless. Serve with guacamole and Spanish rice or refried beans.

One 13x9x2-inch baking dish

1 cup (½ pint) Knudsen Hampshire Sour Cream
1½ cups Knudsen Cottage Cheese
½ teaspoon salt
⅛ teaspoon pepper
1 (7-oz.) can green chilies
¼ cup (½ stick) Knudsen Butter
10 corn tortillas
¾ pound Jack cheese, cut in strips
2 (7-oz.) cans green chili salsa OR 1¾ cups enchilada sauce prepared from mix

1. Blend sour cream, cottage cheese, salt and pepper.
2. Remove seeds from chilies, cut in strips.
3. Sauté tortillas in butter a few seconds on each side to soften; drain on paper towels.
4. Top each tortilla with about 2 spoonfuls cottage cheese mixture, reserve excess for topping. Reserve ⅓ of the Jack cheese and chili strips for garnish. Divide remaining among 10 tortillas.
5. Spread 1 can chili salsa evenly over bottom of baking dish. Roll filled tortillas and arrange in baking dish; pour remaining can chili salsa over all.
6. Cover baking dish with foil and bake at 350°F. 30 minutes or until very hot.
7. Just before serving, spoon reserved cottage cheese mixture over top and garnish with reserved chili and cheese strips. Broil until cheese is bubbly.

Makes 5 servings.

South of the Border Chili Casserole

This is a strictly gringo concoction of Mexican flavors and California convenience foods.

One 1½-quart casserole, buttered

1 (3-oz.) package Knudsen Cream Cheese, at room temperature
¾ cup Knudsen Cottage Cheese
½ cup Knudsen Hampshire Sour Cream
3 tablespoons minced green onion
2 tablespoons diced green chilies
¼ teaspoon salt
1 cup (8-oz. can) chili and beans
1 (2¼-oz.) can sliced ripe olives
2 cups corn chips
½ cup crushed corn chips
½ cup grated sharp Cheddar cheese

1. Preheat oven to 350° F.
2. Blend cream cheese until smooth; add cottage cheese, sour cream, onion, green chilies and salt; mix well.
3. Combine chili and beans with olives.
4. Layer in casserole, in order, 1 cup corn chips, cheese mixture, 1 cup corn chips, chili-olive mixture. Sprinkle with crushed chips.
5. Bake 25 minutes. Remove from oven; sprinkle with cheese and bake 5 to 8 minutes longer or until cheese is melted.

Makes 4 servings.

Chilimex Casserole

Let your teen-agers cook their own supper. They'll love this.

One 11x7x2-inch baking dish

1 cup corn bread mix
1 cup (½ pint) Knudsen Cottage Cheese
⅓ cup water
2 (15-oz.) cans chili con carne with beans
1 (12-oz.) can Mexican style corn
Pimiento strips (optional)

1. Preheat oven to 425°F.
2. In medium bowl, blend corn bread mix, cottage cheese and water. Set aside.
3. Blend chili and corn in baking dish. If chili is thin, drain the corn.
4. Drop corn bread mix by spoonfuls onto chili. Garnish with pimiento strips.
5. Bake 30 minutes or until browned and bubbling.

Makes 4 to 6 servings.

Knudsen Lasagne

This delicious Italian dish and its many variations will become a regular at your house. Great for a no-time-to-cook evening. It tastes even better if it is assembled and refrigerated for a day or two before baking.

One 11x7x2-inch baking dish

4 ounces lasagne noodles
½ pound ground beef
1½ cups thick spaghetti sauce*
2 eggs
1 cup (½ pint) Knudsen Cottage Cheese
3 tablespoons minced green onion
1 tablespoon minced parsley
¾ teaspoon salt
½ pound Mozzarella cheese, thinly sliced
¼ cup shredded Parmesan cheese

1. Cook noodles according to package directions adding 1 tablespoon butter or oil to water; drain.
2. Brown beef, breaking into pieces; drain excess fat.
3. Cover bottom of baking dish with thin layer of sauce; add beef to remaining sauce.
4. Beat eggs in medium bowl; blend in cottage cheese, green onion, parsley and salt.
5. In baking dish, layer in order half the following: noodles, cottage cheese mixture, Mozzarella slices and sauce. Repeat with remaining ingredients. Top with Parmesan cheese. At this point, lasagne may be baked or it may be covered and refrigerated for one or two days.
6. Bake at 350°F. 30 to 35 minutes (slightly longer if refrigerated) or until bubbly. Let stand 10 minutes before cutting.

Makes 4 to 6 servings.

MEATLESS LASAGNE: Omit ground beef.

TUNA LASAGNE: Omit ground beef. Add to sauce 1 (6½-oz.) can white tuna, drained and flaked.

SHRIMP LASAGNE: Omit ground beef. Cook and drain 1 (12-oz.) package frozen shrimp. Cut into pieces and add to sauce.

ITALIAN SAUSAGE LASAGNE: Omit ground beef. Add to sauce ¾-pound fresh Italian sausage, cooked and chopped.

LASAGNE FLORENTINE: Cook 1 (10-oz.) package frozen chopped spinach according to package directions. Drain thoroughly and add to cottage cheese mixture.

KNUDSEN LASAGNE FOR A CROWD: Double recipe and bake in a 13x9x2-inch baking dish.

*Use spaghetti sauce from a mix, canned or homemade. One package spaghetti sauce mix makes 2½ to 3 cups sauce. To make your own, sauté 1½ cloves minced garlic in 2 tablespoons olive oil or butter. Add 1 (1-pound) can tomato purée, 1 (6-oz.) can tomato paste, 2¼ cups water (3 tomato paste canfuls), ½ teaspoon each brown sugar, salt and basil, ¼ teaspoon oregano and ⅛ teaspoon tarragon. Simmer gently, uncovered, about 1½ hours. Makes about 3 cups.

Knudsen Manicotti

Delicious! Well worth the extra trouble.

One 13x9x2-inch baking dish

1 (5-oz.) package manicotti (12 pieces)
1 (8-oz.) package Knudsen Cream Cheese, at room temperature
1 cup (½ pint) Knudsen Cottage Cheese
¼ pound Mozzarella cheese, diced
2 eggs
1 tablespoon chopped parsley
½ teaspoon salt
⅛ teaspoon pepper
⅛ teaspoon nutmeg
½ cup sauterne wine
2½ cups meatless spaghetti sauce (canned, homemade or from mix, see page 92)
1 (3-oz.) can sliced mushrooms, drained
Grated Parmesan cheese

1. Cook manicotti, 4 at a time, in boiling salted water 5 to 6 minutes or until just done but still firm; drain.
2. Blend cream cheese with fork until smooth; mix in cottage cheese. Stir in Mozarella cheese, eggs, chopped parsley, salt, pepper and nutmeg.
3. Combine wine and spaghetti sauce; pour half into baking dish.
4. Using a knife, fill each manicotti with about ¼ cup cheese mixture; arrange in baking dish.
5. Pour remaining sauce over all. Garnish with mushroom slices.
6. Bake at 350°F. 20 to 25 minutes or until bubbly.
7. Serve with Parmesan cheese.

Makes 6 servings.

Simple Sirloin Dish

A dinner party casserole from the freezer.

One 1½ -quart casserole, buttered

1 (14-oz.) package frozen mushroom sauce with sirloin tips
4 ounces medium egg noodles
1 (3-oz.) package Knudsen Cream Cheese, at room temperature
1 cup (½ pint) Knudsen Cottage Cheese
¼ teaspoon thyme
¼ to ½ teaspoon tarragon
½ teaspoon salt
Dash pepper
¼ cup Buttered Bread Crumbs, page 107

1. Thaw or heat sirloin tips to separate meat.
2. Cook noodles according to package directions adding 1 tablespoon butter or oil to water; drain.
3. In medium bowl, blend cream cheese to smooth; blend in remaining ingredients except crumbs. Fold in noodles.
4. Layer in casserole, half the noodle-cheese mixture, all the sirloin tips and remaining half noodle-cheese mixture; sprinkle with crumbs.
5. Bake at 400°F., uncovered, 20 minutes.

Makes 4 servings.

All-in-one Dinner

For a quick meal, always have these ingredients on hand.

One 1½ -quart casserole

*¼ cup (½ stick) Knudsen Butter,
   melted*
½ cup crushed corn flakes
1 package au gratin potato mix
2 cups boiling water
*1 (1-pound) can salmon, drained,
   boned and skinned*
*1 (10-oz.) package frozen
   peas, thawed*
*1 cup (½ pint) Knudsen Cottage
   Cheese*

1. Melt butter and toss with crushed corn flakes; set aside.
2. In large bowl, blend remaining ingredients and spoon into casserole; sprinkle with buttered corn flake crumbs.
3. Bake at 400°F. 35 minutes.

   Makes 4 to 6 servings.

Pasta and Potato Dishes

Even dieters will have no reason to pass up potatoes and noodles when they are made with cottage cheese. Cottage cheese makes these dishes more moist and flavorful in addition to replacing some of the starchy foods with essential protein.

Noodles Romanoff

The perfect accompaniment for a prime rib. You'll enjoy making it.

One 2-quart casserole, buttered

*1 (8-oz.) package wide egg
   noodles*
¼ medium onion, finely chopped
2 tablespoons Knudsen Butter
2 tablespoons flour
½ teaspoon dry mustard
¾ teaspoon salt
Dash cayenne
1 cup Knudsen Milk
*½ teaspoon Worcestershire
   sauce*
Dash Tabasco sauce
*¼ cup grated sharp Cheddar
   cheese*
*1 cup (½ pint) Knudsen
   Hampshire Sour Cream,
   at room temperature*
*1 cup (½ pint) Knudsen Farmer
   Style Cottage Cheese*
*¼ cup crushed croutons or
   Buttered Bread Crumbs,
   page 107*

1. Cook noodles according to package directions adding 1 tablespoon butter or oil to water*; drain.
2. Over medium heat, sauté onion in butter until transparent. Stir in
   flour and seasonings; cook 1 minute.
3. Add milk all at once, stirring constantly, until sauce thickens. Add
   Worcestershire sauce, Tabasco sauce and Cheddar cheese; stir
   until cheese melts.
4. Empty sour cream and cottage cheese into large bowl; gradually
   add hot sauce, stirring constantly.
5. Fold noodles into sauce, spoon into casserole and sprinkle with
   crumbs.
6. Bake at 350°F. 15 minutes.

   Makes 6 to 8 servings.

A little butter or oil added to the cooking water prevents vegetables, macaroni or rice from boiling over.

Knudsen Noodle Ring

No last minute worries about sticky noodles with this attractive ring.

*One 1½-quart ring mold,
generously buttered*

4 ounces medium egg noodles
1½ cups soft bread crumbs
  (about 2 slices), page 25
2 tablespoons Knudsen Butter
2 eggs
¾ cup Knudsen Cottage Cheese
1 cup (½ pint) Knudsen
  Hampshire Sour Cream,
  at room temperature
3 tablespoons minced green
  onion
2 tablespoons minced green
  pepper
2 tablespoons minced pimiento
1 tablespoon minced parsley
½ teaspoon Worcestershire
  sauce
1 teaspoon salt
Dash pepper
Dash garlic powder

1. Preheat oven to 350°F.
2. Cook noodles according to package directions adding 1 tablespoon butter or oil to water; drain.
3. Sauté bread crumbs in butter until golden. Press crumbs firmly onto bottom and sides of ring mold.
4. Beat eggs in large bowl; blend in remaining ingredients.
5. Fold noodles into sauce and pour into mold.
6. Bake 30 minutes and unmold *immediately*. Loosen edge with knife and invert onto warmed serving plate. If desired, garnish with parsley and fill with peas or creamed meat, chicken or seafood.

Makes 4 to 6 servings.

Secret Treasure Potato Casserole

Your guests will notice the unusually good flavor of this recipe. Only *you* will know it's protein-rich *and* made from instant mashed potatoes.

One 13x9x2-inch baking dish

*Instant mashed potatoes (dry)
  for 8 servings*
2 cups (1 pint) Knudsen Farmer
  Style Cottage Cheese
½ cup Knudsen Hampshire Sour
  Cream
1 egg, slightly beaten
2 tablespoons grated onion
1½ teaspoons salt
¼ teaspoon white pepper
2 tablespoons Knudsen Butter,
  melted
½ cup toasted sliced almonds*

1. Preheat oven to 350°F.
2. Prepare potatoes according to package directions EXCEPT omit any salt, butter or milk; blend in remaining ingredients except butter and almonds.
3. Spoon into baking dish, level surface and brush with melted butter.
4. Bake 30 minutes. Lightly brown under broiler, if desired. Sprinkle with toasted almonds.

Makes 10 to 12 servings.

*To toast almonds, spread on baking sheet and bake at 325°F. until golden, about 5 minutes.

Vegetable Dishes

These vegetable dishes are so full of protein they can double as main dishes. More important than this —they taste great and add real interest to a part of the meal that is too often taken for granted.

Green and Gold Casserole

You'll want this again and again. Have it as a vegetable or a colorful meatless main dish.

One 1-quart casserole, buttered

1 pound fresh zucchini, sliced
1 (1-pound) can kernel corn
1½ cups Knudsen Farmer Style
   Cottage Cheese
2 tablespoons Knudsen
   Hampshire Sour Cream
2 tablespoons flour
¾ teaspoon salt
Dash pepper
2 dashes Tabasco sauce
2 eggs
1 to 2 tablespoons diced green
   chilies
½ cup grated Cheddar cheese
½ cup Buttered Bread Crumbs,
   page 107

1. Preheat oven to 350°F.
2. Cook zucchini in boiling salted water until just tender; drain. Drain corn.
3. In mixer bowl or blender jar, combine cottage cheese, sour cream, flour, seasonings and eggs; beat or blend until smooth. Fold in vegetables and chilies.
4. Pour into casserole; top with Cheddar cheese and Buttered Bread Crumbs. Bake 45 minutes.

Makes 4 main dish servings OR 6 protein-rich vegetable servings.

Vegetable Bake

Planned-over vegetables are the basis for this meatless casserole. Try it with frozen mixed vegetables, peas, corn, green beans, carrots, zucchini, summer squash, chopped spinach.

One 1-quart casserole, buttered

1 (3-oz.) package Knudsen
   Cream Cheese, at room
   temperature
1 cup (½ pint) Knudsen Cottage
   Cheese
2 teaspoons lemon juice
1 teaspoon salt
½ teaspoon paprika
¼ teaspoon marjoram
2 eggs, beaten
½ cup soft bread crumbs, page 25
1 tablespoon minced onion
2 cups cooked vegetables

1. Preheat oven to 350°F.
2. Blend cream cheese until smooth; mix in remaining ingredients except vegetables. Fold in vegetables and spoon into casserole.
3. Bake 20 to 25 minutes. Serve immediately.

NOTE: One (10-oz.) package frozen vegetables cooked and drained, can be used instead of 2 cups cooked vegetables.

Makes 4 main dish luncheon servings OR 6 protein-rich vegetable servings.

Italian Style Eggplant

An exciting and delicious way to give your family their first taste of eggplant.

One 11x7x2-inch baking dish

1 small eggplant, about 1 pound
Salt and pepper to taste
6 tablespoons (¾ stick) Knudsen
   Butter
1 (8-oz.) can tomato sauce
½ cup grated Swiss cheese
1 cup (½ pint) Knudsen Cottage
   Cheese
¼ cup Buttered Bread Crumbs,
   page 107

1. Preheat oven to 325°F.
2. Peel eggplant and cut into ½-inch slices; season with salt and pepper.
3. Sauté half the eggplant in half the butter until lightly browned on both sides. Repeat with remaining halves.
4. In baking dish, layer in order, half the following: eggplant, tomato sauce, Swiss cheese and cottage cheese. Repeat with remaining halves of ingredients. Top with crumbs.
5. Bake 30 minutes or until hot and bubbly.

Makes 6 servings.

Breads & Butters

It wasn't so terribly long ago that a family wouldn't have considered sitting down at the table without a plate of bread being there. The bread went on right along with the salt and the pepper —even if the menu already included potatoes, rice, *and* pasta! But times and eating habits do change. Between the calorie counters, the carbohydrate calculators and the rebels against supersoft and overwhipped bread, we have come close to cutting a major source of important nutrients out of our diet.

It certainly isn't necessary, or even desirable, to have bread, pasta and potatoes all in the same meal. But, diet or no diet, every meal should include at least one bread or cereal food. Bread isn't a frill food. Breads and cereal foods are one of the Basic Four Food Groups. They provide B vitamins and iron necessary to a balanced diet. Nutritionally a real injustice is done by severely restricting the amount of bread in the diet. It is much better to control weight by eating *all* foods in moderation.

Having to limit the amount of food we eat makes it all the more important to get maximum enjoyment from what we do eat. One way to do this is to stop treating bread like a stepchild in the menu. Plan it as part of the total balanced meal. And select it carefully to enhance the entrée. There are so many delicious breads to choose. Until the late eighteenth century breads were, for the most part, leavened with yeast. At that time a chemical was discovered in America that eventually evolved to baking soda and baking powder as we know them today. Out of this discovery came a whole new repertoire of uniquely American breads. Each area developed its own favorites to go with available meats and vegetables. Brown bread to go with baked beans. Biscuits for fried chicken. Corn bread with ham. With such a heritage, it is not difficult to find just the right bread to fit any menu.

After you have selected the right bread, make it absolutely irresistible by serving it hot, right out of the oven. Don't hesitate to bake up generous batches. Just serve what is to be eaten at one meal and freeze the rest. Reheat it for a later meal. Breads freeze beautifully and can be thawed and refrozen without damage.

Make the act of selecting and baking the right bread worthwhile by using a really good recipe —like the ones on the pages that follow! Like their early American models, they are made with baking soda and buttermilk or sour cream. This means delicious flavor and moist tender texture. It also means that little or no baking powder is used. Why this means better flavor is explained on page 116. Then give the final touch of glorious enjoyment by serving these delicious breads with real butter. After all, when you can't let yourself eat all you want, shouldn't every bite be the very best?

Preceding page: Orange Yogurt Muffins, page 100; Crusty Cheese Bread, page 103; Butter Balls, page 105; Boston Brown Bread, page 102.

Biscuits

Making biscuits from scratch is an enjoyable cooking skill that pays off in great texture and flavor. Start with Fabulous Biscuits if you're a novice and graduate to the buttermilk and sour cream versions. That magic combination of cultured dairy products and baking soda means better flavor in biscuits just as it does in cakes.

Fabulous Biscuits

This biscuit is so outstanding you'll be creating new uses for it. Besides that, it's a great way to use whipping cream that is just a little less than fresh.

2 cups biscuit mix (do not over-measure)
1 cup (½ pint) Knudsen Whipping Cream

1. Preheat oven to 450°F.
2. Combine biscuit mix and cream in mixing bowl. Mix just until dough holds together.
3. Turn onto floured board and knead lightly until smooth and elastic, about 10 strokes. Roll to ½-inch thickness and cut into 2-inch biscuits or smaller.
4. Bake on ungreased baking sheet 10 minutes.

   Makes 16 two-inch biscuits.

Buttermilk Biscuits

There isn't a time of day when these biscuits don't seem just right.

5 tablespoons Knudsen Butter, melted
2 cups sifted flour
2 teaspoons sugar
2½ teaspoons baking powder
½ teaspoon salt
¼ teaspoon baking soda
⅔ to ¾ cup Knudsen Buttermilk

1. Preheat oven to 450°F. Put butter on to melt.
2. Sift and measure flour; sift again into mixing bowl with remaining dry ingredients.
3. Make a well in center of dry ingredients; pour in buttermilk and melted butter. Stir with fork *only* until dry ingredients are moistened and dough follows fork around bowl.
4. Turn dough onto lightly floured board and knead gently about 10 strokes; roll or pat to ½-inch thickness. Using a 2-inch biscuit cutter, cut biscuits without twisting cutter.
5. Bake on ungreased baking sheet 10 to 12 minutes.

   Makes 14 two-inch biscuits.

Soft as a Cloud Sour Cream Biscuits

The name speaks for itself.

1 cup sifted flour
2 teaspoons baking powder
1 teaspoon sugar
¼ teaspoon baking soda
¼ teaspoon salt
½ cup Knudsen Hampshire Sour Cream
¼ cup Knudsen Half and Half

1. Preheat oven to 450°F.
2. Sift and measure flour; sift again with remaining dry ingredients into medium bowl.
3. In small bowl, blend sour cream and Half and Half. Make a well in center of dry ingredients; pour in sour cream mixture and stir just until dough follows fork around bowl. If too dry, add more Half and Half.
4. Turn dough onto lightly floured board and knead gently 10 to 12 strokes. Roll or pat dough to ½-inch thickness. Using 2-inch biscuit cutter, cut biscuits without twisting cutter.
5. Bake on ungreased baking sheet 10 minutes.

   Makes 8 or 9 two-inch biscuits.

Muffins

A muffin is one of the easiest quick breads there is to make. Take advantage of its simplicity by adding your own special touches. Fold raisins, chopped dates, chopped nuts, diced prunes or grated citrus peel into the finished batter. Just don't complicate things by mixing the batter too much. Muffins will only get tough.

Fluffy Buttermilk Muffins

Molasses gives the special color and flavor to this muffin.

2 tablespoons Knudsen Butter, melted
2 cups sifted flour
1 teaspoon baking powder
½ teaspoon baking soda
½ teaspoon salt
2 tablespoons sugar
1 egg
½ cup Knudsen Buttermilk
½ cup light molasses

1. Preheat oven to 400°F. Put butter on to melt.
2. Sift and measure flour; sift again with baking powder, soda, salt and sugar.
3. Beat egg in medium bowl; blend in buttermilk and molasses. Add dry ingredients and melted butter all at once, stirring just until moistened.
4. Butter muffin pan or line with paper bake cups; fill two-thirds full.
5. Bake 25 minutes.

Makes 12 medium muffins.

Sour Cream Muffins

A basic muffin to go with any meal.

2 tablespoons Knudsen Butter, melted
2 cups sifted flour
⅓ cup sugar
1 teaspoon baking powder
½ teaspoon baking soda
½ teaspoon salt
1 egg
1 cup (½ pint) Knudsen Hampshire Sour Cream
¼ cup Knudsen Milk

1. Preheat oven to 400°F. Put butter on to melt.
2. Sift and measure flour; sift again with remaining dry ingredients.
3. Beat egg in medium bowl; blend in sour cream and milk. Add dry ingredients and melted butter all at once, stirring just until moistened.
4. Butter muffin pan or line with paper bake cups; fill two-thirds full.
5. Bake 15 to 20 minutes.

Makes 12 medium muffins.

Orange Yogurt Muffins

A treat for any time or any meal of the day.

¼ cup (½ stick) Knudsen Butter, melted OR ¼ cup cooking oil
2 cups biscuit mix
¼ cup sugar
½ teaspoon baking soda
1 egg, beaten
1 (8-oz.) carton Knudsen Orange Fruit-Blended Yogurt

1. Preheat oven to 400°F. Put butter on to melt.
2. In large bowl, stir all dry ingredients until soda is evenly distributed.
3. Add egg, yogurt and melted butter; stir just until dry ingredients are moistened. Mixture will resemble soft dough.
4. Butter muffin pan or line with paper bake cups; fill two-thirds full.
5. Bake 15 minutes.

Makes 12 muffins.

ALOHA MUFFINS: Add ½ cup flaked coconut to dry ingredients and substitute Knudsen Pineapple Fruit-Blended Yogurt for orange.

PRUNE MUFFINS: Substitute Knudsen Prune Fruit-Blended Yogurt for orange.

SPICED APPLE MUFFINS: Substitute Knudsen Spiced Apple Fruit-Blended Yogurt for orange.

Buttermilk Bran Muffins

You'll make these the first time because they are so good for you. After that—just because you love them!

¼ cup (½ stick) Knudsen Butter,
   melted
1 egg
¾ cup Knudsen Buttermilk
⅓ cup light molasses
2 cups Bran Buds or All-Bran
⅔ cup sifted flour
⅓ cup sugar
1 teaspoon baking powder
½ teaspoon baking soda
½ teaspoon salt
⅛ to ¼ teaspoon allspice
⅓ cup raisins

1. Preheat oven to 400°F. Put butter on to melt.
2. Beat egg in medium bowl; blend in buttermilk and molasses.
3. Stir in bran and let stand 3 to 5 minutes.
4. Sift and measure flour; sift again with remaining dry ingredients; stir in raisins.
5. Stir melted butter into bran mixture. Add dry ingredients all at once, mixing just until moistened.
6. Butter muffin pan or line with paper bake cups; fill two-thirds full.
7. Bake 20 to 25 minutes.

   Makes 12 medium muffins.

Miscellaneous Quick Breads

All three of these breads were developed by the American colonists from foods that were uniquely available to them. They took corn from the Indians and molasses and bananas from the West Indies and combined them with their own baking powder and baking soda. The end results have become a permanent part of our American cuisine—corn bread, brown bread and banana bread.

Buttermilk Corn Bread

There are many variations for corn bread and even more names. Spider Corn Bread is named for the three legged cast iron fry pan it is baked in. This corn bread is special because it doesn't fall apart! And it is delicious, too.

One 8x8x2-inch baking dish,
   buttered and floured*

¼ cup Knudsen Butter, melted
2 eggs
¼ cup sugar
1 cup flour
⅔ cup cornmeal
2 teaspoons baking powder
¼ teaspoon baking soda
¾ teaspoon salt
1 cup Knudsen Buttermilk

1. Preheat oven to 400°F. Put butter on to melt.
2. Beat eggs in large bowl; add sugar and mix well.
3. Sift and measure flour; sift again with cornmeal, baking powder, baking soda and salt.
4. Add dry ingredients alternately with buttermilk to egg-sugar mixture.
5. Stir in melted butter and pour into baking dish.
6. Bake about 25 minutes or until a toothpick inserted in the center comes out dry.

   Makes 8 to 12 servings.

YOGURT CORN BREAD: Increase baking soda to ½ teaspoon. Substitute 1 (8-oz.) carton Knudsen Plain Yogurt for buttermilk.

SPIDER CORN BREAD: Double recipe and bake about 30 minutes in preheated buttered 10-inch cast iron fry pan.

CORN STICKS: Bake about 18 minutes in well buttered cast iron corn stick pans. Makes 12.

*For a good crust, corn bread must be baked in a glass, cast iron or dark metal pan.

Boston Brown Bread

Boston Brown Bread has been a "must" with baked beans and cole slaw since the days of the Pilgrims. Have fun baking your own.

One 9x5x2¾-inch loaf pan,
   buttered and floured

1 cup sifted flour
1 cup sifted whole-wheat flour
2 tablespoons sugar
½ teaspoon baking soda
¾ teaspoon salt
¾ cup raisins
1 egg
1 cup light or dark molasses
¾ cup Knudsen Buttermilk

1. Preheat oven to 350° F.
2. Sift and measure regular and whole-wheat flours; sift again with sugar, soda and salt. Toss raisins in flour.
3. Beat egg in large bowl; blend in molasses and buttermilk. Add dry ingredients all at once and blend well.
4. Pour into prepared loaf pan and bake 1 hour or until a toothpick inserted in crusty portion of center comes out clean.

Makes 1 loaf.

Banana Nut Bread

A great way to use those overripe bananas.

One 9x5x2¾-inch loaf pan,
   buttered and floured

2¼ cups sifted flour
¾ teaspoon baking soda
½ teaspoon salt
¼ cup (½ stick) Knudsen
   Butter, at room temperature
¾ cup sugar
2 eggs
¾ cup mashed, very ripe banana
   (2 to 3 medium bananas)
½ cup Knudsen Hampshire
   Sour Cream
½ cup finely chopped walnuts

1. Preheat oven to 350°F.
2. Sift and measure flour; sift again with soda and salt.
3. In large bowl, cream butter and sugar until light and fluffy; beat in eggs.
4. Add sifted dry ingredients alternately with banana and sour cream, mixing just until blended; stir in nuts and pour into pan.
5. Bake 1 hour or until a toothpick inserted in crusty portion of center comes out clean. Remove from pan; cool on rack.

Makes 1 loaf.

Yeast Breads

The making of yeast breads is usually reserved for those leisurely chilly days when everyone is around to enjoy the aroma of the dough while it rises and bakes. The delicious fragrance is second only to the flavor and texture of the generously buttered bread right out of the oven.

If you're a first-timer at making yeast breads, you'll want to know the following:

HOW TO SOFTEN YEAST: Dry yeast is soaked in *warm* water to reactivate it. If the water is too hot, the yeast will be destroyed. Sprinkle the dry yeast over warm water (about 110°F.) and let stand for five minutes. Before adding it to the flour, stir gently to moisten any dry particles remaining on top.

PROVIDING WARMTH FOR RISING DOUGH: The heat from the pilot in a gas oven makes a good atmosphere for yeast growth. Another good place is the top of a refrigerator or freezer that vents at the back. To use an electric oven, turn on for two minutes and turn off; wait five minutes before putting dough in oven.

Wonderful flavor! Make Hampshire Yeast Crescent dough into any conventional yeast roll shape or into the Old-Fashioned Cinnamon Rolls on page 21. In any case, don't plan on leftovers!

1 package active dry yeast
¼ cup warm water
4 cups sifted flour
1 teaspoon salt
¼ cup sugar
½ cup (1 stick) Knudsen Butter, at room temperature
2 eggs, slightly beaten
¾ cup Knudsen Hampshire Sour Cream
¾ teaspoon vanilla

1. Soften yeast in water, page 102.
2. Sift and measure flour; sift again with salt and sugar into large mixer bowl.
3. Using electric mixer, cut butter into dry ingredients until mixture resembles fine crumbs.
4. Stir in yeast, eggs, sour cream and vanilla to make a smooth dough; shape into a ball.
5. Wrap in plastic wrap and refrigerate at least 3 hours or overnight.
6. Divide dough in quarters. On well floured board, roll one quarter into a 12-inch circle; cut in 8 equal wedges. Roll each wedge starting at the wide end; curve into crescent shape. Place with point on bottom on ungreased baking sheet. Repeat with remaining dough.
7. Set pan in warm place; allow rolls to rise until doubled in size. Preheat oven to 375°F.
8. Bake 12 to 15 minutes or until golden brown.

Makes 32 crescent rolls.

Crusty Cheese Bread

Crusty, chewy and full of protein.

One 1½-quart casserole, buttered

1 package active dry yeast
¼ cup warm water
1 cup (½ pint) Knudsen Farmer Style Cottage Cheese, at room temperature
1 tablespoon sugar
1½ teaspoons salt
1 egg
2¼ to 2½ cups unsifted flour
1 tablespoon Knudsen Butter, at room temperature

1. Soften yeast in water, page 102.
2. Using electric mixer, blend softened yeast with remaining ingredients except flour and butter.
3. Add flour in ½ cup portions to form stiff dough; beat well, by hand, after each addition.
4. Cover dough and let rise in warm place until doubled in size (about 1 hour).
5. Stir down dough and turn into casserole; let rise 30 to 40 minutes longer or until almost doubled in size. Preheat oven to 350°F.
6. Bake 40 to 50 minutes or until golden brown. Brush crust with butter and serve.

Makes 1 loaf.

CHEESE-ONION BREAD: Add 1 tablespoon grated onion and 2 tablespoons toasted sesame seeds in step 2; mix in 1 cup grated sharp Cheddar cheese when stirring down dough in step 5.

Specialty Breads

Start with a ready-mix bread and turn it into a real meal-stopper. Fun and easy!

Herbed Tomato-Cheese Bread

Sour cream enhances this moist yummy bread. Serve it with steaks, chops or hamburger patties. Wrap left-over Herbed Tomato-Cheese Bread in foil and refrigerate. It reheats beautifully.

One 13x9x2-inch baking dish, buttered

Sour Cream Topping:
1 medium onion, minced
2 tablespoons Knudsen Butter
¾ cup Knudsen Hampshire Sour Cream
⅓ cup mayonnaise
4 ounces (about 1 cup) grated Cheddar cheese
¾ teaspoon salt
¼ teaspoon pepper
¼ teaspoon leaf oregano
Pinch sage

Bread Base:
2 cups biscuit mix
⅔ cup Knudsen Milk
3 medium tomatoes, peeled and sliced ¼ -inch thick
Paprika

1. Preheat oven to 400°F.
2. Sauté onion in butter until tender; blend with remaining topping ingredients and set aside.
3. Stir milk into biscuit mix to make soft dough. Turn dough onto well floured board and knead lightly 10 to 12 strokes.
4. Pat dough over bottom of baking dish, pushing dough up sides of dish to form a shallow rim.
5. Arrange tomato slices over dough. Spoon on sour cream topping and sprinkle with paprika.
6. Bake 20 to 25 minutes. Let stand about 10 minutes before cutting.

Makes 12 servings.

ITALIAN ONION CREAM BREAD: Reduce salt to ½ teaspoon. Omit Cheddar cheese, oregano, sage and tomatoes. Add to topping: 3 tablespoons minced pimiento, 2 tablespoons shredded Parmesan cheese, 1½ teaspoons minced parsley and ⅛ teaspoon basil.

Cottage Pizza Bread

Bubbly and crisp on the outside, moist and delicious on the inside. Enjoy these pizza flavors with any meal.

One 13x9x2-inch baking dish, buttered

1 (1-pound) loaf frozen ready-to-bake yeast bread
Filling:
1 egg
1 cup (½ pint) Knudsen Cottage Cheese
2 tablespoons grated Parmesan cheese
½ teaspoon basil
½ teaspoon oregano
¼ teaspoon garlic salt
¼ teaspoon pepper
1 (6-oz.) can pizza topping
½ cup grated Mozzarella cheese

1. Thaw bread and divide in half. Stretch half to fit baking dish. Press into place, forming slight rim.
2. Beat egg and blend in remaining filling ingredients. Spread evenly over dough.
3. Stretch remaining half of dough to fit pan. Place over filling and press edges to seal. Let rise until doubled in volume, about 1 hour. Preheat oven to 350°F.
4. Spread pizza topping evenly over bread. Sprinkle with Mozzarella cheese.
5. Bake 30 minutes. Let stand 5 minutes, cut in squares and serve.

Makes 9 to 12 servings.

Butter

The delightful and satisfying flavor of real butter makes almost any food taste better. The flavor of mushrooms and other vegetables sauced and sautéed in butter is incomparable. Cakes and breads made with butter have a special flavor and texture. Eggs and seafood are complemented by its flavor. And, of course, as a spread for coffeecakes, pancakes, breads and crackers, it stands alone.

Such a treasured food deserves the best of care. Like other dairy foods, butter should be kept cold and covered to protect it from oxidation and drying. Careful wrapping or covering also seals out other flavors in the refrigerator. Butter eagerly assumes most flavors—whether you want it to or not.

Many refrigerators have a special warmer compartment for storing butter at spreading consistency. This is a wonderful convenience, but it is important to store only as much butter in this area as will be used in a day or two. The warmer temperature speeds up flavor change and dries the butter. Butter in its wrapper keeps in the coldest part of the refrigerator for several weeks. For longer storage, wrap the original package with foil and freeze for up to six months. It will stay in perfect condition. Sweet (unsalted) butter should be used within a week or two or frozen for longer storage.

Butter Balls

Have Butter Balls on hand and escape showing a jam and crumb smeared stick of butter to your drop-in guests!

1 stick Knudsen Butter
Butter ball paddle set
Kettle of boiling water
Large bowl ice water
Small bowl ice water
Airtight storage container

1. Cut cold butter in half lengthwise. Cut each half in half lengthwise again, forming 4 long butter sticks. Cut each stick into 4 equal cubes.
2. Pour boiling water over ridged face of butter paddle and plunge into ice water. Repeat for second paddle. The scalding process kills any mold growths.
3. Place cold butter cube between ridged faces of paddles and revolve paddles against each other until butter cube forms a sphere.
4. Drop formed butter ball into ice water just until set. Refrigerate in airtight container. Freeze for long storage.

Makes 16 Butter Balls, 1½ teaspoons each.

Whipped Butter

Wonderful for pancakes, waffles and toast.

1. One or more sticks of butter may be whipped at one time.
2. Place butter in small bowl and leave at room temperature until slightly softened.
3. While butter is still slightly firm, beat with electric mixer on high speed until it becomes very light in color and nearly doubles in volume.
4. Spoon into serving bowl and serve, or refrigerate until serving time.

Garlic Butter

The basic of all flavored butters. It's more subtle because the garlic is par-boiled. Serve it on French bread, lamp chops, steak or hamburger.

2 to 4 cloves garlic
½ cup (1 stick) Knudsen Butter,
* at room temperature*
¼ teaspoon salt
1 tablespoon minced parsley

1. Peel garlic and drop into boiling water for 30 seconds; drain and crush.
2. Blend all ingredients well and refrigerate.

Tip: To soften butter quickly: Fill a bowl with boiling water. Empty and invert over butter dish. Butter will be spreading soft in minutes. Save butter wrappers to butter casseroles and baking pans.

Herbed Butters

Keep these butters on hand for serving on the many meats, vegetables and breads they complement so well. Form the chilled herbed butters into balls or pats and freeze.

Herb Butter

Use on mushrooms, zucchini, chicken, bread.

½ cup (1 stick) Knudsen Butter, at room temperature
2 teaspoons minced parsley
1 tablespoon minced pimiento
¼ teaspoon oregano
¼ teaspoon salt

1. Combine butter and seasonings; beat until light and fluffy.

Italian Butter

Use on zucchini, green beans, chicken, veal, bread.

½ cup (1 stick) Knudsen Butter, at room temperature
2 teaspoons lemon juice
1 tablespoon basil
½ teaspoon oregano
½ teaspoon garlic salt

1. Combine butter and seasonings; beat until light and fluffy.

Blue Cheese Butter

Use on hamburger patties, steak, bread, canapés.

½ cup (1 stick) Knudsen Butter, at room temperature
1½ ounces blue cheese
2 teaspoons dry sherry
1 tablespoon minced parsley
½ teaspoon garlic salt

1. Combine butter and seasonings; beat until light and fluffy.

Parmesan Butter

Use on French bread, zucchini, peas, pasta.

½ cup (1 stick) Knudsen Butter, at room temperature
2 teaspoons grated Parmesan cheese
1½ teaspoons basil
1½ teaspoons marjoram
¼ teaspoon salt

1. Combine butter and seasonings; beat until light and fluffy.

Lemon Butter

Use on baked or broiled fish, broccoli, spinach.

½ cup (1 stick) Knudsen Butter, at room temperature
1 tablespoon lemon juice
¼ teaspoon grated lemon peel
¼ teaspoon garlic salt
⅛ teaspoon pepper

1. Combine butter and seasonings; beat until light and fluffy.

Horseradish Butter

Use on roast beef, hamburger patties.

½ cup (1 stick) Knudsen Butter, at room temperature
2 tablespoons horseradish
¼ teaspoon garlic salt

1. Combine butter and seasonings; beat until light and fluffy.

Clarified or Drawn Butter

The common complaint about frying in butter is that it burns. It is possible to have the wonderful flavor of butter in fried foods without this problem. Clarified butter is the answer. Clarified butter is also referred to as drawn butter or in the Orient as ghee.

Butter is 80.5% fat. The remainder is milk, and, in the case of salted butter, salt. It is the protein in the milk that browns when the water evaporates. If the milky residue is removed, the butterfat can be used for frying and sautéeing without burning.

Once you have used clarified butter for frying, you'll find many more uses for it. You'll discover it coats vegetables better than unclarified butter. Serve it hot with artichokes or lobster. Most of all, you will love it for cooking eggs and for sautéeing vegetables, seafood and chicken. You won't want to be without it.

TO MAKE CLARIFIED BUTTER

1. Salted or unsalted butter can be clarified. Salt is removed in clarification.

2. Any amount of butter can be clarified at one time.

3. Melt butter in heavy pan over *low* heat. Butter separates into milky portion on the bottom and oily portion on the top.

4. Cook butter until liquid from milky portion boils off. Clear yellow oil and white fluffs of protein and salt remain. Remove from heat before browning starts.

5. Pour through fine strainer or 4 layers of cheesecloth into a glass or pottery jar that can be sealed.

6. Refrigerate, covered, until use. It will keep several weeks. For longer storage, freeze it.

BROWNED BUTTER FOR NOODLES: Melt clarified butter in saucepan. Heat until it browns slightly. Toss with freshly cooked noodles. Keeps noodles from sticking and imparts a special flavor.

TO BUTTER HOT VEGETABLES: Drain cooked vegetables thoroughly. (Save juices for soups or sauces if you like.) Add clarified butter and return to heat to evaporate excess moisture and melt butter. Hold lid on pan and toss vegetables in melted butter. Season and serve. Each piece of vegetable will be gleaming.

Buttered Bread Crumbs

Once you've had Buttered Bread Crumbs on hand, you won't be able to present a "bald" casserole again. Make up several recipes and freeze them in an airtight container. Very handy to have around.

1 slice bread (not thin slice)
1 tablespoon Knudsen Butter
1 tablespoon minced parsley (optional)

1. Tear bread into blender jar*; blend until crumbly. Tear into small bits with fingers if no blender is available.

2. Melt butter in fry pan over medium heat; toss crumbs in butter until lightly browned. Remove from heat and add parsley.

Makes ½ cup buttered crumbs.

PARMESAN CRUMBS: Add 1 to 2 tablespoons shredded Parmesan cheese.

HERBED CRUMBS: Add ½ teaspoon appropriate herb—oregano, sage, basil or marjoram.

*For best results, crumb only one slice bread at a time in blender.

Cheesecakes & Cheese Pies

Finding a clear definition of the terms "cheesecake" and "cheese pie" is very difficult. It depends on where you are, how much liberty you are willing to take with the classic recipes and how imaginative you wish to be. The origins are buried in history. The first cheesecakes may have been made by the ancient Greeks. They were mentioned in a Greek cookbook dated 250 A.D. There were so many versions on the Greek island of Samos that it came to be known as The Cheesecake Island.

To many, cheesecake is the light dry German variety made with cottage cheese. The favorite of Californians seems to be the moist, solid variety made with cream cheese. Cheese pies are almost universally made from cream cheese and may or may not be baked. There are other variations in both cheesecakes and cheese pies. The only consistent difference between them seems to be in the pan that is used. A cheese pie is baked in a pie plate and usually makes from 8 to 10 servings. A cheesecake is baked in a straight sided round cake pan and is *usually* large enough and rich enough to serve 16 to 20. An investment in a 9-inch springform pan will be enjoyed for cheesecakes and many other recipes. The big advantage of this pan is that the removable sides make it possible to unmold a dessert without turning it upside down.

Baked cheesecakes and cheese pies are actually custards. The delicate egg mixtures should be baked at low temperatures just long enough for them to "set." Overbaking or too high heat causes them to puff and brown too much during baking and to shrink too much on cooling. As with any custard, they will water-off or weep if overbaked. When cooled, these cheesecakes will become level, leaving room for a sour cream topping and a glaze. All cheesecakes and cheese pies should be thoroughly chilled before cutting and refrigerated to protect the delicate egg custards from spoilage.

There is no need to get into a rut with your favorite cheesecake or cheese pie. You can have infinite variety by adding and changing glazes and garnishes. The chocolate topping and fruit glazes at the end of the chapter are flavor and color touches to glamorize your first cheesecake or give new interest to your pet cheese pie recipe.

Preceding page: Elegant Cheesecake Ring (Knudsen No-Bake Cheesecake), page 113; Knudsen Cream Cheese Pie, page 111; Instant Cheese Pie, page 111, with Apricot Glaze, page 114; Grasshopper Cream Cheese Pie, page 112; Traditional Cheesecake, page 112, with Raspberry Glaze (Strawberry Glaze), page 114.

Your favorite and ours! Make several and keep them in the freezer for impromptu company. Knudsen Cream Cheese Pie freezes beautifully.

One 9-inch glass pie plate

Crust:
    ¼ cup (½ stick) Knudsen Butter, melted
    ¼ cup sugar
    1½ cups graham cracker crumbs (about 18 crackers)
Filling:
    4 (3-oz.) packages Knudsen Cream Cheese, at room temperature
    ¾ cup sugar
    2 eggs
    2 teaspoons vanilla
    1 teaspoon lemon juice
    1 teaspoon grated lemon peel
Topping:
    1 cup (½ pint) Knudsen Hampshire Sour Cream, at room temperature
    ¼ cup sugar
    1 teaspoon vanilla

1. Preheat oven to 300°F. Put butter for crust on to melt.
2. Blend crust ingredients; press onto bottom and sides of pie plate. Bake 10 minutes. See instructions for making a perfect crumb crust on page 133.
3. In large bowl, beat cream cheese until smooth; add remaining filling ingredients and beat until blended. Pour into crust.
4. Bake 40 minutes or until center of pie is no longer wet. The filling may crack around the edge but it should not brown. Remove from oven and cool 10 minutes.
5. Blend topping ingredients and spread evenly over entire surface. Return to oven 5 minutes.
6. Cool to room temperature and refrigerate at least 5 hours before serving. Top with glaze, if desired. For freezing, omit glaze and place layer of plastic wrap directly over sour cream topping. Wrap drugstore style with heavy aluminum foil. Freeze. To thaw, let stand at room temperature about 3 hours.

Makes 8 to 10 servings.

KNUDSEN CREAM CHEESECAKE: Substitute one 9-inch springform pan for pie plate. Press crumb crust mixture onto bottom and sides of pan and bake as directed above. Prepare double recipe of filling; pour into crust and bake 1 hour 15 minutes or until set. Prepare topping: Increase sour cream to 1½ cups and sugar to ⅓ cup. Proceed according to recipe directions. Makes 16 to 20 servings. For a less flavorful, less sweet cheesecake crust, use the zwieback crust from the Traditional Cheesecake recipe, page 112.

When you just must taste cheese pie *now!*

One 9-inch graham cracker crust

1 (8-oz.) package Knudsen Cream Cheese, at room temperature
1⅓ cups Knudsen Half and Half
1 (3¼ -oz.) package instant lemon or vanilla pudding mix

1. Blend cream cheese until smooth; gradually beat in Half and Half until creamy.
2. Add pudding mix and beat until smooth.
3. Pour into crumb crust and chill until set. When set, top with desired glaze.

Makes 8 servings.

Traditional Cheesecake

Appreciate the subtle flavor of the cheese!

*One 9-inch springform pan,
buttered and floured*

Crust:
  *¼ cup (½ stick) Knudsen
    Butter, melted*
  *1½ cups zwieback crumbs
    (6-oz. package)*
  1½ teaspoons cinnamon
Filling:
  4 eggs, separated
  ½ teaspoon salt
  2 tablespoons lemon juice
  1 teaspoon vanilla
  1 teaspoon almond extract
  1 cup sugar
  ⅔ cup sifted flour
  *1½ teaspoons grated lemon
    peel*
  *2 cups (1 pint) Knudsen
    Cottage Cheese*
  *1 cup (½ pint) Knudsen
    Hampshire Sour Cream*

1. Preheat oven to 300°F. Put butter for crust on to melt.
2. Blend crust ingredients; press onto sides and bottom of pan. Tilt pan to press crumbs onto sides.
3. In medium bowl, beat egg yolks until light; blend in remaining filling ingredients except cottage cheese, sour cream and egg whites.
4. Empty cottage cheese into large bowl; add small amount of egg mixture and beat on high speed until curd is broken and nearly smooth. Add remaining egg mixture and sour cream; beat until blended.
5. Beat egg whites until stiff but not dry; fold into cheese mixture.
6. Pour into crumb lined pan and bake 1 hour.
7. Turn oven off and let cake cool in oven, with door ajar, 1 hour.
8. Refrigerate 5 hours before serving.

NOTE: If desired, reserve up to ¼ cup crumb crust mixture for cheesecake garnish. After the cake has baked 30 minutes, sprinkle crumbs over top and return to oven for remaining 30 minutes.

Makes 12 to 16 servings.

HOOP CHEESE CHEESECAKE: Increase salt to 1 teaspoon. Substitute 2 (8-oz.) packages Knudsen Hoop Cheese for cottage cheese.

Grasshopper Cream Cheese Pie

Spectacular! This will perk up even a jaded cheese pie palate.

One 9-inch glass pie plate

Chocolate crumb crust:
  *¼ cup (½ stick) Knudsen
    Butter, melted*
  *1¼ cups chocolate cookie
    crumbs*
Filling:
  *4 (3-oz.) packages
    Knudsen Cream Cheese,
    at room temperature*
  ⅔ cup sugar
  2 eggs
  *¼ cup green crème
    de menthe*
  *2 teaspoons white crème
    de cacao*
*1 recipe Chocolate Sour Cream
  Topping, page 114*

1. Preheat oven to 300°F. Put butter for crust on to melt.
2. Combine crust ingredients and press onto bottom and sides of pie plate.
3. In large bowl, beat cream cheese until smooth; blend in remaining filling ingredients and pour into crust.
4. Bake 40 minutes; cool.
5. Spread chocolate glaze over surface of cooled pie and refrigerate at least 5 hours before serving.

Makes 8 to 10 servings.

The classic in its category.

One 9-inch springform pan

Filling:
- *2 envelopes unflavored gelatin*
- *¾ cup sugar*
- *¼ teaspoon salt*
- *2 eggs, separated*
- *1 cup Knudsen Milk*
- *1 tablespoon lemon juice*
- *1 teaspoon grated lemon peel*
- *1 teaspoon vanilla*
- *¼ cup sugar*
- *1 cup (½ pint) Knudsen Whipping Cream*
- *3 cups (1½ pints) Knudsen Cottage Cheese*

Crust:
- *3 tablespoons Knudsen Butter, melted*
- *2 tablespoons sugar*
- *1 cup graham cracker crumbs*
- *½ teaspoon cinnamon*
- *½ teaspoon nutmeg*

1. Mix gelatin, ¾ cup sugar and salt in top of double boiler. Add egg yolks and milk; beat until well blended. Cook over boiling water, stirring constantly, until gelatin is dissolved.
2. Remove from heat; stir in lemon juice, peel and vanilla. Refrigerate, stirring occasionally, until mixture mounds slightly when dropped from spoon.
3. While mixture is chilling, blend crust ingredients. Reserve 2 tablespoons crumb mixture; press remaining onto bottom of pan.
4. Beat egg whites until frothy; gradually add ¼ cup sugar and continue beating until stiff and glossy. Whip cream until stiff. Set both aside.
5. In large bowl, beat cottage cheese with electric mixer on high speed until curd breaks. Blend in thickened gelatin mixture; fold in whipped cream and then beaten egg whites.
6. Turn into crumb lined pan; sprinkle with reserved crumbs. Refrigerate about 4 hours or until firm.

Makes 10 to 12 servings.

ELEGANT CHEESECAKE RING: Press crust mixture onto bottom and part way up side of large bundt pan. Prepare one and one-half times filling, pour into crumb lined pan and chill until set. Unmold carefully.

Although these delicately flavored desserts need no embellishing at all, the addition of a beautiful glaze or topping will bring new excitement to them. The new flavor complement, the jewel colors and the added dimension will make a new recipe out of your favorite cheesecake or cheese pie. A glaze can be as simple as a can of prepared pie filling or beautifully colored fruit preserves spread over the top of a cheesecake. A ring of well-drained fresh or canned fruit is a beautiful and simple garnish. If you have a little more time, you will want to try one of these glazes designed just for these most delightful of desserts.

As nice to look at as it is to eat, Apricot Glaze is a perfect complement for cheesecake.

- *1 (16-oz.) can apricot halves*
- *3 tablespoons sugar*
- *1 tablespoon cornstarch*
- *1 teaspoon lemon juice*
- *Yellow and red food coloring*

1. Drain apricots, reserving ¾ cup syrup. In small saucepan, blend sugar and cornstarch to remove lumps; blend in reserved syrup.
2. Cook over medium heat until thickened and clear.
3. Remove from heat; stir in remaining ingredients.
4. Place wax paper directly on top of hot glaze; refrigerate until cool.
5. Arrange apricot halves, cut side down, in a ring over surface of chilled cheesecake or cheese pie. Spoon cooled glaze over.

Makes glaze for 1 nine-inch cheesecake or cheese pie.

Strawberry Glaze

Our favorite is the raspberry variation. All three flavors complement any cheesecake or cheese pie.

1 (10-oz.) package frozen
  strawberries, thawed
1 tablespoon cornstarch
¼ cup sugar
Dash salt
½ teaspoon lemon juice
½ teaspoon vanilla
1 to 2 drops red food coloring

1. Combine first four ingredients in saucepan; blend. Cook until clear and thickened.
2. Remove from heat and stir in remaining ingredients.
3. Place wax paper directly on top of hot glaze; refrigerate. When cool, spread over chilled cheesecake or cheese pie. Refrigerate until set.

Makes glaze for 1 nine-inch cheesecake or cheese pie.

RASPBERRY GLAZE: Substitute 1 (10-oz.) package frozen raspberries for strawberries. Before cooling, press through fine strainer or cheesecloth to remove seeds. Omit food coloring.

PINEAPPLE GLAZE: Substitute 1 (8½-oz.) can crushed pineapple for strawberries; drain. Use drained syrup to cook with sugar, etc. Fold in pineapple after syrup cools. Use yellow food coloring.

Cranberry Glaze

A special glaze for the fall and winter season.

3 tablespoons sugar
1 tablespoon cornstarch
1 (1-pound) can whole
  cranberry sauce
½ teaspoon grated lemon peel

1. In stainless steel, glass or enamel saucepan, blend sugar and cornstarch to remove lumps.
2. Gradually blend in cranberry sauce and lemon peel. Cook, stirring constantly, until thickened and clear; refrigerate. When cooled, spread over chilled cheesecake or cheese pie and refrigerate.

Makes glaze for 1 nine-inch cheesecake or cheese pie.

Cherries Jubilee Glaze

When you want to be really special—serve Cherries Jubilee Cheesecake.

1 (1-pound) can dark sweet
  pitted cherries
2 tablespoons sugar
5 cloves
1 cinnamon stick
Peel of ½ lemon (removed with
  vegetable peeler)
1 tablespoon cornstarch
2 tablespoons Kirsch (optional)

1. Drain syrup from cherries into saucepan. Add sugar, seasonings, and lemon peel; simmer, covered, 15 minutes.
2. Strain off cloves, cinnamon and lemon peel. The syrup remaining should measure about ⅔ cup. Add water or reduce as necessary.
3. Remove about 2 tablespoons syrup; cool and blend thoroughly with cornstarch. Add slowly to hot syrup, stirring constantly, until mixture boils and becomes clear and thickened.
4. For real "Jubilee" flavor, warm Kirsch in ladle over candle or burner. Tip ladle into flame to ignite. When flame dies, add to sauce. Fold in drained cherries and cool.
5. Spread over chilled cheesecake. Refrigerate until set.

Makes glaze for 1 nine- or ten-inch cheesecake or cheese pie.

Chocolate Sour Cream Topping

Use this topping instead of the usual sour cream one. It makes any cheesecake a chocolate cheesecake.

4 ounces semi-sweet or milk
  chocolate
½ cup Knudsen Hampshire Sour
  Cream, at room temperature

1. Melt chocolate over hot water or on very low heat. When melted, remove from heat and blend in sour cream.
2. Spread over surface of cooled cheesecake or cheese pie; refrigerate until firm. *Do not bake!*

Makes topping for 1 nine-inch cheesecake or cheese pie.

Cakes & Frostings

One of the first cooking projects most little girls want to attempt is baking a cake. There is something deeply satisfying about hearing your family rave over the cake *you* baked—whether you are 8, 18 or 80. With so many mixes available today, it is not difficult to bake a very satisfactory cake. But the Mmmmmmms and Ahhhhhhs will be even more fervent when they experience the greater moistness, better flavor and better keeping qualities of a homemade cake made with real butter and buttermilk, sour cream or yogurt. Find out by baking some of the cakes in this chapter.

These cakes are especially delicious for several reasons. To start with, they are made with butter. This immediately suggests delightful flavor. But that's not all. Butter makes cakes more moist and rich tasting, too. This is because it doesn't contain emulsifiers. Emulsifiers are added to the vegetable shortenings used in many cake mixes and recipes because they allow more air to be whipped into the batters. This greater volume of air and greater dispersion of the fat detract from the moistness of the cake. Even though a cake made with butter may actually have less fat, it will have a richer taste and texture.

Another reason that these cakes are better is that they are made with cultured dairy products. The characteristic flavor, aroma and texture of cakes and breads made with sour cream, buttermilk and yogurt are well known and appreciated. In addition to this, the fact that recipes made with cultured dairy products contain little or no baking powder further enhances their flavor. Were you aware that baking powder had a flavor? Some describe it as metallic, others as bitter or burning. Notice the difference when you use baking soda and cultured dairy products. There is no off flavor to cover the subtle flavors of the other ingredients.

You can enjoy this advantage in any standard cake recipe you now use. Convert it to buttermilk or yogurt by following the method described on the next page. If you already have an old-fashioned recipe calling for sour milk, just use buttermilk. No other changes are necessary. Sour milk recipes come from the days when milk soured naturally because it was not pasteurized. Another point about old-fashioned recipes—many of them call for the soda to be stirred into the buttermilk to dissolve it. This procedure is all right, but because soda is ground finer now and dissolves readily, it is usually sifted with the flour.

The finishing touch you put on these cakes is another reason why they are going to be better. Top your better flavored, better textured cake with one of our very special cream cheese or sour cream frostings. Or with whipped cream. Cater to your family's whims by baking cakes in their favorite flavors and frosting them to match. Start with the recipes as they are given here and then branch out and create your own variations. You'll be the most in-demand cake baker in the neighborhood.

Prune Sheet Cake (Prune Cake), page 121, served with Whipped Cream Topping, page 123.

A cake recipe is really a formula. It combines ingredients to achieve a particular rising power and level of acidity so that the finished cake will be light, moist and delicately browned. If a batter is too acid, the cake will shrink and fall, taste doughy and never brown properly. If a batter has too much soda, the cake will be dry, crumbly, grayish in color and have a soapy taste. To arrive at a good formula, the acid ingredients must be balanced by baking soda or, to a lesser degree, egg whites. Although most foods are on the acid side, the level is not high enough to affect the results. Only the highly acid foods, such as yogurt, buttermilk, sour cream, citrus juices, honey, molasses, brown sugar and cream of tartar need to be balanced. By adding soda to recipes containing these ingredients, a proper acid level can be achieved and a good amount of rising power can be obtained.

The easiest way to get a properly balanced cake is, of course, to use a tested recipe like the ones in this chapter. But it is possible to take a promising standard plain milk or water cake and convert it to an even better flavored buttermilk or yogurt cake. This is done simply by adding soda to balance the acid of these ingredients and subtracting baking powder.

A rough rule is to decrease the baking powder by twice the amount of soda you are adding.

If a recipe calls for 1 cup of milk or water you may:

> Substitute 1 cup of buttermilk and: Add ½ teaspoon baking soda. Subtract 1 teaspoon baking powder.

> Substitute 1 cup of plain yogurt and: Add 1 teaspoon baking soda. Subtract 2 teaspoons baking powder.

If a recipe calls for 1 cup of buttermilk you may:

> Substitute 1 cup of plain yogurt and: Add ½ teaspoon baking soda. Subtract 1 teaspoon baking powder if present.

> Substitute ½ cup of plain yogurt and ½ cup water. Do not change the baking soda or baking powder quantities.

Substituting sour cream for plain milk or water is more complicated because sour cream is both higher in fat and lower in liquid than these products. The substitution can be made, but a little trial and error may be necessary. Here is a rule to guide you.

If a recipe calls for 1 cup plain milk or water you can:

> Substitute 1 cup sour cream and: Add 2 or 3 tablespoons milk or water. Add ½ teaspoon baking soda. Subtract 1 teaspoon baking powder. (It may be necessary to subtract 2 or 3 tablespoons of fat from recipe.)

Converting Cakes to Buttermilk, Yogurt or Sour Cream

General Rules for Cake Baking

1. Have all ingredients at room temperature — eggs, butter, buttermilk, sour cream. Sugar and baking soda dissolve better and faster.

2. Measure accurately — especially acid ingredients and soda. See the inside front cover for instructions on measuring dairy foods. If substitutions are necessary, follow rules to the letter.

3. Butter and flour the baking pans on the bottom only, except when indicated otherwise. Save butter wrappers for this purpose.

4. Preheat oven well in advance and do not open oven door until last third of baking time.

5. Do not overbake cakes. Overbaking causes drying. A cake is fully baked when it shows one of the following signs: The edges begin to pull away from the pan OR the surface springs back when lightly tapped with finger OR a toothpick inserted in the center comes out dry — except in the case of fruit pulp cakes.

Basic Buttermilk Cake

Being basic doesn't keep this cake from being great! Try the variations, too.

*Two 9-inch round cake pans, wax
    paper lined*

*2¼ cups sifted cake flour
¾ teaspoon baking powder
¾ teaspoon baking soda
¼ teaspoon salt
½ cup (1 stick) Knudsen butter,
    at room temperature
1½ cups sugar
2 eggs
1 teaspoon vanilla
1 cup Knudsen Buttermilk*

1. Preheat oven to 375°F.
2. Sift and measure flour; sift again with baking powder, baking soda and salt.
3. Cream butter and sugar in large bowl; beat in eggs, one at a time; add vanilla and beat until light and fluffy.
4. Add dry ingredients in three portions alternating with buttermilk, beating well after each addition. When all ingredients have been added, beat on medium speed 1 minute.
5. Pour into prepared pans and bake 20 to 25 minutes or until a toothpick inserted in center comes out dry.
6. Cool on racks 15 minutes; remove from pans and cool completely before frosting. Frost with any variation of Creamy Butter-Cheese Frosting, page 122, Superb Chocolate Frosting, page 121 or Easiest Hampshire Chocolate Frosting, page 122.

Makes 12 to 16 servings.

EXTRA-RICH BUTTERMILK CAKE: Increase butter to ¾ cup (1½ sticks).

BUTTERMILK CHOCOLATE CAKE: Reduce sifted flour to 2 cups. Omit baking powder and increase baking soda to 1 teaspoon. Either granulated or light brown sugar may be used. Add 2 ounces baking chocolate, melted, to butter-sugar mixture.

GOLD CAKE: Substitute 6 egg yolks for 2 whole eggs.

SPICE CAKE: Sift following spices with dry ingredients: 1 teaspoon cinnamon, ½ teaspoon cloves, ¼ teaspoon nutmeg. Substitute light brown sugar for half the granulated sugar. Frost with Panocha variation of Creamy Butter-Cheese Frosting, page 122.

SHEET CAKE: Bake in 13x9x2-inch baking pan about 30 minutes.

Scrumptious Yellow Cake

Yogurt is great for cake baking. Let this recipe prove it to you.

*Two 9-inch round cake pans, wax
    paper lined*

*2½ cups sifted cake flour
1 teaspoon baking soda
½ teaspoon baking powder
½ teaspoon salt
¾ cup (1½ sticks) Knudsen
    Butter, at room temperature
1 cup sugar
2 eggs
1½ teaspoons vanilla
1 (8-oz.) carton Knudsen Plain
    Yogurt*

1. Preheat oven to 350°F.
2. Sift and measure flour; sift again with baking soda, baking powder and salt.
3. Cream butter and sugar in large bowl; add eggs, one at a time, beating well after each addition. Add vanilla and beat until light and fluffy.
4. Add dry ingredients in three portions alternating with yogurt. When all ingredients have been added, beat on medium speed 1 minute.
5. Pour into cake pans and bake 25 to 30 minutes or until a toothpick inserted in center comes out dry.
6. Cool on racks 15 minutes; remove from pans and cool completely before frosting. Frost with Citrus variation of Creamy Butter-Cheese Frosting, page 122.

Makes 12 to 16 servings.

A heavenly cake with very special variations.

Two 9-inch round cake pans, wax paper lined

2 cups sifted cake flour
¾ teaspoon baking powder
½ teaspoon baking soda
¼ teaspoon salt
½ cup (1 stick) Knudsen Butter, at room temperature
1½ cups sugar
2 eggs
1 teaspoon vanilla
1 cup (½ pint) Knudsen Hampshire Sour Cream, at room temperature

1. Preheat oven to 375°F.
2. Sift and measure flour; sift again with baking powder, baking soda and salt.
3. Cream butter and sugar in large bowl; beat in eggs, one at a time; add vanilla and beat until fluffy and light in color.
4. Add sifted dry ingredients in three portions, alternating with sour cream. When all ingredients have been added, beat on medium speed 1 minute.
5. Pour batter into pans and bake about 25 minutes or until a tooth-pick inserted in center comes out dry.
6. Cool on racks 15 minutes; remove from pans and cool completely before frosting.

Makes 12 to 16 servings.

DELUXE SOUR CREAM CHOCOLATE CAKE: Add 2 ounces melted baking chocolate to butter-sugar mixture. Omit baking powder and increase baking soda to ¾ teaspoon.

DELUXE DATE CAKE: Substitute light brown sugar for half the granulated sugar. Sift ⅛ teaspoon allspice with dry ingredients. Fold ¾ cup chopped dates and ½ cup finely chopped walnuts into finished batter.

DELUXE PINEAPPLE CAKE: Stir well-drained contents of 1 (8¾-oz.) can crushed pineapple into finished batter.

FIFTIETH ANNIVERSARY CAKE: Substitute light brown sugar for half the granulated sugar. Beat 2 table-spoons grated orange peel into finished batter and fold in ¾ cup diced pecans. Bake in buttered and floured 9-inch *tube pan at 350°F. 45 minutes* or until toothpick inserted in cake comes out dry. Before cooling and removing cake from pan, poke with holes at ½-inch intervals; spoon dissolved mixture of ¼ cup orange juice, ¼ cup sugar and 2 or 3 tablespoons Cointreau (optional) over cake. Cool completely before removing from pan. Wrap carefully in foil or plastic wrap and store at least 24 hours before cutting.

When you have three bananas so ripe they are about to pour out of their skins, make this great cake.

Two 9-inch round cake pans, wax paper lined

2½ cups sifted cake flour
1¾ cups sugar
2¼ teaspoons baking powder
¾ teaspoon baking soda
1 teaspoon salt
¾ cup (1½ sticks) Knudsen Butter, at room temperature
1¼ cups mashed, very ripe banana (about 3 medium)
⅔ cup Knudsen Buttermilk
2 eggs
⅔ cup finely chopped walnuts

1. Preheat oven to 350°F.
2. Sift and measure flour; sift again into large bowl with sugar, baking powder, baking soda and salt.
3. Add butter, banana and ⅓ cup buttermilk; beat 2 minutes.
4. Add remaining buttermilk and 2 eggs; beat 2 minutes.
5. Fold in nuts and pour into pans.
6. Bake 30 to 35 minutes or until a toothpick inserted in center comes out dry.
7. Cool on racks 15 minutes; remove from pans and cool completely before frosting. Frost with Creamy Butter-Cheese Frosting, page 122, or Banana variation.

Makes 12 to 16 servings.

BANANA SHEET CAKE: Bake in 13x9x2-inch buttered and floured baking pan 40 minutes at 350°F. (325°F. for glass baking pan.)

Knudsen Gingerbread

John Adams once expressed the thought that molasses was an essential ingredient in the American Independence. Along with ginger it is most certainly essential in Early American cooking. What could be more natural than Gingerbread made with buttermilk. You'll *know* that this one is not from a mix. It's moist and delicious.

*One 13x9x2-inch baking pan,
buttered and floured*

*2½ cups sifted flour
1 teaspoon baking powder
1½ teaspoons baking soda
1 teaspoon ginger
2 teaspoons cinnamon
½ cup (1 stick) Knudsen Butter,
at room temperature
¾ cup firmly packed light brown
sugar
2 eggs
¾ cup light molasses*
1 cup Knudsen Buttermilk*

1. Preheat oven to 350°F. (325°F. for glass pan.)
2. Sift and measure flour; sift again with baking powder, baking soda, ginger and cinnamon.
3. Cream butter and sugar in large bowl. Beat in eggs, one at a time, mixing well after each addition; blend in molasses.
4. Add dry ingredients in three portions alternating with buttermilk, beating well after each addition.
5. Pour into prepared pan and bake 35 to 40 minutes or until a toothpick inserted in center comes out dry.
6. Serve warm or cooled with Hampshire Crème Fraîche, page 142, Whipped Cream Topping, page 123, or Hampshire Sour Cream sweetened with brown sugar.

Makes 16 to 20 servings.

*Butter the cup before measuring honey, molasses or syrup. You'll get every drop.

Old-Fashioned Devil's Food Cake

Moist and dark! This is a cake that will taste the way Devil's Food Cake tasted when you were a child!

*Two 9-inch round cake pans,
wax paper lined*

*3 ounces unsweetened baking
chocolate, melted*
2¼ cups sifted cake flour
2 teaspoons baking soda
½ teaspoon salt
½ cup (1 stick) Knudsen Butter,
at room temperature
1 (1-pound) box or 2⅓ cups
firmly packed light brown
sugar**
3 eggs
2 teaspoons vanilla
¾ cup Knudsen Buttermilk
¾ cup boiling water*

1. Preheat oven to 375°F. Put chocolate on to melt.
2. Sift and measure flour; sift again with baking soda and salt.
3. Cream butter and sugar in large bowl; beat in eggs, one at a time, beating well after each addition. Add vanilla and melted chocolate; beat until light and fluffy.
4. Add dry ingredients in three portions alternating with buttermilk, mixing well after each addition. Blend in boiling water and pour into prepared pans. (Batter will be very thin.)
5. Bake 25 to 30 minutes or until a toothpick inserted in center comes out dry.
6. Cool on racks 15 minutes; remove from pans and cool completely before frosting.

Makes 12 to 16 servings.

DEVIL'S FOOD SHEET CAKE: Bake in 13x9x2-inch buttered and floured baking pan 35 minutes at 375°F. (350°F. for glass pan).

*Melt baking chocolate in double boiler or use premelted unsweetened chocolate.

**Light brown sugar and dark brown sugar give very different results in cakes. Dark brown sugar makes a dryer, less sweet cake.

An old-fashioned cake with a new yogurt twist.

Two 9-inch round cake pans, wax paper lined

2 ounces unsweetened baking chocolate, melted
2 eggs, separated
1½ cups sugar
1¾ cups sifted cake flour
1½ teaspoons baking soda
¾ teaspoon salt
⅓ cup cooking oil
1 (8-oz.) carton Knudsen Plain Yogurt
⅓ cup Knudsen Milk

1. Preheat oven to 350°F. Put chocolate on to melt.
2. Beat egg whites until frothy. Gradually add ½ cup of the sugar, beating constantly until stiff and glossy. Set aside.
3. Sift and measure flour; sift again into large bowl with baking soda, salt and remaining sugar.
4. Add oil and about half the yogurt; beat 1 minute. Add remaining yogurt, milk, egg yolks and melted chocolate; beat 1 minute.
5. Fold in beaten egg whites and pour into pans.
6. Bake 25 to 30 minutes or until a toothpick inserted in center comes out dry. Cool on racks 15 minutes. Remove from pans and cool completely before frosting.

Makes 12 to 16 servings.

This is a moist and delicious cake that men love—and ladies, too!

Two 8-inch round cake pans, wax paper lined

Prunes
1½ cups sifted flour
1 teaspoon baking soda
¼ teaspoon salt
½ teaspoon cinnamon
½ teaspoon nutmeg
½ teaspoon allspice
¼ teaspoon cloves
½ cup (1 stick) Knudsen Butter, at room temperature
1½ cups sugar
2 eggs
⅔ cup Knudsen Buttermilk
⅓ cup chopped walnuts

1. Cook dry prunes according to package directions; remove from syrup, pit, chop and measure ⅔ cup.
2. Preheat oven to 350°F.
3. Sift and measure flour; sift again with baking soda, salt and spices.
4. Cream butter and sugar in large bowl; beat in eggs, one at a time, mixing well after each addition. Blend in prune pulp.
5. Add dry ingredients in three portions alternating with buttermilk, beating well after each addition. Stir in nuts and pour into pans.
6. Bake 30 to 35 minutes or until a toothpick inserted in center comes out dry.
7. Cool on racks 15 minutes; remove from pans and cool completely before frosting. Frost with Creamy Butter-Cheese Frosting, page 122.

Makes 12 to 16 servings.

PRUNE SHEET CAKE: Bake in 9x9x2-inch baking pan 45 to 50 minutes. Reduce heat 25°F. for glass pan.

Found yourself in a frosting rut? Felt that too many frostings were just too sweet? Knudsen Cream Cheese and Knudsen Hampshire Sour Cream are the answer. Don't overlook whipped cream, either.

Smooth and creamy. Hampshire Sour Cream takes the edge off the sweetness.

1 (6-oz.) package semi-sweet chocolate morsels
½ cup Knudsen Hampshire Sour Cream
1 teaspoon vanilla
¼ teaspoon salt
2½ cups powdered sugar

1. Melt chocolate over hot water or on very low heat.
2. Remove from heat; blend in sour cream, vanilla and salt.
3. Gradually beat in sugar until smooth. Refrigerate briefly if too soft to spread.

Makes filling and frosting for 2 eight- or nine-inch layers.

Easiest Hampshire Chocolate Frosting

Absolutely the easiest chocolate frosting ever. Beautiful to work with and not *too* sweet.

10 to 12 ounces semi-sweet or milk chocolate or a combination
2 cups (1 pint) Knudsen Hampshire Sour Cream, at room temperature

1. Melt chocolate over boiling water or on very low heat.
2. Stir melted chocolate to smooth; remove from heat and blend in sour cream. Refrigerate briefly if too soft to spread.

Makes filling and frosting for 2 nine-inch layers.

Creamy Butter-Cheese Frosting

Our very finest basic frosting. Try your own variations.

1 (3-oz.) package Knudsen Cream Cheese, at room temperature
¼ cup (½ stick) Knudsen Butter, at room temperature
2 tablespoons Knudsen Milk
1 teaspoon vanilla
⅛ teaspoon salt
1 (1-pound) box powdered sugar

1. Beat cream cheese and butter until fluffy; blend in milk, vanilla and salt.
2. Gradually add sugar and beat until smooth and creamy.

Makes filling and frosting for 2 or 3 nine-inch layers.

CHOCOLATE BUTTER-CHEESE FROSTING: Beat 2 ounces melted unsweetened chocolate into finished frosting. Add milk or cream as necessary.

ORANGE BUTTER-CHEESE FROSTING: Substitute 3 tablespoons frozen orange juice concentrate for milk.

BANANA BUTTER-CHEESE FROSTING: Substitute ½ teaspoon banana extract for ½ teaspoon of the vanilla.

MARASCHINO BUTTER-CHEESE FROSTING: Substitute 2 tablespoons maraschino cherry juice for milk. Stir in 3 tablespoons minced maraschino cherries. Add red food coloring.

CITRUS FROSTING: Add 1½ teaspoons grated orange, lime, grapefruit or lemon peel to finished frosting.

PANOCHA FROSTING: Omit ½ cup of the powdered sugar. Heat ½ cup packed brown sugar with butter and milk until sugar melts; cool. Beat in cream cheese and remaining ingredients.

COCONUT BUTTER-CHEESE FROSTING: Toast 1 cup or 1 (3½-oz.) can flaked coconut. Crumble half and stir into finished frosting. Garnish with remaining half.

Whipped Chocolate Cheese Frosting

Especially for angel or sponge cakes. Really luscious!

1 (6-oz.) package semi-sweet chocolate morsels
1 cup (½ pint) Knudsen Whipping Cream
1 (3-oz.) package Knudsen Cream Cheese, at room temperature
1 tablespoon Knudsen Half and Half or Milk
⅛ teaspoon salt
¾ cup firmly packed light brown sugar
1 teaspoon vanilla

1. Melt chocolate over boiling water or on very low heat. Smooth melted chocolate with rubber scraper and cool to room temperature.
2. Whip cream until stiff; refrigerate.
3. Beat cream cheese, Half and Half and salt until blended; gradually add brown sugar and beat until smooth.
4. Blend in vanilla and melted chocolate; refrigerate until mixture mounds when dropped from spoon.
5. Fold in whipped cream. Refrigerate briefly if too soft to spread.

Makes frosting for 1 ten-inch angel food, chiffon or sponge cake.

WHIPPED BUTTERSCOTCH CHEESE FROSTING: Substitute butterscotch morsels for chocolate morsels. Add 2 tablespoons water to melted butterscotch; blend well. Increase salt to ¼ teaspoon.

Saucy Angel Frosting

An easy and delicious whipped cream frosting. Especially good for angel cake. Double the recipe for a large angel cake.

1 cup (½ pint) Knudsen Whipping Cream
2 tablespoons sugar
1 teaspoon vanilla
1 (8-oz.) carton Knudsen Pineapple Fruit-Blended Yogurt

1. Pour cream into small mixer bowl; refrigerate with beaters until well chilled.
2. Whip cream until frothy; gradually add sugar and continue beating until stiff. Add vanilla and yogurt and fold until well blended.
3. Split angel cake; fill and frost; refrigerate. Serve within 2 hours.

Makes filling and frosting for one small loaf angel cake.

ASSORTED SAUCY ANGEL FROSTING FLAVORS: Substitute Knudsen Cherry, Boysenberry, Orange or Lime Fruit-Blended Yogurt for pineapple.

24 HOUR SAUCY ANGEL FROSTING: Add gelatin as instructed in Whipped Cream Frosting below.

Whipped Cream

Few dessert toppings are as simple to make as whipped cream. A few tips will help guarantee your complete satisfaction every time.

TIPS ON WHIPPING CREAM

1. A day or two (or longer) age on cream thickens it and improves its whipping qualities.
2. The cream, bowl and beaters should be thoroughly chilled before beating.
3. Use *fine* granulated sugar, if available.
4. The more sugar added to whipped cream, the less firm it will whip. Add as little sugar as possible to get the flavor you want. For greatest stability, add the sugar gradually after whipping has begun.
5. Whip cream in a deep narrow bowl to prevent spattering and to speed whipping.
6. One cup of whipping cream yields approximately 2 cups of whipped cream.

Whipped Cream Topping

No substitute topping tastes as good as real whipped cream. Try some of our special flavor variations.

1 cup (½ pint) Knudsen Whipping Cream
Dash salt
½ teaspoon vanilla, peppermint, almond or other flavor extract
1 to 2 tablespoons sugar
Food coloring (optional)

1. Combine cream, salt and vanilla in small bowl; refrigerate with beaters until well chilled.
2. Beat cream until frothy; gradually add sugar and continue beating until stiff. Add a few drops food coloring, if desired.
3. Refrigerate. Will maintain consistency 2 or 3 hours.

Makes 2 cups.

WHIPPED CREAM FROSTING: Double recipe to frost 1 ten-inch angel cake. Soften 1 teaspoon gelatin in 2 tablespoons water in a cup. Place cup in pan of simmering water until gelatin is dissolved. Cool. As soon as sugar is added to cream, drizzle in dissolved gelatin. Continue beating until stiff. Frosting will hold 24 hours in refrigerator without weeping.

CINNAMON WHIPPED CREAM: Substitute brown sugar for white. Add ½ teaspoon ground cinnamon.

CINNAMON RED HOT WHIPPED CREAM: Omit sugar and vanilla. Boil ¼ cup cinnamon redhots in ¼ cup water until dissolved; continue boiling until thickened. Cool and add to cream before whipping. Holds well.

CHOCOLATE WHIPPED CREAM: Use 1 tablespoon sugar only. Add ¼ cup instant hot chocolate powder.

MOCHA WHIPPED CREAM: Add 1 teaspoon instant coffee to chocolate variation.

CRÈME DE MENTHE WHIPPED CREAM: Fold 2 tablespoons Crème de Menthe into finished topping.

Pies & Pastries

Baking a great pie is one of the most convincing ways for a woman to showcase her ingenuity and talent in the kitchen. There is no question about it, pie baking is a test of skill—not just one skill, but many skills. After all, a pie is not a simple concoction. It is a crust, a filling, perhaps a topping and a lot of coordination. Pies are baked or unbaked. There are custard pies, cream pies, chiffon pies, gelled pies, fruit pies, double-crust pies, lattice-topped pies, deep-dish pies, tarts, etc., etc. Each variety demands its own special techniques. Great pie bakers may be born —but more than likely they are developed out of good training, lots of experience, more than a fragment of experimentation and, of course, a lot of recipes with potential for greatness.

Here is a chapter full of recipes to let you display your skill. As you first scan them you may think that they compose a simple collection of favored classic pies. Investigate more closely, eye the ingredients, follow the procedure and you'll see that somewhere in each is locked a surprise element. There may be a hidden layer of delightfully flavored cream cheese giving creamy softness to the nip of a fresh fruit pie. Or some fruit-blended yogurt giving a zing to an unexpectedly *un*rich cream pie. Maybe the surprise is a background of sour cream rounding out the flavor of a fruit pie. The recipes in this chapter are unique enough to open up new avenues of interest and variation for even the most experienced pie baker. But in their originality, some are still simple enough for the novice to enjoy success with on a first try.

It is usually the crust of the pie that makes the new pie baker uneasy. With the many pre-baked crusts, ready-to-bake frozen crusts and ready-to-roll pie crust mixes, it is possible to bake a pie without coping with all the problems of crust making. The main thing is to let your family enjoy the fabulous fillings. If you are ready to try your hand at a pie crust from scratch, there are recipes for standard pastry and crumb crusts at the end of the chapter. For a new flavor pleasure, try the cream cheese and cottage cheese crusts.

Tucked in among the pie recipes is a recipe for cream puffs. Elegant, delicious, impressive cream puffs! Here is the answer for the new cook who wants to "do it herself" but doesn't have the experience or equipment to bake a pie. Cream puffs are so simple to make and they can be the stage for an unlimited number of luscious things—including most of the cream pie fillings in this chapter.

So, no matter who you are, there are many delightful creations in this chapter for you to make to please and impress the PTA Board, the neighbors, your mother-in-law or, most especially, the eager following that sits at your table every day.

Custard Pies

Custard pies are really the easiest of baked pies. And no dessert could be more nourishing. Just take care not to overbake them.

Buttermilk Custard Pie

Brown on top, light and lemony inside. After you've made and served this delicious pie you'll wonder why you've been neglecting custard pies.

One 9-inch unbaked pastry crust

⅓ cup Knudsen Butter, at room temperature
1 cup sugar
3 eggs, separated
3 tablespoons flour
¼ teaspoon salt
1 teaspoon lemon juice
½ teaspoon grated lemon peel
1½ cups Knudsen Buttermilk

1. Preheat oven to 450°F.
2. In large bowl, cream butter and sugar until light; beat in egg yolks.
3. Add flour, salt, lemon juice and peel; beat until well blended. Blend in buttermilk.
4. Beat egg whites until stiff but not dry; fold into liquid ingredients.
5. Pour filling into crust and bake 10 minutes. Reduce oven temperature to 350°F. and bake 40 minutes longer. Cool.

Makes 6 to 8 servings.

Cottage Cheese Custard Pie

Even desserts can boost protein counts. This old farm recipe, especially.

One 9-inch unbaked pastry crust

2 cups (1 pint) Knudsen Cottage Cheese
3 eggs
¾ cup sugar
2 tablespoons flour
Juice and grated peel of one lemon

1. Preheat oven to 450°F.
2. Bake pastry 6 minutes; cool. Reduce oven temperature to 350°F.
3. In large bowl, beat cottage cheese to smooth curd. Add eggs, sugar, flour, lemon juice and peel; beat until well blended. OR put all ingredients in blender jar; blend until smooth.
4. Pour into crust and bake 50 to 60 minutes or until a knife inserted in pie just off center comes out clean.
5. Cool 1 hour before serving.

Makes 6 servings.

Baked Fruit Pies

These are the favorite pies of the American male—with a new twist. Sour cream is the unexpected flavor enhancer.

Peaches 'n' Cream Pie

Canned peaches make this an easy year-round pie.

1 recipe Standard Pastry Crust, page 133, Double Crust variation

Filling:
1 (1-pound) can sliced peaches AND
1 (1-pound 13-oz.) can sliced peaches
1 cup (½ pint) Knudsen Hampshire Sour Cream, at room temperature
½ cup sugar
2 tablespoons flour
½ teaspoon grated lemon peel
½ teaspoon vanilla
¼ teaspoon almond extract
⅛ teaspoon salt

1. Preheat oven to 450°F. Drain peaches thoroughly in collander.
2. Blend remaining ingredients; fold in well-drained peach slices.
3. Pour filling into pastry lined pie plate. Cover with top crust and seal edges carefully; crimp edges and cut design in center.
4. Bake 10 minutes. Reduce oven temperature to 350°F. and bake 30 minutes longer. Serve warm or cool.

Makes 6 to 8 servings.

This is apple pie with the "à la mode" built in. Delicious!

One 9-inch unbaked pastry crust

Filling:
1 egg
1 cup (½ pint) Knudsen
Hampshire Sour Cream,
at room temperature
¾ cup sugar
2 tablespoons flour
¼ teaspoon vanilla
Dash salt
2¼ cups finely chopped,
peeled cooking apple
(2 to 3 apples)
¼ teaspoon grated lemon peel
Crumb Topping:
¼ cup (½ stick) Knudsen
Butter
½ cup sugar
⅓ cup flour
¾ teaspoon cinnamon

1. Preheat oven to 450°F.
2. Beat egg in large bowl; blend in sour cream, sugar, flour, vanilla and salt. Fold in apple and lemon peel.
3. Pour filling into crust and bake 10 minutes. Reduce oven temperature to 350°F. and bake 30 minutes longer or until crust is golden brown.
4. Meanwhile, prepare topping by cutting butter into sugar, flour and cinnamon. Electric mixer can be used.
5. After 30 minute baking period, sprinkle topping over pie and bake 15 minutes longer. Serve warm or cool.

Makes 6 to 8 servings.

For the men in your life—a really hearty pie!

1 recipe Standard Pastry Crust,
page 133, Double Crust
variation

Filling:
1½ cups seedless raisins
1 egg
1 cup (½ pint) Knudsen
Hampshire Sour Cream,
at room temperature
1 cup firmly packed light brown
sugar
3 tablespoons flour
2 teaspoons champagne
vinegar
1 teaspoon cinnamon
¼ teaspoon nutmeg
¼ teaspoon salt

1. Preheat oven to 450°F.
2. Place raisins in saucepan with water to cover. Cover and simmer 5 minutes or until raisins have plumped; drain.
3. Beat egg in medium bowl; blend in remaining ingredients. Fold in drained raisins.
4. Pour filling into pastry lined pie plate. Top with pastry or lattice pastry strips and seal edges carefully. Crimp edges and cut design in center of plain top crust.
5. Bake 10 minutes. Reduce oven temperature to 350°F. and bake 25 minutes longer. Serve warm for fullest flavor.

Makes 6 to 8 servings.

No-Bake Pies

Pretty is the word to describe these delicious refrigerator pies. If you serve them at an all-girl affair, you had better make enough for the family, too. You'll never be forgiven otherwise. Hold any whipped cream toppings until you are ready to serve.

Lime Divine Pie

A favorite of ours. Try it one of these warm days.

One 9-inch fully baked pastry crust or graham cracker crust

1 (3-oz.) package lime gelatin
1 cup boiling water
1 (8-oz.) package Knudsen Cream Cheese, at room temperature
1 (8-oz.) carton Knudsen Lime Fruit-Blended Yogurt
1 recipe Whipped Cream Topping, page 123

1. Dissolve gelatin in boiling water; cool to room temperature.
2. In large bowl, beat cream cheese until smooth; gradually blend in yogurt. Add gelatin slowly, beating until smooth.
3. Pour into crust; chill until firm. Frost with Whipped Cream Topping and garnish with chocolate curls.

   Makes 6 to 8 servings.

ASSORTED DIVINE PIE FLAVORS: Substitute Knudsen Boysenberry, Cherry, Strawberry or Orange Fruit-Blended Yogurts and a matching flavored gelatin for the lime flavor. Use raspberry gelatin with boysenberry yogurt.

HAMPSHIRE LIME DIVINE PIE: Substitute 1 cup (½ pint) Knudsen Hampshire Sour Cream for cream cheese for a softer, more tangy pie at about 40 calories less per serving.

Cool Lemon Pie

A lemon pie without the problems. It is beautiful and delicious.

One 9-inch fully baked pie crust (graham cracker, standard pastry or cream cheese pastry) OR 6 to 8 tart shells

Filling:
  1 (3½ -oz.) package lemon pudding and pie filling mix
  ¾ cup sugar
  ¼ cup water
  3 egg yolks
  1 cup boiling water
  1 cup (½ pint) Knudsen Hampshire Sour Cream
  2 tablespoons lemon juice
  1 teaspoon grated lemon peel
1 recipe Whipped Cream Topping, page 123
¼ to ½ cup chopped nuts or several pieces sugared lemon peel

1. In stainless steel, glass or enamel saucepan combine pudding mix with sugar and ¼ cup water; blend in egg yolks.
2. Add boiling water and cook, stirring constantly, until mixture thickens and first bubbles appear. Cool slightly at room temperature. Pudding will stiffen if cooled too much.
3. Meanwhile, empty sour cream into small mixer bowl and put in freezer with beaters until *very* cold. Beat 4 to 5 minutes on high speed until doubled in volume. (See page 141 for detailed instructions.)
4. Stir lemon juice and peel into warm pudding. Fold in whipped sour cream. Pour into crust and refrigerate 4 to 5 hours.
5. Garnish with Whipped Cream Topping and chopped nuts or sugared lemon peel.

   Makes 6 to 8 servings.

Chocolate "Marsh-Mello" Pie

A *great* chocolate pie!

One 9-inch fully baked
pastry crust

Filling:
1 (4-oz.) bar German sweet
chocolate
2 cups miniature
marshmallows
2 tablespoons sugar
Dash salt
½ cup Knudsen Milk
1 (8-oz.) package Knudsen
Cream Cheese, at room
temperature
1 cup (½ pint) Knudsen
Whipping Cream
¼ teaspoon vanilla
1 recipe Whipped Cream
Topping, page 123 (optional)

1. Melt chocolate and marshmallows with sugar, salt and milk in top of double boiler.
2. In large bowl, beat cream cheese until smooth; gradually add hot chocolate mixture, blending well. Refrigerate until cool.
3. Whip cream with vanilla; fold into cooled chocolate mixture. Refrigerate until mixture mounds when dropped from spoon.
4. Spoon into crust and shape into decorative swirls; refrigerate until set.
5. Garnish with Whipped Cream Topping, if desired, and serve.

Makes 6 to 8 servings.

Strawberry Surprise Pie

A beautiful pie—glazed fresh strawberries set on a snowy layer of moist cream cheese. Delicious, too!

One 9-inch fully baked pastry
crust OR 8 individual tart shells

Glaze:
½ basket strawberries,
washed and hulled
¾ cup water
½ cup sugar
1 tablespoon cornstarch
1 teaspoon unflavored gelatin
Red food coloring

Filling:
1 (8-oz.) package Knudsen
Cream Cheese, at room
temperature
⅓ cup sugar
2 tablespoons Knudsen Half
and Half
1 tablespoon lemon juice
½ teaspoon grated lemon peel
1½ baskets strawberries, washed
and hulled
½ recipe Whipped Hampshire
Crème Fraîche, page 142

1. In medium saucepan, crush strawberries for glaze with potato masher. Add water and sugar; simmer 5 minutes. Press through strainer to remove pulp.
2. Blend cornstarch and gelatin with ¼ cup cooled strawberry juice to remove lumps. Add to remaining strawberry juice in pan.
3. Cook over medium heat, stirring constantly, just until thickened and clear. Add food coloring as desired and cool to room temperature.
4. Prepare filling. In medium bowl, beat cream cheese with sugar, Half and Half, lemon juice and peel until light and fluffy. Spread in cooled crust(s).
5. Arrange strawberries, stem-end down, over cream cheese layer. Pour cooled glaze over all.
6. Refrigerate 3 to 4 hours. Serve garnished with a dollop of Whipped Hampshire Crème Fraîche.

Makes 8 servings.

RED, WHITE AND WOW CHERRY PIE: Omit glaze, strawberries and Whipped Hampshire Crème Fraîche. Spoon contents of 1 (1-pound 5-oz.) can cherry pie filling over cream cheese filling in crust.

Tropical Banana Cream Pie

Absolutely delicious in banana or coconut. So easy you won't mind baking it over and over!

One 9-inch graham cracker or fully baked pastry crust

Filling:
1 (3¾-oz.) package instant vanilla pudding mix
1 cup (½ pint) Knudsen Hampshire Sour Cream
¾ cup Knudsen Half and Half
3 to 4 bananas
1 recipe Whipped Cream Topping, page 123

1. Combine instant pudding, sour cream and Half and Half; mix according to package directions.
2. Pour about ⅓ of pudding into crust. Arrange cut or whole bananas over. Cover with remaining pudding. Chill until firm.
3. Garnish with Whipped Cream Topping and serve.

   Makes 6 to 8 servings.

COCONUT CREAM PIE: Substitute 1 (3½-oz.) can flaked coconut for bananas. Fold all but ¼ cup coconut into pudding. Toast reserved coconut, if desired, and sprinkle over Whipped Cream Topping.

Strawberry Parfait Pie

You've made this pie with ice cream before. Try it now with fewer calories and a new zing.

One 9-inch fully baked pastry crust or graham cracker crust

1 (3-oz.) package strawberry gelatin
1 cup boiling water
1 basket strawberries
2 (8-oz.) cartons Knudsen Strawberry Fruit-Blended Yogurt
1 recipe Whipped Cream Topping, page 123 (optional)

1. Dissolve gelatin in boiling water; cool to room temperature.
2. Wash and stem strawberries. Reserve 6 attractive berries for garnish; slice remaining berries.
3. Gradually blend cooled gelatin into yogurt; chill until mixture mounds when dropped from spoon.
4. Fold in sliced strawberries and spoon into crust; chill until set.
5. Garnish with Whipped Cream Topping, if desired, and whole strawberries.

   Makes 6 servings.

ASSORTED PARFAIT PIE FLAVORS: Omit strawberries. Substitute Knudsen Boysenberry, Lemon, Lime or Orange Fruit-Blended Yogurts and a matching flavored gelatin for the strawberry flavor. Use raspberry gelatin with boysenberry yogurt. Fold well-drained mandarin orange segments into orange variation.

Luscious Cherry-Cheese Pie

A beautiful pie—and so easy!

One 9-inch pie plate

Crust:
2 tablespoons Knudsen Butter
2 (2¾-oz.) boxes chocolate snaps

Filling:
1 (3-oz.) package cherry flavored gelatin
¾ cup boiling water
1 cup (½ pint) Knudsen Cottage Cheese
1 cup (½ pint) Knudsen Whipping Cream
½ can (1-pound 5-oz. size) cherry pie filling

1. Preheat oven to 425°F. Put butter for crust on to melt. Dissolve gelatin for filling in boiling water; cool.
2. Prepare crust. Reserve 16 snaps; crush remaining snaps and mix with melted butter. Press onto bottom of pie plate. Arrange reserved snaps around side. Bake 5 minutes; cool.
3. Combine cooled gelatin with cottage cheese in blender jar; blend on low speed until smooth. Refrigerate until slightly thickened.
4. Whip cream until stiff; fold into cheese-gelatin mixture. Refrigerate until mixture mounds when dropped from spoon.
5. Spread canned pie filling into crust; fill with whipped mixture and shape into decorative swirls. Refrigerate until firm.

   Makes 8 servings.

Cream puffs always create a sensation. They are so simple to make you'll wonder why the mixes were ever created.

Cream Puffs

Absolutely delicious—and not too sweet.

Cream Puffs à la Knudsen

Filling:
2 cups (two ½ pints)
    Knudsen Whipping Cream
¼ teaspoon salt
½ teaspoon vanilla
¼ cup sugar
2 (8-oz.) cartons
    Knudsen Boysenberry
    Fruit-Blended Yogurt
1 recipe Cream Puffs, below
Powdered sugar

1. Combine cream, salt and vanilla in medium bowl. Refrigerate with beaters until well chilled.
2. Beat cream until frothy; gradually add sugar and continue beating until stiff. Fold in yogurt.
3. Spoon boysenberry mixture into cream puffs; refrigerate until serving time.
4. Sift powdered sugar over puffs before serving.

Makes 12 large puffs.

MISCELLANEOUS CREAM PUFFS À LA KNUDSEN: Substitute Knudsen Lime, Orange, Pineapple or Strawberry Fruit-Blended Yogurt for Boysenberry.

Cream Puffs

In addition to the dessert fillings, cream puffs are wonderful holders for seafood or chicken salads.

1 cup water
½ teaspoon salt
½ cup (1 stick) Knudsen Butter
1 cup sifted flour
4 eggs, at room temperature

1. Preheat oven to 425°F.
2. Bring water to boil with salt and butter.
3. As soon as butter melts and a full boil begins, add flour all at once and stir rapidly. Remove from heat as soon as mixture holds together and looks like corn meal mush.
4. Add eggs, one at a time, beating well after each addition.
5. Drop by tablespoonfuls onto cookie sheet. Allow for expansion.
6. Bake 20 minutes; reduce heat to 325°F. and bake 20 minutes longer or until golden and crisp.
7. Remove from oven and make slit in each puff or cut off tops to allow steam to escape. Cool on racks and fill.

Makes 12 large puffs.

APPETIZER OR TEA PUFFS: Drop by half teaspoonfuls onto cookie sheet. Bake at 400°F. for about 15 minutes. Makes about 60 puffs.

Fillings for Cream Puffs

Let your imagination go wild when you look for cream puff fillings. Here are a few suggestions for one recipe of cream puffs.

WHIPPED CREAM: Fill puffs with 2 recipes Whipped Cream Topping, page 123.

BANANA OR COCONUT: Fill puffs with 2 recipes Tropical Banana Cream Pie filling or coconut variation, page 130.

CHOCOLATE "MARSH-MELLO": Fill puffs with 1 recipe Chocolate "Marsh-Mello" Pie filling, page 129.

LEMON: Fill puffs with 1 recipe Cool Lemon Pie filling, page 128.

ICE CREAM: Fill puffs with any flavor Knudsen Ice Cream.

Pie Crusts

Show your real cooking skill by making homemade pie crusts. Here are our favorite cream cheese and cottage cheese pastries along with the standard pastry and crumb crusts.

Cream Cheese Pastry

Knudsen Cream Cheese Pastry is excellent for small sweet or savory tarts as well as for pies. See the recipe for Petite Pâtes, page 27.

One 9-inch pie plate

½ cup (1 stick) Knudsen Butter
1 (3-oz.) package Knudsen Cream Cheese, at room temperature
1¼ cups sifted flour
¼ teaspoon salt

1. In large bowl, blend butter and cream cheese with electric mixer.
2. Add flour and salt, all at once, and beat on low speed, just until mixture leaves sides of bowl and forms a ball.
3. For pie crust: Turn dough onto well floured board and roll to an 11-inch circle. Fit into pie plate according to instructions 4 through 6 for Pastry Crust, page 133.
4. Pierce sides and bottom of pastry with fork; refrigerate 1 hour.
5. Bake in preheated 450°F. oven 8 minutes or until golden.

Makes pastry for 1 nine-inch pie.

Cottage Cheese Pastry

Surprised? A little extra protein never hurt anyone. Actually, the cottage cheese is here for its special flavor.

One 9-inch pie plate

1½ cups sifted flour
⅛ teaspoon salt
½ cup (1 stick) Knudsen Butter, at room temperature
¼ cup Knudsen Cottage Cheese

1. Combine all ingredients in electric mixer bowl and beat on low speed just until dough leaves sides of mixer bowl and forms a ball.
2. For pie crust: Follow basic instructions 3 through 6 for rolling and shaping pastry crust, page 133. Chill 3 hours.
3. Preheat oven to 450°F. Bake 10 to 12 minutes or until golden.

Makes pastry for 1 nine-inch crust.

Graham Cracker Crumb Crust

A great crust for a beginner.

One 9-inch pie plate

¼ cup (½ stick) Knudsen Butter, melted
1½ cups graham cracker crumbs (18 crackers)
¼ cup sugar

1. Preheat oven to 375°F. Put butter on to melt.
2. Blend graham cracker crumbs, sugar and melted butter.
3. Distribute crumbs evenly over bottom and sides of pie plate with fork. Press into place.
4. For perfectly shaped crust, press 8-inch pie plate onto crumbs sliding it against sides to pack and smooth. Form rim by pressing side of finger between two pie plate rims. Proceed around pie. Edges of crumb crusts formed this way do not burn as readily.
5. Bake 8 minutes. Cool on rack before filling.

Makes 1 nine-inch graham cracker crust.

This is a classic pastry crust recipe with an option to use some butter. Try it and discover the delightful flavor and color difference.

One 9-inch pie plate

1½ cups sifted flour
¾ teaspoon salt
½ cup shortening OR ¼ cup
  shortening and ¼ cup
  (½ stick) Knudsen Butter
3 to 4 tablespoons ice water

1. Using pastry blender or two knives, cut shortening into flour and salt in large bowl. Mixture should look like coarse meal.

2. Sprinkle ice water, 1 tablespoon at a time, over mixture, tossing rapidly with fork. Dough should clump together. Add more water only if mixture is still *very* dry and crumbly.

3. Turn dough onto wax paper. Press together into a ball and flatten on lightly floured board. Roll to an 11-inch circle.

4. Roll onto rolling pin or fold in quarters and transfer to pie plate. Ease pastry into pie plate. Stretching causes shrinkage during baking.

5. Trim pastry ½-inch from rim of pie plate. Patch pastry with excess pieces. Moisten surfaces to be joined and press together.

6. Moisten underside of overhanging pastry. Fold overhanging edge in half and press together. Crimp edge of crust.

7. For pre-baked pastry crust: Pierce sides and bottom of crust with fork about every inch. Bake in preheated 450°F. oven 10 to 12 minutes or until golden. Cool on rack.

Makes 1 nine-inch pastry crust.

PASTRY FOR DOUBLE CRUST PIE: Use 2 cups sifted flour, 1 teaspoon salt, ⅔ cup shortening and 4 to 6 tablespoons water.

Tip: Problems with soggy crusts on custard or baked fruit pies? Try this solution. Prepare bottom crust and stick generously with fork tines. Bake 8 minutes in preheated 425°F. oven. Remove from oven, brush entire inner surface with beaten egg and return to oven for 2 minutes. Fill the pie and bake at about 350°F. until done. Also, shiny pans, such as those made of aluminum foil, reflect heat and therefore encourage soggy crusts. Place them on a dark cookie sheet for baking. Or, better yet, use a glass or dull metal pie pan to start with.

Tip: So-called standard 9-inch pie pans vary tremendously in actual diameter and in amount of filling they will hold. The prepared crusts available in the freezer section of the market are particularly small. If your pans are of the larger variety, you may want to prepare 1½ times the filling with some pies, gelled pies in particular, in order to fill the shells generously.

Tip: If you are not ready to tackle a pie crust from scratch, there are many alternatives: Buy prebaked shells or tart shells. Buy preformed ready-to-bake shells in the freezer section of the market. Buy ready-to-roll pastry sticks. Or make cream puffs instead. No special equipment necessary.

Tip: Ready-made crusts and some homemade crusts have very thin edges that burn easily. As soon as these crusts are fully cooked and browned nicely, wrap a strip of aluminum foil around the pie rim to cover edge of crust. Complete baking.

More Desserts

The dessert that follows a beautiful meal is somewhat like the finale to a sensitive play. It is the ending that is preceded by a careful weaving of characters around a message. When the curtain drops, it should drop on a line that completes and clarifies the meaning of the entire production. The central message of a meal revolves around the entrée. The appetizer sets the stage. The vegetables, pastas, breads and garnishes support and complement it. The dessert, then, must close the performance. If it is too rich and heavy, it overwhelms and dominates the carefully built theme. If it is too mundane, it is anti-climactic. The dessert that ends a rich and beautiful meal must be light and simple, yet glamorous and dramatic. This chapter is full of recipes to be cast in the role!

There are the light and airy production numbers that great hotel chefs choose to conclude sumptuous banquets. If you have thought that these desserts — the Charlotte Russes, the Bavarian Creams and the cool, airy soufflés — took a chef's skill to prepare, read the recipes. They take no special skills. And as the chef knows so well, they can be prepared in advance and are no trouble to serve to the biggest crowd.

With an elegant serving dish and garnish, few desserts are as glamorous as those of fruit. The jewel colors and natural shapes of the fruit shining through crystal stemware are beautiful simplicity. The glamour comes from the garnish of a soft creamy sauce — such as the ones in this chapter. Expect a little murmur of appreciation when your guests discover the marvelous flavor complement that sour cream is to fruit.

The penetrating chill of a frozen dessert provides a refreshing punch line to a filling dinner. The very special frozen desserts that you make yourself from the recipes in this chapter have a surprise quality that comes from their uniquely delicious flavor.

So, that's the synopsis of the recipes in this chapter. (Except for a few cookies and candies reserved for after-the-performance munching.) Make one of them soon. Your guests will shower compliments on you when you make the final act of your next dinner a dessert that allows them to remember the enjoyment of the *entire* production. But remember one thing. They'll be expecting you to top your performance next time.

Preceding page: Fresh strawberries served with Hampshire Sour Cream.

These are desserts to be served after a filling and satisfying meal. Admittedly they are not all willing to tell their calories, but many are made with whipped sour cream at about half the calories of whipped cream. They are all beautiful and delicious!

Chocolate Rum Mousse

Many dishes go under the name of "mousse"—from hot, savory dishes to cold or frozen sweet ones. All are light and fluffy because the French word "mousse" actually means "froth." This dessert mousse is for the chocolate lovers. It's light enough to follow a big dinner.

One 1-quart serving dish OR
8 individual sherbets

1 cup (½ pint) Knudsen
Hampshire Sour Cream
1 cup (½ pint) Knudsen
Whipping Cream
1½ teaspoons unflavored
gelatin
2 tablespoons water
2 tablespoons Knudsen Milk
¼ cup light brown sugar
⅛ teaspoon salt
1 (6-oz.) package
chocolate morsels
1 teaspoon rum extract
½ teaspoon vanilla
2 egg whites

1. In large mixing bowl, combine creams and refrigerate.
2. Soften gelatin in water in a cup. Place cup in pan of simmering water until gelatin is dissolved.
3. Heat milk with half the sugar and the salt in top of double boiler until sugar dissolves. Add chocolate and continue heating until melted. Remove from heat and blend in rum extract, vanilla and dissolved gelatin.
4. Beat egg whites until frothy; gradually add remaining sugar, beating until stiff but not dry.
5. Stir about one-fourth of the beaten egg whites into chocolate mixture until blended. Fold in remaining egg whites.
6. Without cleaning beaters, whip the cream mixture until stiff. Add chocolate mixture and fold until well blended.
7. Spoon into serving dish or sherbets; chill until set.

   Makes 8 servings, ½ cup each.

CHOCOLATE CHARLOTTE: Line one 9-inch springform pan with split lady fingers, cut side in. Fill with double recipe Chocolate Rum Mousse prepared according to recipe directions. Makes 16 servings.

CHOCOLATE SOUFFLÉ Fasten a 2½-inch wide sturdy foil collar around a 6-cup soufflé dish. Fill with double recipe Chocolate Rum Mousse. When set, remove foil collar. Makes 16 servings.

CHOCOLATE RUM MOUSSE PIE: Fill one 9-inch fully baked pastry crust with 1 recipe Chocolate Rum Mousse. Makes 8 servings.

For individual servings, spoon into puff pastry, cream puff or tart shells.

Berry Bavarian

A traditional Bavarian Cream is a gelatin thickened custard with whipped cream, and perhaps beaten egg whites, folded in. This recipe strays from the traditional but only to lower the calories a bit. It sacrifices none of the elegant flavor or texture. And it's PINK.

One 1-quart mold

1 (10-oz.) package frozen
raspberries, thawed
2 teaspoons unflavored gelatin
2 tablespoons water
1 cup Knudsen Half and Half
½ cup sugar
2 teaspoons lemon juice
1 cup (½ pint) Knudsen
Hampshire Sour Cream

1. Drain raspberries; reserve syrup. Soften gelatin in water.
2. In top of double boiler, combine Half and Half, sugar and softened gelatin. Heat, stirring constantly, just until sugar and gelatin have dissolved; add 2 tablespoons reserved raspberry syrup. Cool to room temperature.
3. Press raspberries through strainer to remove seeds; stir lemon juice into purée.
4. Whip sour cream according to directions on page 141. Fold whipped sour cream and raspberry purée into cooled Half and Half mixture. Pour into mold; refrigerate until set. Unmold to serve.

   Makes 6 to 8 servings.

STRAWBERRY BAVARIAN: Substitute frozen strawberries for raspberries. Decrease sugar to ⅓ cup.

Lemon Cheese Soufflé

A genuine soufflé is made from beaten egg whites and a white sauce. And it's baked. This "mock" soufflé is an elegant light dessert that could double as a glamorous molded salad.

One 1-quart soufflé dish

2 envelopes unflavored gelatin
⅓ cup water
1 (3½- or 4-oz.) package lemon pudding and pie filling mix (not "instant")
¼ cup sugar
2 eggs, separated
2 tablespoons lemon juice
1 teaspoon grated lemon peel
2 cups (1 pint) Knudsen Farmer Style Cottage Cheese
⅓ cup diced pecans
1 cup (½ pint) Knudsen Hampshire Sour Cream

1. Fasten a 2½-inch wide aluminum foil collar around top of soufflé dish. Soften gelatin in water in a cup.
2. Cook pudding according to package directions; stir in softened gelatin and sugar until dissolved.
3. Beat egg yolks in large bowl; gradually add hot pudding, lemon juice and peel, stirring constantly. Cover surface of pudding with wax paper and cool to room temperature. Do not refrigerate or gelatin will set.
4. When cooled*, blend in cottage cheese and nuts.
5. Beat egg whites until stiff but not dry. With same beater, whip sour cream according to directions on page 141; fold into egg whites.
6. Fold whipped mixture into pudding and pour into soufflé dish; refrigerate until set.

Makes 8 to 10 servings.

Cottage cheese curd toughens when added to hot sweet mixtures. Cool puddings and gelatins thoroughly before adding cottage cheese.

Hampshire Charlotte Russe

A Charlotte Russe is a Bavarian Cream molded in a lady finger lined mold. A very special dessert.

One 9-inch springform pan

11 or 12 lady fingers, split lengthwise
4 eggs, separated
2 cups Knudsen Milk
2 envelopes unflavored gelatin
½ cup sugar
¼ teaspoon salt
½ teaspoon vanilla
¼ cup fresh lemon juice
1 tablespoon grated lemon peel
2 cups (1 pint) Knudsen Hampshire Sour Cream
¼ cup sugar

1. Line sides of springform pan with split lady fingers, cut side in.
2. Beat egg yolks and milk in top of double boiler; blend in gelatin, ½ cup sugar and salt.
3. Cook over boiling water, stirring constantly, until custard coats a metal spoon; remove from heat and stir in vanilla, lemon juice and peel. Let stand at room temperature.
4. Empty sour cream into large mixer bowl; place with beaters in freezer to chill.
5. Beat egg whites until frothy; gradually add ¼ cup sugar, beating until stiff and glossy. Using same beater, whip sour cream until doubled in volume, about 5 minutes.
6. Combine egg whites, whipped sour cream and custard; fold until well blended. Pour into lady finger lined pan; refrigerate until set.
7. Remove sides from pan and serve.

Makes 12 to 14 servings.

Strawberry Yogurt Shimmy

For calorie watchers — and people who just enjoy eating. Try other flavors of yogurt and gelatin for fun.

1 (3-oz.) package strawberry gelatin
¾ cup boiling water
¾ cup ice water
1 (8-oz.) carton Knudsen Strawberry Fruit-Blended Yogurt

1. Dissolve gelatin in boiling water.
2. Add ice water and chill to consistency of unbeaten egg white.
3. Whip thickened gelatin until fluffy; fold in yogurt until blended. Refrigerate until set.
4. Spoon into dessert dishes and top with Hampshire Sour Cream.

Makes 4 to 6 servings.

Confetti Cream Cake

A spectacular dessert for a special occasion party. Choose other flavors of gelatin for "confetti" to match your party color scheme.

One 9-inch springform pan

"Confetti":
1 (3-oz.) package EACH
orange, lime and strawberry
gelatin

Crust:
1 cup graham cracker crumbs
(12 crackers)
1 tablespoon sugar
2 tablespoons Knudsen
Butter, melted

Filling:
1 (3-oz.) package lemon
gelatin
¼ cup sugar
1 cup boiling water
1 cup (½ pint) Knudsen
Whipping Cream
1 (8-oz.) package Knudsen
Cream Cheese, at room
temperature
1½ recipes Whipped
Cream Topping, page 123

1. Prepare "confetti" by dissolving each package of gelatin in 1¾ cups boiling water. Pour each into a shallow pan and chill until set. Cut into small cubes.
2. Combine crust ingredients and press onto bottom of springform pan.
3. Prepare filling by dissolving gelatin and sugar in boiling water; cool to room temperature.
4. Whip cream until stiff; refrigerate.
5. In large bowl, beat cream cheese until smooth; gradually beat in cooled gelatin. Fold in whipped cream; blend well.
6. Using a spatula, scoop "confetti" into cream cheese mixture. Gently fold together and pour into springform pan. Refrigerate several hours until set.
7. Before serving, prepare Whipped Cream Topping.
8. Remove sides from springform pan and frost cake with topping. Refrigerate until serving time. Frosting will hold several hours. To hold frosted cake for 24 hours, add 1 teaspoon unflavored gelatin, softened in 2 tablespoons water, to topping according to directions for Whipped Cream Frosting on page 123.

Makes 16 servings.

Boysenberry Torte

To call the following recipe a torte is taking some liberties. It has the ingredients, the beauty and the delicious flavor. Perhaps that's enough. For a cool look, substitute lime yogurt for boysenberry.

One 9-inch square or 11x7x2-
inch baking dish

1 (8½ -oz.) package
chocolate wafers, crushed
(about 2 cups)
½ cup (1 stick) Knudsen Butter,
at room temperature
2 cups powdered sugar
2 eggs
1 teaspoon grated lemon peel
1 (2⅛ -oz.) package chopped
pecans (½ cup)
2 cups (two ½ -pint cartons)
Knudsen Whipping Cream
¼ cup sugar
2 (8-oz.) cartons Knudsen
Boysenberry Fruit-Blended
Yogurt

1. Reserve ½ cup crushed wafers; press remaining onto bottom of baking dish. (For a firmer crust, blend crumbs with 2 tablespoons melted butter.)
2. Cream butter with powdered sugar; add eggs, one at a time, beating until smooth and creamy. Stir in lemon peel.
3. Drop creamed mixture by tablespoonfuls onto crushed wafers; spread carefully to prevent mixing with crumbs. Sprinkle pecans over creamed mixture.
4. Pour cream in small bowl; refrigerate with beaters until well chilled. Whip cream until frothy; gradually add sugar and beat until stiff. Fold in yogurt and spread evenly over nuts.
5. Sprinkle reserved crushed wafers over all and refrigerate 1 to 2 hours. Cut in squares to serve.

Makes 9 to 12 servings.

Fruit Desserts

Refreshing fruit paired with cheese or a cream topping is simple elegance—and appreciated after a heavy meal.

Coeur à la Crème

A Coeur à la Crème is a heart shaped mold of drained fresh cheeses and cream. The mild flavor and soft, spreadable texture make it a perfect foil for other delicately flavored foods. At the same time it provides the richness to soften tart or strong flavors. Surrounded with colorful cut fresh fruit it is a beautiful ending to a filling dinner.

1 (8-oz.) package Knudsen
   Cream Cheese, at room
   temperature
2 cups (1 pint) Knudsen Farmer
   Style Cottage Cheese
¼ cup Knudsen Whipping Cream
Fresh cut fruit (strawberries,
   peaches, pears, pineapple,
   apples)

1. Blend cream cheese; beat in cottage cheese until smooth.
2. Whip cream until stiff; fold into cheese mixture.
3. Line a large strainer or coeur à la crème mold with 3 layers of cheesecloth; fill with cheese mixture. Cover with cheesecloth and a flat plate; place a heavy object on top. Support strainer or mold in large deep bowl; refrigerate and drain at least 12 hours.
4. To serve, invert strainer or mold onto serving platter; remove cheesecloth. Surround with selected cut fruit.

Makes 6 to 8 servings.

PASHKA: Add ⅓ cup sugar and ½ teaspoon vanilla with cheeses. Fold in 1 cup chopped candied or dried fruit and ½ cup blanched slivered almonds before pressing into mold. Serve garnished with candied fruit and nuts. Pashka is a traditional Russian Orthodox Easter dessert. It is molded in a pyramid shape and decorated in Easter motifs.

Quick Hampshire Brûlée

Crème Brûlée is another French sounding recipe not to be found in a French cookbook. It is actually a Creole invention. The original is a custard made from whipping cream topped with a layer of brown sugar and broiled. Quick Hampshire Brûlée is a simple variation of the original. Lower in calories because it is made with sour cream. The tangy flavor of sour cream is a pleasant combination with the fruit.

One 9-inch glass pie plate

1 (1-pound 13-oz.) can
   peach halves, well-drained
2 cups (1 pint) Knudsen
   Hampshire Sour Cream,
   at room temperature
1 tablespoon sugar
½ teaspoon grated orange
   or lemon peel
¾ cup light brown sugar

1. Arrange peach halves in pie plate.
2. Blend sour cream, sugar and peel; spread over fruit.
3. *Just* before serving, sprinkle brown sugar evenly over sour cream, being careful to completely cover entire surface.
4. Broil 3 inches from broiler 1 to 3 minutes or until sugar melts. *Serve immediately* or surface will become very liquid.

Makes 6 to 8 servings.

Strawberries Juliet

Our version of Strawberries Romanoff. It's not only easier, but lower in calories.

2 baskets fresh strawberries
¼ cup sugar
1 tablespoon lemon juice
1 tablespoon Cointreau (optional)
1 pint Knudsen Vanilla Ice Cream
1 (8-oz.) carton Knudsen
   Strawberry Fruit-Blended
   Yogurt

1. Wash and hull strawberries. Reserve 8 attractive berries for garnish. Halve remaining berries and mix with sugar, lemon juice and Cointreau, if desired. Refrigerate.
2. At serving time, spoon halved strawberries into sherbet glasses.
3. Beat ice cream until soft; fold in yogurt to achieve marbled effect.
4. Spoon sauce over berries immediately and garnish with whole strawberries.

Makes 8 servings.

Hampshire Ambrosia

Ambrosia was the food of the mythological Greek gods. To partake of it was to achieve some level of immortality and divinity. Obviously such a food must have a very special aroma and flavor. Luscious and fragrant!

2 medium oranges, peeled and
   sectioned
1 basket strawberries, hulled
   and halved
1 (15¾-oz.) can pineapple
   chunks OR ½ small fresh
   pineapple, chunked
1 large banana, sliced

Topping:
  ¾ cup Knudsen Hampshire
    Sour Cream
  2 tablespoons light brown
    sugar
  ¾ teaspoon grated orange
    peel
  Dash salt
½ cup toasted coconut,
   page 145

1. Prepare fruits except banana; refrigerate.
2. Combine topping ingredients in small bowl; place with beaters in freezer until well chilled.
3. Whip topping mixture until doubled in volume, about 5 minutes.
4. At serving time, slice banana and add to prepared fruit. Alternate layers of fruit with coconut and sour cream topping in 4-ounce parfait glasses.

Makes 6 servings.

Fruit Dessert Toppings

Sour cream—whether it is plain, whipped or combined with other ingredients—brings out the full flavor of fresh, frozen or canned fruit. Grapes, peaches, nectarines, bananas, apples, strawberries and blueberries get particularly enthusiastic responses. For a change — one of special interest to the calorie watchers — try a mound of Knudsen Plain or Fruit-Blended Yogurt. Pineapple, lime and lemon are especially compatible.

Whipped Sour Cream Topping

Whipped sour cream is a soft and beautiful topping — perfect for fruit and lower in calories than whipped cream.

1 cup (½ pint) Knudsen
  Hampshire Sour Cream
2 tablespoons sugar
Dash salt
½ teaspoon vanilla

1. Combine all ingredients in small bowl; place with beaters in freezer.
2. When ice crystals begin to form around outside of sour cream, remove from freezer and begin beating on high speed.
3. Continue beating 4 or 5 minutes or until double in volume. The sour cream will thin at first.

Makes about 2 cups.

TIPS ON WHIPPING SOUR CREAM

1. One cup of Hampshire Sour Cream makes 1¾ to 2½ cups whipped sour cream.
2. Sour cream whips best if it is *very* cold.
3. It takes 4 or 5 minutes to whip sour cream. This is considerably longer than sweet cream. If it takes longer than 5 minutes, the cream probably is not cold enough. Rechill and whip again.
4. Sour cream whips to soft peaks. It will never become very stiff or turn to butter—no matter how long it is whipped.
5. Whipped sour cream can be rewhipped—several times if necessary. Chill completely each time and whip as before.

Whipped Hampshire Crème Fraîche

Crème fraîche is what the French call unpasteurized heavy cream (about 30% fat) that has been allowed to culture slightly. The French serve it in many ways, particularly on fruit. Whipped Hampshire Crème Fraîche is a combination of whipping cream (36% fat) and sour cream (20% fat). The end product is much like crème fraîche in fat content and flavor. You'll love it on shortcake, fruit pies or fruit compotes. It is a beautiful combination of the advantages of whipped cream and sour cream. The best of both.

½ cup Knudsen Hampshire
   Sour Cream
½ cup Knudsen
   Whipping Cream
2 tablespoons sugar
½ teaspoon vanilla
Dash salt

1. Combine creams in small bowl. Refrigerate with beaters until well chilled.
2. Beat creams until frothy; gradually add sugar, vanilla and salt, beating until quite stiff.
3. Refrigerate until used. Will maintain consistency 1 to 2 hours.

Makes about 2 cups.

ORANGE HAMPSHIRE CRÈME FRAÎCHE: Add 1 tablespoon orange juice, 1 teaspoon lemon juice and ½ teaspoon grated orange peel.

Cottage Cheese Fluff

A delicious and high protein topping for peaches, pineapple, berries, pears or grapes. Try the special parfait variations.

1 cup (½ pint) Knudsen
   Hampshire Sour Cream
¼ cup sugar
½ teaspoon lemon juice
⅛ teaspoon cinnamon
1 cup (½ pint) Knudsen Farmer
   Style Cottage Cheese

1. Combine sour cream, sugar, lemon juice and cinnamon in small bowl; place with beaters in freezer until *very* cold.
2. Beat sour cream until thick and doubled in volume, about 5 minutes; fold in cottage cheese and refrigerate. Will maintain consistency several hours.

Makes about 2½ cups sauce.

CHERRY COTTAGE CHEESE FLUFF PARFAIT: Add ½ teaspoon nutmeg to topping and alternate with cherry pie filling (one 1-pound 5-oz. can) and graham cracker crumbs (1 cup or 12 crackers, crushed) in 8 parfait glasses.

HINDU COTTAGE CHEESE FLUFF PARFAIT: Omit cinnamon and lemon juice; add ¼ teaspoon each almond extract, lemon extract and ground cardamon. Spoon into dessert glasses; add drained peach halves and additional topping. Garnish with toasted slivered almonds.

Frozen Desserts

Pull out that neglected ice cream freezer and have some simple old-fashioned fun making homemade ice cream or sherbet. If you don't have a mechanical freezer, use the freezer section of your refrigerator.

Fast freezing is the most important factor in making smooth textured ice cream. Follow mechanical freezer instructions for icing and salting to give the best freezing conditions. If the freezer section of a refrigerator is used, it should be set to the coldest setting and the freezing tray should be placed in the coldest spot. Even under the best circumstances home freezers cannot begin to match the sub-zero temperatures used in freezing ice creams commercially. Homemade ice cream recipes attempt to compensate for this by requiring you to beat them as they freeze. This happens automatically in mechanical ice cream freezers. If you are freezing ice cream in the freezer section of a refrigerator, you must beat partially frozen ice cream to a mush two or three times during the freezing process. This will keep the ice crystals small and the texture creamy. Ingredients like gelatin, egg white, cream and fruit pulp promote creaminess, also.

Ice creams and sherbets will not keep forever—particularly the homemade ones. Eat them as soon as they are made. That's the fun of it and that's when they're the best.

Lemon Buttermilk Ice Cream

An easy and delicious ice cream to make in your mechanical ice cream freezer.

1 envelope unflavored gelatin
¼ cup water
3 cups Knudsen Buttermilk
2 cups (two ½-pint cartons)
   Knudsen Whipping Cream
1 (6-oz.) can frozen lemonade
   concentrate, thawed
¾ cup sugar
2 tablespoons vanilla
1½ teaspoons grated lemon peel
¼ teaspoon salt
10 drops yellow food coloring

1. Soften gelatin in water in a cup. Place cup in pan of simmering water until gelatin is dissolved.
2. Blend remaining ingredients; stir in dissolved gelatin.
3. Pour into ice cream freezer container. Allow can to revolve a few minutes to dissolve sugar before adding ice.
4. Ice and salt freezer; complete freezing process following equipment instructions.

Makes 2½ quarts ice cream.

Hampshire Peach Ice Cream

Peaches and sour cream team up again.

One 9-inch square baking dish
   OR two ice trays

1 egg
1 cup (½ pint) Knudsen
   Hampshire Sour Cream
1 cup (½ pint) Knudsen
   Whipping Cream
1 cup sugar
2 tablespoons lemon juice
½ teaspoon vanilla
2 cups diced fresh peaches
   (about 4 or 5 medium)

1. Turn freezer control to coldest setting.
2. Beat egg in large bowl; blend in remaining ingredients.
3. Pour into baking dish or trays and freeze.
4. When ice crystals begin to form, turn into bowl and beat with electric mixer to consistency of soft mush. Return to freezer container and freeze. Repeat two or three times for best texture.

Note: This may also be made in a mechanical ice cream freezer. Fill freezer container with ice cream mixture and freeze according to freezer instructions.

Makes 6 to 8 servings.

Bali Hai Ice Cream

You'll never find this exotic flavor in a carton. Every taste reminds you of your own special island.

One 9-inch square baking dish
   OR two ice trays

1 egg, separated
1 (6-oz.) can frozen lemonade
   concentrate, thawed
½ cup sugar
2 tablespoons lemon juice
2 cups (1 pint) Knudsen
   Hampshire Sour Cream
2 ripe medium papayas, mashed
   (about 1½ cups)
2 small bananas, mashed

1. Turn freezer control to coldest setting.
2. In large bowl, beat egg yolk; blend in lemonade concentrate, sugar and lemon juice. Blend in sour cream and fruit.
3. Beat egg white until soft peaks form; fold into sour cream mixture.
4. Pour into baking dish or ice trays and freeze.
5. When ice crystals begin to form, turn into bowl and beat with electric mixer to consistency of soft mush; return to pan and freeze. Repeat two or three times for best texture.
6. Serve garnished with toasted shredded coconut or chopped Macadamia nuts.

Note: If ice cream seems pale, add food coloring.

Makes 1½ quarts ice cream.

Cool Orange Sherbet

Serve this refreshing and different orange sherbet from hollowed out orange cups.

One 9-inch square baking dish
  OR two ice trays

1½ teaspoons unflavored gelatin
2 tablespoons water
2½ cups Knudsen Buttermilk
½ cup sugar
1 (6-oz.) can frozen orange
  juice concentrate
2 tablespoons lemon juice
1 egg, separated
5 drops yellow food coloring
1 drop red food coloring

1. Turn freezer control to coldest setting.
2. Soften gelatin in water in a cup. Place cup in pan of simmering water until gelatin is dissolved.
3. Strain buttermilk to remove butter chunks; blend with sugar, juice concentrate, lemon juice, egg yolk and food coloring. Stir in dissolved gelatin.
4. Beat egg white until soft peaks form; fold into buttermilk mixture.
5. Pour into baking dish or trays and freeze. When ice crystals begin to form, turn into bowl and beat with electric mixer to consistency of soft mush; return to pan and freeze. Repeat two or three times for best texture.

Makes 6 to 8 servings.

Lime Sherbet

Cool and refreshing nourishment. Buttermilk gives the protein and calcium bonus.

One 9-inch square baking dish
  OR two ice trays

1 (3-oz.) package lime gelatin
⅔ cup sugar
1 cup boiling water
2 cups Knudsen Buttermilk
1 tablespoon lemon juice
1 teaspoon grated lemon peel

1. Turn freezer control to coldest setting.
2. In large bowl, combine gelatin, sugar and boiling water. Stir to dissolve and cool to room temperature.
3. Strain buttermilk to remove butter chunks. Blend buttermilk and remaining ingredients into gelatin mixture.
4. Pour into baking dish or trays and freeze. When ice crystals begin to form, turn into bowl and beat with electric mixer to consistency of soft mush; return to pan and freeze. Repeat two or three times for best texture.

Makes 6 to 8 servings.

Buttermilk Pineapple Sherbet

We get regular requests for this all time favorite!

One 9-inch square baking dish
  OR two ice trays

1 (8¾-oz.) can crushed
  pineapple
½ cup sugar
¼ teaspoon salt
1 teaspoon unflavored gelatin
1 egg, separated
1 tablespoon lemon juice
2½ cups Knudsen Buttermilk

1. Turn freezer control to coldest setting.
2. Drain pineapple; reserve syrup.
3. Combine reserved syrup, sugar, salt and gelatin in saucepan; heat until sugar and gelatin are completely dissolved. Cool.
4. Beat egg yolk in large bowl; blend in cooled syrup, lemon juice and buttermilk. Fold in drained pineapple.
5. Beat egg white until soft peaks form; fold into pineapple mixture.
6. Pour into baking dish or ice trays and freeze.
7. When ice crystals begin to form, turn into bowl and beat with electric mixer to consistency of soft mush; return to pan and freeze. Repeat two or three times for best texture.

Makes 6 to 8 servings.

Tip: Move sherbet trays from freezer to refrigerator section 15 minutes before serving.

Orange Freeze

A special dessert treat with a minimum of calories.

One ice tray

½ cup orange juice
¼ cup honey
1 (8-oz.) carton Knudsen
    Orange Fruit-Blended Yogurt
¼ teaspoon salt
1 tablespoon lemon juice
2 egg whites

1. Turn freezer control to coldest setting.
2. Blend orange juice with honey; add remaining ingredients, except egg whites, and mix thoroughly.
3. Pour into ice tray and freeze until nearly firm.
4. When orange mixture is nearly frozen, beat egg whites until stiff but not dry.
5. Turn frozen mixture into large bowl and beat to consistency of soft mush. Fold in beaten egg whites; return to ice tray and freeze.

Makes 4 to 6 servings.

Coconut Boysenberry Mousse

A light frozen dessert to top a heavy meal. Try it with orange yogurt for a change.

One ice tray

1 cup (½ pint) Knudsen
    Whipping Cream
1 egg white
2 tablespoons sugar
¼ teaspoon vanilla
1 (8-oz.) carton Knudsen
    Boysenberry Fruit-Blended
    Yogurt
1 cup (3½-oz. can) coconut,
    toasted

1. Turn freezer control to coldest setting.
2. Combine cream, egg white, sugar and vanilla in bowl and beat until stiff; fold in yogurt and toasted coconut. Reserve some coconut for garnish.
3. Spoon into ice tray; freeze until firm.

Note: To toast coconut: Spread evenly over shallow pan; bake at 350°F., stirring often, 8 to 12 minutes or until golden.

Makes 4 to 6 servings.

Cookies and Candies

Here are our favorite cookie and candy recipes. Each one is delicious enough to be on your family's request list and special enough to be served at a fancy tea.

Frosted Lemon Cookies

A tender, lemony, mouth-watering cookie.

Cookie:
    2 cups sifted flour
    ½ teaspoon baking soda
    ½ teaspoon baking powder
    1 cup sugar
    ½ cup (1 stick) Knudsen Butter
    2 eggs
    ½ cup Knudsen Buttermilk
Frosting:
    2 tablespoons Knudsen Butter
    2 cups powdered sugar
    3 tablespoons lemon juice
    Grated peel of ½ lemon
    2 to 3 drops yellow food
        coloring

1. Preheat oven to 375°F.
2. Sift and measure flour; sift again with baking soda and baking powder.
3. Cream sugar and butter; beat in eggs one at a time.
4. Blend buttermilk into creamed mixture. Add dry ingredients and mix thoroughly.
5. Drop by teaspoonfuls onto greased cookie sheet. Allow room for expansion.
6. Bake 8 to 10 minutes or until edges are barely browned; cool on rack.
7. Combine frosting ingredients and beat until light and creamy.
8. Frost cooled cookies. Store in airtight containers with wax paper between layers.

Makes 4 dozen cookies.

Vanilla Cream Cheese Cookies

Our favorite buttery crisp cookie. They keep very well stored in airtight containers.

1 cup (2 sticks) Knudsen Butter
1 (3-oz.) package Knudsen Cream Cheese
1 cup sugar
1 egg yolk
2 tablespoons vanilla
2½ cups sifted cake flour

1. Cream butter, cream cheese and sugar; blend in egg yolk and vanilla. Mix in flour.
2. Form dough into a log 1½-inches in diameter and roll in wax paper. Refrigerate at least 2 hours.
3. Preheat oven to 325°F. Cut into ¼-inch slices and bake 25 minutes or until edges are golden. Cool on rack.

Makes 5 dozen cookies.

SPARKLY CREAM CHEESE COOKIES: Press colored sugar crystals into rounds before baking.

CHOCOLATE DIP CREAM CHEESE COOKIES: Dip rims of cooled baked cookies in melted chocolate morsels.

Marbled Brownies

The children may ask for these but they are really intended for an adult taste.

One 9-inch square baking pan, buttered

Cream Cheese Layer:
1 (8-oz.) package Knudsen Cream Cheese, at room temperature
¼ cup sugar
1 egg
½ teaspoon vanilla

1 (15½ - or 16-oz.) package brownie mix
1 recipe Chocolate Sour Cream Topping, page 114

1. Preheat oven to 350°F.
2. Beat cream cheese until smooth; blend in sugar, egg and vanilla.
3. Prepare cake version of brownie mix according to package directions.
4. Spread half the prepared brownie batter in pan and pour cream cheese mixture over. Top with remaining brownie batter and swirl through cream cheese mixture to create marbled effect.
5. Bake 45 minutes. Cool on rack 2 hours.
6. Frost with Chocolate Sour Cream Topping. When topping is set, cut in squares and serve.

Makes 16 brownies.

Golden Nuggets

This delicious cookie will be enjoyed by everyone.

3 cups sifted flour
1 teaspoon baking powder
¼ teaspoon baking soda
1 teaspoon salt
1 cup (2 sticks) Knudsen Butter, at room temperature
½ cup firmly packed light brown sugar
1 cup sugar
1 teaspoon vanilla
1 tablespoon lemon juice
½ cup Knudsen Hampshire Sour Cream
1 (3½ -oz.) can flaked coconut

1. Sift and measure flour; sift again with baking powder, baking soda and salt.
2. In large bowl, cream butter and sugars until fluffy; mix in vanilla and lemon juice.
3. Add dry ingredients alternately with sour cream, mixing just until well blended.
4. Cover and refrigerate at least 2 hours. May be refrigerated for as long as one week. Freeze for longer storage.
5. Preheat oven to 400°F. Shape teaspoonfuls of dough into balls and roll in flaked coconut.
6. Bake 10 to 12 minutes or until golden. Cool on rack.

Makes about 6 dozen cookies.

HAMPSHIRE DROP COOKIES: Stir ½ cup chopped nuts into dough with dry ingredients. Omit chilling period. Drop by teaspoonfuls onto cookie sheet. Bake 8 to 10 minutes or until edges are golden.

Kipfel

You'll love these tiny nut filled tarts! Fill them with your favorite jam or preserves for a change.

Pastry:
  2½ cups sifted flour
  ¼ teaspoon salt
  *1 cup (2 sticks) Knudsen
    Butter*
  *1 cup (½ pint) Knudsen
    Cottage Cheese*
Nut Filling:
  ⅓ cup Knudsen Milk
  2 cups ground walnuts
  ⅔ cup sugar
  ½ teaspoon vanilla
  Dash salt

1. Sift and measure flour; combine with salt in mixing bowl.
2. Using pastry blender, cut butter into flour until mixture resembles coarse meal.
3. Add cottage cheese and mix until dough holds together; shape into ball, wrap in plastic wrap and chill 1 hour.
4. Combine all filling ingredients and blend.
5. Preheat oven to 425°F.
6. On well floured board, roll dough ⅛-inch thick. Cut into 2½- or 3-inch rounds. Center dab (less than 1 level teaspoon) of filling on each round; moisten edge, fold in half and press to seal. Crimp curved edge and pierce top with fork tines.
7. Bake on ungreased cookie sheet 10 to 12 minutes or until nicely browned. Cool on rack.

Makes about 40 small tarts.

Chocolate Cream Cheese Fudge

The "unbeatable" fudge.

One pie plate, buttered

*1 (3-oz.) package Knudsen
  Cream Cheese*
¼ cup (½ stick) Knudsen Butter
1 teaspoon Knudsen Milk
*1 (13-oz.) package walnut
  fudge frosting mix*

1. Combine cream cheese, butter and milk in stainless steel or enamel saucepan; stir over low heat until melted and well blended.
2. Remove from heat and stir in frosting mix; return to medium heat and cook, stirring, until smooth and glossy.
3. Turn into pie plate and refrigerate until firm. Cut into squares.

Makes about 1 pound fudge.

Pecan Chocolate Log

The Pecan Chocolate Log is a really "special" candy that even men and children can make.

*1 (6-oz.) package chocolate
  morsels*
*1 (8-oz.) package Knudsen
  Cream Cheese, at room
  temperature*
1 teaspoon vanilla
1 (1-pound) box powdered sugar
2 cups minced pecans

1. Melt chocolate over boiling water or on very low heat. Remove from heat and stir with rubber scraper to smooth.
2. Blend in cream cheese and vanilla. Mixture becomes glossy and seems to separate.
3. Blend powdered sugar into chocolate mixture and refrigerate until firm. Electric mixer may be used.
4. Place half of chocolate mixture on wax paper. Form into log 1½-inches in diameter; roll in pecans. Repeat with remaining half. Wrap in foil or plastic wrap and refrigerate until firm.
5. Cut in ½-inch slices. Store in refrigerator.

Makes 2 pounds candy.

CHOCOLATE SPHERES: Shape teaspoonfuls of chilled chocolate mixture into balls and roll in chopped nuts or grated milk chocolate.

CHOCOLATE DROPS: Drop teaspoonfuls of warm chocolate mixture onto wax paper and top with whole nuts, cherries or dried fruits.

PECAN BUTTERSCOTCH LOG: Substitute butterscotch morsels for chocolate.

Nutrition & Dairy Foods

Good nutrition is not the only factor important in promoting general good health. Adequate rest and exercise, sunshine and fresh air, regularity in life habits, freedom from excessive physical or emotional stress and proper medical attention all play important roles. However, nutrition is one factor that can be changed from bad to good without the expenditure of additional time or money. In fact, food costs and preparation time may actually be cut. The major effort is merely a matter of keeping the principles of good nutrition in mind when planning meals and shopping for food.

The signs of being well-nourished are similar to the signs of good general health: healthy tissues and skin, good muscle tone, adequate energy for life, a good appetite and a positive outlook. The symptoms of bad nutrition are illusive. They could indicate many disorders. They are: susceptibility to illness, aches and pains, poor muscle tone, lack of energy, poor teeth, poor skin, poor hair and fingernail condition, depression, loss of appetite or unusual appetite. As a matter of fact, one of our most serious and noticeable nutrition problems is caused by *over* eating. Overweight!

Good nutrition is important everyday to help us all enjoy good general health, but it is even more important during times of stress. The body needs more nutrients when under emotional or physical stress and at these times it may use what it gets inefficiently. Illness, injury, surgery, immobility, extreme physical exertion, exposure to extreme temperatures—even pregnancy, obesity and growth—are forms of physical stress. Any individual may be subject to one or several of these stresses at any one time. The best preventive or preparation for stress is a well-nourished body—one that has been well-nourished for many years.

Although many factors affect the mental and physical development of children, a great many studies are indicating that inadequate nutrition, particularly in the early years, is responsible for retarding both physical and mental growth.[1] These studies have been conducted primarily in the developing countries, but studies here confirm the same conclusions. Studies also indicate that once serious retardation has occurred, full potential will never be reached, no matter how good the nutritional level is in later years.

The importance of good nutrition for a happy, productive life is certain.

What is Good Nutrition?

The science of nutrition is very young. Historically it is still a new idea that one can become sick from something one *didn't* eat! As in the other sciences our knowledge is mushrooming and being refined continually.

The National Research Council's 1968 revision of the Recommended Dietary Allowances[2] lists ten vitamins and five minerals in addition to protein and calories now known to be essential to good human nutrition. The recommended allowances of these nutrients vary according to the age, sex and size of the individual. Additional allowances are recommended for pregnant and lactating women. The Council stresses that these allowances can be attained by eating a variety of common foods. In this way, other nutrients for which human requirements are less well defined, will also be provided.

Eating a variety of nutritious foods is only the beginning of good nutrition. The body is not truly nourished until the nutrients have been absorbed in the digestive system and actually used in the cells of the body. Many things can inhibit this process. For one thing, the essential nutrients are dependent on each other for most efficient absorption and use.

For example, the absorption and use of iron is greatly improved by the presence of vitamin C, protein, copper and several of the B vitamins. Calcium absorption is improved by the presence of phosphorus, protein, butterfat and vitamins A, C and D (the sunshine vitamin). The conclusion to this is: a variety of foods should be eaten at the same time to provide a mixture of wide ranges of nutrients. The vitamins and minerals in a pill taken with a cup of coffee for breakfast are not nearly as effective as the vitamins in foods provided in a well-balanced meal.

How to Achieve Good Nutrition

Eating regular, well-balanced meals is the first step in the process of providing good nutrition. The easiest way to assure that a meal is well-balanced is to plan it according to the Basic Four Food Guide[3]. The Basic Four Food Guide divides ordinary foods into four groups according to the essential nutrients each contains. When a menu contains one or more foods from each group, most or all of these essential nutrients are almost sure to be present. In this way they can work together to promote their mutual absorption and use in the body. Here is a simplified Basic Four chart.

THE BASIC FOUR FOOD GUIDE

THE MILK GROUP — *3 or more glasses daily — children; 4 or more glasses daily — teen-agers; 2 or more glasses daily — adults*
Whole, low fat or nonfat milk
Buttermilk or yogurt
(Ice cream can supply part)

THE MEAT GROUP — *2 or more servings daily.*
Meat, fish, poultry or eggs
Cottage cheese or ripe cheese
(Dry beans, peas, nuts as alternates)

BREADS AND CEREALS — *4 or more servings daily.*
Enriched or whole grain breads
or cereals

VEGETABLES AND FRUITS — *4 or more servings daily.*
Include dark green or yellow vegetables
Include vitamin C fruits or vegetables

Why is Milk So Important?

It is self-deceptive to think that it is easy to have a well-balanced diet without milk. Milk supplies more necessary nutrients in good amounts than any other food. Without it, it would be very difficult for anyone, no matter what his age, to get an adequate supply of calcium — and troublesome to get enough riboflavin. Protein, phosphorus, vitamin A and thiamine contributions are significant, too. A recent government survey[4] indicates that the diets of many Americans are significantly lacking in calcium, vitamin A and vitamin C. Including more dairy foods in the diets of these people would easily correct the calcium and vitamin A deficiencies.

Calcium

Calcium is the most important nutrient that milk provides. Although many foods contain small amounts of calcium, milk is the only common food that, in normal quantities, can begin to provide the recommended daily calcium allowance for children, teen-agers and adults. Actually, three quarters of the calcium in the American diet comes from dairy foods.

The need for calcium for building strong bones and teeth is well known. What is less known is that the body uses calcium in many other equally essential processes throughout life. Muscle and nerve tissues, the heart especially, need calcium in the fluids surrounding them for smooth passage of nerve impulses and muscle contraction. Calcium is essential for the normal clotting of blood. It is used and lost in digestive fluids and perspiration. The body loses calcium daily, no matter how little is consumed in the diet. These losses are greater during emotional upset and with perspiration during extreme physical effort, heat or fever. Calcium is lost whenever the body is immobile or extremely inactive. This was made dramatically clear through our manned space flights. Astronauts rapidly lost bone calcium when in a weightless state. To reduce this tendency, exercises are required as a part of flight procedures. To stay healthy, skeletal bones need to support the weight of the body and to resist the pull of the muscles.

If calcium for these needs is not provided in the diet, the body has a mechanism to withdraw it from the skeleton. Even when calcium intakes are high this mechanism allows the constant exchange of new calcium for old in the bones. The process, which is extremely complex, involves the hormone from the parathyroid gland. It is this hormone that maintains the constant calcium level of the blood by regulating its withdrawal from the bones. And as long as the needs of the body are greater than the intake, calcium will be withdrawn to perform essential life functions. A diet adequate in calcium—and the nutrients that promote its absorption and use—is the best way to prevent this loss. Inadequate calcium during the growing years results in slower growth, smaller stature and possible rickets. There is even evidence of actual bone loss in children with inadequate calcium in their diets. In later years the results are osteomalacia and osteoporosis. The most prevalent is osteoporosis—a disorder which causes the gradual decrease in the amount and strength of the bone tissue.

About 30 percent of the population in the United States over sixty years old have osteoporosis, four out of five of whom are women. The causes of osteoporosis are as complicated as calcium metabolism itself. Hormones, age, activity level and nutrition are all involved. A life long dietary shortage of calcium is perhaps the most important factor. Several studies have indicated that the calcium intakes of people who have osteoporosis have been low over periods of years. Increasing the intakes of calcium and the nutrients associated with its absorption has been a major means of arresting osteoporosis. But no treatment has been found to return the skeleton to its original condition once severe damage has been done.

Calcium metabolism is a very complex process. Vitamin D, parathyroid hormone, milk fat and phosphorus are all important to good absorption. In addition, protein, vitamin A and vitamin C are needed for the conversion of calcium to bone. *In milk, calcium is provided in a unique medium that promotes its optimum absorption and use.* Milk provides phosphorus in the most workable proportion for the absorption and use of calcium. It also supplies butterfat which contains not only vitamin A but an enzyme that has been shown to stimulate the absorption of calcium. Milk protein contains two amino acids that also aid in this process.

The vitamin D necessary for calcium absorption and bone building is available naturally in only a few foods. Fortunately the human body has the ability to produce its own supply in any bare skin that is exposed to ultraviolet light. This is just one of the many advantages of walking, playing, gardening or just sitting in the warm sunshine. It is not necessary to be out daily or for great lengths of time to get enough vitamin D. Your body can store it for future use. During their greatest growing years, children may require a vitamin D supplement. The family doctor should be consulted for guidance as to the exact amount because too much, as well as too little, vitamin D can be harmful. For this reason vitamin compounds are not added to Knudsen products. This is one of the factors responsible for the fresh natural flavor of Knudsen milk.

All considered, dairy foods are not only the best source of calcium but they provide for its best use. Women and teen-age girls take special note! A recent government survey indicates that you are most likely to be deficient![4]

Protein

Recent trends in dieting and meal planning have made Americans aware of the need for protein. Something that is not so well known is that dairy foods provide generous amounts of it. Either a cup of cottage cheese or a quart of milk will provide about 30 grams of protein, over half the recommended daily allowance for an adult woman. That same 30 grams of protein makes a significant contribution to the requirements of men and teen-agers. And for very few calories!

Most of the protein in milk is casein—a protein unique in milk. All milk protein is easy to digest and is complete—containing some of each of the essential amino acids. The relationship of these amino acids is excellent for body building and repair. As with calcium, protein requirements are increased when the body is under emotional or physical stress. Injury and surgery increase requirements. Losses are increased during infection, fever and immobilization. Just about any time that there is a loss of calcium, there is a companion loss of protein. The need to replace calcium and protein losses makes eating dairy products a very sensible, as well as satisfying, decision.

Riboflavin

More than 50% of the riboflavin in the United States food supply comes from dairy foods. Riboflavin is water soluble and is therefore not present in the fat portion of milk products. Riboflavin is closely associated and necessary to the process of converting food to energy. Because of this, needs are greater during times of increased physical or metabolic activity. Skin and eye health, as well as general health, are adversely affected by riboflavin deficiencies. Riboflavin can be destroyed by exposure to artificial or natural light. Dairy product cartons are designed to protect these foods from such losses.

Vitamin A

A quart of whole milk provides about half the vitamin A requirement for children and about a quarter of the requirement of teen-agers and adults. Because vitamin A is fat soluble, the products with higher milk fat content contain relatively more. Just one tablespoon of butter provides almost 10% of the adult daily allowance. Vitamin A does not occur naturally, except in trace amounts, in the nonfat milk products. It occurs in two forms—either as pure vitamin A or as carotene, which can be converted to vitamin A in the body. In milk fat it is primarily in the "ready-to-use" form. Vitamin A helps prevent infection by maintaining healthy skin and mucous membranes. It prevents night blindness which can be caused by a deficiency of vitamin A.

Planning Meals to Include Dairy Foods

Even though the importance of milk in the diet may be totally accepted, it still may seem difficult to put the acceptance into action. Fortunately, our American meal pattern helps. We *are* milk drinkers! It doesn't matter a great deal whether we drink regular, extra rich, low fat or nonfat milk. Or buttermilk, chocolate milk or any other beverages made from these milks. Eight ounces of any of them provide about a third of the daily adult calcium allowance. For those who just won't drink their two to four glasses a day, there are other solutions. A carton of yogurt can be a breakfast, a snack, a sack lunch, a fruit salad dressing or a dessert. Ice cream provides good milk nutrients, too. Beyond this, all you have to do is browse through this book to find hundreds of ways that milk products can be incorporated into practically every course of every meal. Explore the recipes and enjoy making them knowing that they are helping to make your family a healthier family.

For current specific information on the composition of Knudsen products write: Barbara Lane, Home Economics Director, Knudsen Corporation, P.O. Box 2335, Terminal Annex, Los Angeles, California 90054.

Deep appreciation is expressed to the following people who so generously gave their time to counsel the author in the writing of this chapter:

Dr. Zoe Anderson, Home Economics Department—Foods and Nutrition, San Diego State College.

Dr. George Briggs, Chairman, Department of Nutritional Sciences, University of California—Berkeley.

Mrs. Marie Harrington, Home Advisor—Nutrition, University of California, Agricultural Extension Service.

Home Economists of the California Dairy Council, Los Angeles.

[1] Studies in the area of malnutrition in early life and subsequent mental performance and physical growth are summarized in the Dairy Council Digest, Volume 39, No. 3, May-June, 1968.

[2] Food and Nutrition Board, National Academy of Sciences-National Research Council. *Recommended Dietary Allowances*, 1968 Revision.

[3] U. S. Department of Agriculture *Basic Four Food Guide*. Approved by the American Medical Association.

[4] U. S. Department of Agriculture, Agricultural Research Service. *Household Food Consumption Survey 1965-66, Report No. 1.*

How Dairy Foods Are Made

At the Dairy

All dairy products start from milk and high quality milk begins at the dairy farm. A hundred years ago in the state of California, one cow produced enough milk for two and a half people. Today one cow produces milk for nineteen. California cows produce an average of 1,200 gallons of milk per year compared to a national average of 900 gallons. This tremendous increase in milk production is due to scientific breeding and feeding of milk cows. Many cows are bred to be milkers, but only those with the most potential are actually selected. They are fed nutritionally balanced meals of mixed feeds to promote the highest and best milk production. This tremendous technological advance has allowed milk to remain our most economical food buy. Regular inspections of the milk cows by government inspectors insure the health of the cows and the safety of their milk.

The importance of an abundant, safe and economical supply of milk cannot be underestimated. Many state and federal laws exist solely to protect it. Knudsen amplifies this list of regulations with its own more stringent standards to add "appetizing" and "fresh" to the list of words describing our milk products.

The milking procedure has progressed far beyond the three legged stool and bucket. Each cow appears twice daily at the milking stall where she is washed and then machine milked. The milk is transported through stainless steel pipelines directly to a storage tank where it is immediately refrigerated. All milking equipment and storage tanks are thoroughly cleaned and sanitized after each use.

At the Creamery

Every day a refrigerated milk transport picks up the milk from each dairy farm and delivers it to the Knudsen processing plants where it is first subjected to certain laboratory tests. The goal of these tests is to confirm the flavor and the quality of the milk. Knudsen's expert milk tasters sample milk from each farm. Milk is a natural product and therefore does vary with the season, the feed of the cow, the breed of cow and her stage of lactation. Modern technology has made it possible to reduce variations to the point that it takes an expert to detect them. A second test is made to detect the presence of any impurities or microorganisms in the milk. This is one of the areas where the Knudsen standard rises above the legal requirement. Finally, laboratory tests are made to determine the amounts of milk fat and milk solids present in the milk from each dairy. The price to the farmer is determined by the fat and solids content of the milk.

Speed, careful attention to cleanliness and constant refrigeration in the processing of the milk are essentials in getting safe fresh dairy products to the consumer. Standardized tests and procedures are scientifically controlled so that Knudsen products are a consistent high quality from day to day. As much as possible, the Knudsen Cottage Cheese produced today will taste and look like the Knudsen Cottage Cheese produced on any other day.

Basic Processing

Here is an explanation of the basic procedures in getting dairy products ready for the consumer.

SEPARATION of the cream from the nonfat portion of the milk is the first step in the processing of a great deal of the milk. Cream is lighter than nonfat milk and therefore can be separated from it in a centrifuge. The cream and nonfat milk must be separated in order to standardize the fat content of each product.

STANDARDIZATION is the process of blending cream, whole milk and nonfat milk in various combinations to arrive at an exact fat content for the finished product. The fat contents of dairy products are set by law and have a great deal to do with the texture, flavor and the cost of the finished products.

FORTIFICATION is the process of adding nutrients such as concentrated nonfat milk, vitamins, minerals or other nutrients to a food. Concentrated nonfat milk is added to many Knudsen products for additional flavor, body and nutrient value.

HOMOGENIZATION is a process by which the fat particles of the milk are broken into hundreds of smaller particles—particles so small that they no longer tend to float to the surface. This is accomplished by forcing milk or cream which has been heated to 130°F. through very small openings. This extreme pressure causes the fat particles to shatter. The consumer advantages of homogenized milk over unhomogenized milk are many. The flavor is richer, it stays fresh longer, gives more uniform cooking results and is even easier to digest.

Not all products are homogenized. Whipping cream would not whip satisfactorily if the fat particles were too small. The cream used for churning butter and buttermilk is not homogenized.

PASTEURIZATION is a heat treatment to insure freedom from any possible harmful bacteria present in milk. It is accomplished almost simultaneously with homogenization. The first pasteurized milk had a definite cooked flavor. The necessity of a safe milk supply that was still appetizing motivated scientists to develop a more refined process that left the milk tasting fresh. Milk is now heated to a minimum of 161°F., held for a brief period of 15 seconds and then cooled immediately. All of the milk used in Knudsen products is pasteurized.

These are the basic milk processing procedures. They are highly controlled and highly automated—so much so that the milk that is milked from the cow today will be in the store tomorrow.

The processing of cultured products and cheeses is more complicated and takes the standardized, pasteurized and homogenized milk through additional stages.

Cultured Products

Yogurt, sour cream and buttermilk are cultured dairy products. Cheeses are also cultured, but in a different way. Raw (unpasteurized) milk contains natural enzymes and microorganisms. If raw milk were left at room temperature, it would sour and thicken because these organisms would produce lactic acid which causes the casein, the basic protein in milk, to coagulate and form a "custard." Pasteurization kills these organisms and prevents this natural souring.

To manufacture cultured dairy products in the creamery, a culture of selected laboratory controlled microorganisms is added to warm pasteurized milk or cream—depending on the end product—and allowed to develop in temperature controlled rooms. When the right degree of acidity has developed, the product is refrigerated immediately to stop the growth of the "culture."

Specific cultures are chosen for specific products because of the flavor or degree of acidity they will develop. Low fat yogurt and buttermilk are very similar in fat content and yet the acid and flavor differences are great because of the different cultures used. Sour cream and buttermilk are made with similar cultures but still do not have the same flavor or texture because of the difference in fat content. Slight variations in flavor and texture can be noticed from day to day in cultured products. This is because cultures are living things and cannot be completely controlled. The vast experience of Knudsen's research, production and quality control personnel minimizes these differences to the point that most people never detect them.

Cheeses

Cheese making is an ancient and fascinating process. The varieties of cheese on the market are numerous. They vary in flavor, color, shape, texture, caloric content and use. This diversity is created by using milks from different sources (cows, goats, etc.) and of different fat levels and also by varying the cultures used and the length of aging. Cheese can be anything from moist cottage cheese to chewy Mozzarella, hard Parmesan or moldy soft Camembert.

Knudsen specializes in fresh unripened cheeses—cottage cheese, hoop cheese and cream cheese. The processes for making each of these cheeses are very similar. Cream cheese is made from cream. Cottage cheese and hoop cheese are made from nonfat milk. Uncreamed cottage cheese and hoop cheese may be the same or nearly the same as the bakers' cheese, pot cheese or farmer cheese of other parts of the country.

To make cottage or hoop cheese curd, pasteurized nonfat milk is put into a large vat and warmed to about 76°F. A laboratory controlled culture is added and held at a set temperature until a specific acid level develops and the "custard" is set. The natural enzymes, rennet and pepsin, are added with the culture to just the large curd cottage cheese. At this point the "custard" is cut into small cubes with a wire cheese knife. The spacing of the wire blades varies with the size of curd desired. The temperature of the vat is raised to approximately 135°F. to pull the whey from the cheese curd. Experienced cheese makers stir and observe the curds and whey. At the right time they stop the cooking and draw off the clear yellow whey, leaving the white curds. The curds, which are actually a concentration of most of the protein of the milk, are thoroughly washed with clear water and drained. It takes 2⅔ quarts of milk to make a pint of Knudsen Farmer Style Cottage Cheese.

Salt and cream are mixed with drained cottage cheese curd to make Knudsen Farmer Style or Velvet Cottage Cheese. Low fat cottage cheese is only partially creamed. It is made by mixing salt, concentrated nonfat milk and just a small amount of cream with the nonfat cottage cheese curd.

Hoop cheese is plain large curd type cottage cheese curds pressed together and packaged. No salt or cream are added.

Cream cheese is heated, blended, stabilized and packaged. Some salt is added in processing.

Buttermilk

Buttermilk is normally a by-product of the production of *butter*. At Knudsen, where a 50-year reputation for real churned buttermilk exists, the opposite is more true.

Anyone who has overbeaten whipping cream has an idea of how butter is extracted from cream. As the chilled cream is beaten, the fat globules begin to clump together. Soon the smooth cream separates into light yellow creamy butter and a thin liquid called buttermilk. For delicious Knudsen Real Churned Buttermilk, the process is more complicated.

First of all, Knudsen Buttermilk is churned from a light cream that is cultured and *is not* homogenized. The cool cream is agitated in huge revolving churns. As it is churned, the butter particles begin to come together and at the same time shed their thin coating into the buttermilk. This coating of complex phospho-lipid material is important for its nutritional benefits. It is also responsible, along with expert culturing, for the fine, distinctive flavor and the smooth, light texture of Knudsen Buttermilk.

It is the churning of Knudsen Buttermilk that distinguishes it from other buttermilks. The actual churning of buttermilk is so unusual that even government publications list only cultured nonfat milk as buttermilk. Knudsen Buttermilk is cultured in addition to being churned. The culturing gives the refreshing tang and the pleasant body that makes buttermilk taste much richer than it actually is. In reality, buttermilk is lower in fat than low fat milk.

Butter

A word about butter. Knudsen makes both salted and unsalted (sweet) butter. Salted butter is generally preferred in the United States for eating. It has slightly superior keeping qualities. Unsalted butter is preferred on the European table and is wonderful for baking.

Frozen Desserts

Frozen desserts of fine texture and flavor are no accident. Expert formulation, finest quality ingredients and ultra high-speed freezing equipment are responsible for the high quality of Knudsen ice creams, ice milks and sherbets. The primary difference between the various types of frozen desserts is their fat content. Knudsen products range all the way from sherbets at 1.25% milk fat to ice creams as high as 16%. The processing is essentially the same. The liquid ingredient (cream or other liquid), sugar and flavorings are put into huge cylinder freezers resembling oversized home mechanical freezers on their sides. These ingredients are whipped together and frozen until the mixture is the consistency of a soft serve cone. This soft ice cream is poured into formed cartons, sealed and moved immediately to the sub-zero freezing mechanism. There are several types of freezing mechanisms with temperatures as low as −50°F. designed to freeze these desserts as quickly as possible. This ultra-fast freezing is a major factor in the development of the fine creamy texture of Knudsen ice creams and sherbets.

Imitation Dairy Products

Imitation dairy products are a new addition to the dairy line. An imitation dairy product is, by law, a product made from fresh nonfat milk and vegetable fat—like Knudsen Imitation Milk and Knudsen Imitation Sour Cream. It contains the same amount of protein and calcium as the natural milk product because it is made from milk. It is a common misconception that imitation dairy products are lower in fat and calories than natural dairy products. In reality, the amount of fat must be the same and therefore the calories will be about the same, also.

Another misconception is that all vegetable fats are acceptable in diets restricted in saturated fat or cholesterol. Although vegetable fats contain no cholesterol, they may be high in saturated fats. The advantage of imitation dairy products is lower cost.

There are two other modified dairy or milk-like products on the market today, filled products and nondairy products. Neither filled nor nondairy products are required to attempt to provide the nutrients of real milk. A filled product is manufactured from vegetable fat and reconstituted nonfat dry milk or fluid nonfat milk. The completely nondairy products may resemble dairy products in appearance but they are formulated from nondairy ingredients.

Product Labeling

Laws regarding product labeling have become a matter of great public interest. It is the law that all ingredients must be listed on the food container in the order of their decreasing amounts by weight. This is demonstrated on Knudsen salad cartons.

However, most dairy products do not list ingredients. The reason is that definitions and standards of identity for most dairy foods have been set by law under the State of California Agricultural Code. To bear the name of a standardized product, and not list ingredients, a product must contain only the ingredients set forth in the code and it must contain them in the specified amount, shape and form. Ice creams, yogurt, cheeses and all milks are standardized foods. Unless the carton lists a deviation—such as, "artificial sweetener added"—you are assured that the product conforms to the code.

Why don't all brands of standardized foods look and taste alike? First of all, most processing codes offer some tolerance. Ice milk may contain as little as 2% milk fat or as much as 7%. Anything in this range is legally ice milk. The most important differences come from other things. Just as the same recipe prepared by two women can produce two dramatically different dishes, standardized dairy products from two companies can vary. The better product comes from greater "know how," superior ingredients and extra care.

Conclusion

The rules of speed, careful attention to cleanliness and constant refrigeration are rigidly observed throughout the stages of milk processing. All processing equipment is scrupulously cleaned and sanitized with scrub brushes, detergent and steam after each use. The milk and other dairy products are at all times stored at temperatures to preserve their freshness.

The final link in the chain of people involved in providing fresh, consistent and appetizing dairy products is the Knudsen Sales-Driver. He makes regular deliveries to each market from a constantly refrigerated van. He is well trained and able to see that the Knudsen products he delivers are well cared for and always fresh when you select them from the dairy case.

For tips on how you can make that carefully guarded freshness last, see pages 6 to 8.

For current specific information on the composition of Knudsen products write: Barbara Lane, Home Economics Director, Knudsen Corporation, P.O. Box 2335, Terminal Annex, Los Angeles, California 90054.

Processing of Knudsen Dairy Products

Index

*indicates a tip or note.
Items in italics are recipe variations.

Equipment for Cooking with Dairy Foods

Here Are The Things You'll Need! Standard measuring cups and spoons—for accurate measuring. A straight edged spatula, too ☐ Enamel, glass, ceramic, stainless steel or teflon-lined pans—to make creamy white sauces ☐ Double boilers and Bain Maries (a chafing dish with a water bath beneath)—for cooking and holding sour cream sauces and delicate dairy dishes at gentle low temperatures ☐ Accurate thermostatically controlled appliances—for holding delicate sauces and for good baking results ☐ Pyrex, enamel and ceramic